SUCCEEDING
IN
PRIVATE
PRACTICE

SUCCEEDING

A BUSINESS GUIDE FOR PSYCHOTHERAPISTS

IN

PRIVATE PRACTICE

Eileen S. Lenson

SAGE Publications
International Educational and Professional Publisher
Thousand Oaks   London   New Delhi

For information address:

 SAGE Publications, Inc.
2455 Teller Road
Thousand Oaks, California 91320

SAGE Publications Ltd.
6 Bonhill Street
London EC2A 4PU
United Kingdom

SAGE Publications India Pvt. Ltd.
M-32 Market
Greater Kailash I
New Delhi 110 048 India

Printed in the United States of America

Library of Congress Cataloging-in-Publication Data

Lenson, Eileen S.
    Succeeding in private practice: a business guide for
psychotherapists / Eileen S. Lenson.
        p. cm.
    Includes bibliographical references and index.
    ISBN 0-8039-4957-X (cloth). — ISBN 0-8039-4958-8 (pbk.)
    1. Psychotherapy—Practice—United States. I. Title.
    [DNLM: 1. Private Practice. 2. Practice Management, Medical.
3. Psychotherapy—organization & administration. 4. Psychotherapy—
economics—United States. 5. United States. WM 420 L573s 1994]
    RC465.6.L46   1994
    616.89′0068—dc20
    DNLM/DLC   93-11898

94 95 96 97 10 9 8 7 6 5 4 3 2

Sage Production Editor: Diane S. Foster

This book is dedicated to my wonderful and loving husband, Lloyd, in appreciation not only for his understanding, patience, and motivation but also for the special opportunities he has offered me during our marriage.

Contents

Acknowledgments   **xii**

Introduction   **xiii**

**1. Attraction of a Private Practice
     Is It Right for You?**   **1**

Attraction of a Private Practice   1
But Is Private Practice Right for You?   4

2. Selecting Options in Private Practice   **10**

Group Versus Solo   10
Full Versus Part Time   13
Specialized Versus Generalized Practice   14
Buying Versus Starting a New Practice   14
Type of Business Organization   17

3. Setting Up Your Business   **21**

Credentials   21
Financial Status   28
Policy and Procedure Manual   29
Selecting an Office Location   30
Subleasing   31
Home Office   31
Negotiating a Lease   33
Office Construction   34
Soundproofing   35

Furnishings and Equipment   35
Naming Your Practice   43
Stationery   43
Insurance for Your Practice   46
Consultants   51

4. Clinical Record Keeping and Paperwork   54

Appointment Book   54
Telephone Book   55
Confidentiality   55
Legal Requests for Clinical Notes   56
Client Requests for Clinical Notes   56
Intake Forms   56
Clinical Notes   63
Termination Letter   67
Old Files   67
Correspondence   68
Forms   69
Resource File   70

5. Taxes   71

Select Business Entity   71
Taxpayer Identification Number   73
Maintain Records   73
Business Deductions   74
Self-Employment Taxes   76
Employment Taxes   77
Federal Income Tax Withholding   77
Social Security and Medicare Tax   78
Federal Unemployment Tax Act (FUTA)   78
State Unemployment Insurance   79
State Income Taxes   79
County, City, and Other Local Taxes   79
Personal Property Taxes   80
Workers' Compensation Insurance   80
Filing Forms   80
Client Tax Deductions   80
Audits   81

6. Fee Setting, Collections, and Bookkeeping   82

Fee Setting   82
Billing   86

Fee Collection   88
Payment Sources   90
Third-Party Reimbursement   97
Bartering   103
Delinquent Accounts   103
Missed Appointments   107
Bookkeeping   108
Petty Cash   112
Bank Accounts   112

7. Legal Aspects of a Private Practice   114

Malpractice   114
Liability Insurance   115
What to Do If You Are Sued   116
Five Components of a Malpractice Lawsuit   117
Liability in Supervision   117
Liability and Contracts   118
Causes for Malpractice   118
Prevention   121
Privileged Communication   123
Confidentiality   124
Selecting an Attorney   124
Subpoena   124
Depositions   125
Court   125
Fees for Depositions or Courtroom Appearances   127

8. Safety Issues   129

Suicidal Client   129
Battered Client   132
Violent Client   132
Child-Abusing Client   134
Litigious Client   135

9. Marketing   136

Professional Goals and Objectives   137
Referral Development   139
Cold Calls   155
Selling Your Services   159
Maintaining Referrals   162
Soliciting Client Feedback   164
Advertising   164

Personal Image   182
Summary   182

10. Ethical Aspects of a Private Practice   184

Value Differences   185
Confidentiality   185
Privileged Communication   187
Informed Consent   188
Contracts   189
Premature Termination and Abandonment   190
Termination   191
Continuing Nonbenefiting Clients   192
Boundaries   192
Sexual Misconduct   193
Psychiatric Hospitals   193
Group Therapy   194
Availability of Records   194
Supervision   195

11. Retirement Planning   196

Individual Retirement Accounts (IRAs)   197
Simplified Employee Pension (SEP)   197
Keogh Plan   198
Defined Benefit Plan   199
Target Benefit Pension Plan   199
401-K Plan   200
Social Security (FICA)   200
Corporate Pension Plans   201
Tax-Deferred Annuities (TDAs)   201
Single-Premium Deferred Annuity (SPDAs)   201
Considerations in Selecting Retirement Plans   201
Estate Planning   202

12. Employees: Hiring, Managing, Firing   204

Hiring   204
Policy and Procedure Manual   208
Personnel Records   208
Secretarial Tasks   209
Qualifications   214
Managing   215
Firing   219

13. Additional Avenues in Private Practice   **223**

Contracting With Psychiatric Hospitals   223
General Consultation   224
Home Evaluations for Adoptions   225
Supervision   226
Teaching   227
Administering to Private Mental Health Groups   227
Presenting Conferences   227
Forensic Psychotherapy   228
Expert Witness Testimony   229
Jury Selection and Psychological Autopsy   230
Child Custody Evaluations   230
Consultation to Personal Injury Attorneys and
    Workers' Compensation   231
Nonclinical Roles With HMOs   232
Home Visits   233
Telephone Therapy   234
Industrial Psychotherapy   235
Expansion With Therapists and Offices   236
Products   238
Future Opportunities   239

14. Taking Care of Yourself   **240**

Workaholism   241
Social Support   241
Clinical Expertise   242
Time Management   242
Written Communications   243
Organization   243
Realistic Goals   243
Monotony   244
Childhood Messages   244
Isolation   244
Plan for Retirement   245

References   **247**

Recommended Reading   **251**

Index   **253**

About the Author   **267**

Acknowledgments

Special thanks to my father, Dr. Robert R. Stromberg, for his guidance and insight. His meaningful critiques of my writings over the years have been tremendously instrumental to my growth as an author. Also, thanks to my mother, Joyce Stromberg, for always being there to cheer me on.

I also wish to thank Kathy Yoder, Dr. Pierre Haber, Patricia J. Moline, Jeff Taksey, David Dillon, Don Marion, Anne Seiler, John Fellenz, Ben Benson, and other individuals who read parts of this manuscript, for their time and helpful input. A special thanks to my editor, Marquita Flemming, who provided support, focus, and direction during the completion of my manuscript. Also, thanks to my beautiful and lively daughter, Rachel, who patiently (though unknowingly) tolerated my completion of this book during her first year of life.

Introduction

A few years ago a licensed professional counselor working in a hospital mentioned that she had begun a part-time private practice. When I inquired as to whether she had obtained malpractice insurance, she looked surprised at my question and replied that she did not see the need, as she had good relationships with her clients.

A psychologist who was held in high esteem by the psychiatric hospital in which he worked approached me sheepishly one day and asked what he should be doing with regard to marketing in preparation to enter private practice.

A social worker complained to me that her marketing was not working. When asked what she was doing, she replied that she had sent out announcements of her practice, but that referrals were not coming in. She was at a loss as to what to do next.

Over the years I have had master's- and doctoral-degreed therapists— successful, qualified clinicians employed in agency settings—ask how to go about starting a private practice. It is not unusual for psychotherapists with excellent clinical skills not to know how to blend the professional and business aspects required for a private practice.

I urge interested parties to learn all they can about the business of private practice before they go into it. A private practice is a small business. The statistics for survival of new businesses are grim. Although approximately 650,000 new small businesses are incorporated each year, 23% close down within 2 years. Fifty percent close within 4 years, and 60% of all new incorporated businesses close within 6 years (personal communication with Steve

Dixon, Small Business Association, United States Employment and Establishment Microdata, January 1992).

But do remember that some of the successful "greats" in our country bet on themselves to win when the odds were down. Pepsi-Cola went bankrupt three times, and Raytheon lost $5 million on the first microwave oven it produced. You have to make the decision, as did I, that you can emotionally and financially take the risks in starting a private practice.

I have made an assumption in this book that the reader has a high level of clinical expertise and wants to become a private practitioner, or wishes to improve an existing practice. Graduate schools generally fail to teach the business side, or even to acknowledge that having a private practice is a business. They do not consider "economics" to be an academic function. I hope this book will serve as a bridge that will enable the reader to plan properly and to avoid unanticipated problems.

It can be discouraging and hard when starting a private practice. You will need to have emotional as well as financial staying power when starting out. At the time I was considering starting a practice, I attended a seminar given by a well-known consultant on private practice. In an authoritative voice he said, "No one should consider establishing a private practice in Houston at this time because of the economic situation." (Houston was in the deep recession of the 1980s.) Instead of accepting his "wisdom," I chose to become more determined to reach my goals. I prefer to believe that we should bet on ourselves to win, not to lose.

And so I began. I have never worked as hard as when I began my private practice. I went from being employed—with a steady income, health insurance, and a great retirement plan; working 8 hours a day; and enjoying relaxed and pleasant lunches—to working 12- to 13-hour days, having no benefit package, being constantly preoccupied about the unfilled therapy hours, and eating breakfast and lunch in the car between office/hospital/marketing meetings. And yet, because I am doing what I want to do and have the opportunity for an endless expression of creativity and choices, I am personally and professionally happier and my passion for continuing my private practice continues to grow.

Many issues must be considered when starting a private practice. Each will be addressed in the forthcoming chapters. Money is usually a problem to the small business owner; general small-business books make the assumption that burdensome loans from the bank need to be obtained and thus devote disproportionate sections to describing how to get loans, as well as discussing exactly what type of product you should be selling in order to pay back these loans.

Fortunately, as therapists, we know what we are selling: therapy. As therapists we do not have to spend considerable amounts of money on cash registers, light fixtures, inventory, and employee salaries. We do hire staff and we do buy equipment and furniture. Therefore, these topics are covered in this book. Yet, the coverage is slanted differently from most business books.

Chapter 1, "Attraction of a Private Practice: Is It Right for You?" addresses the varied reasons psychotherapists are motivated to enter private practice. The decision to enter the private sector is an individual one, yet 10 primary attractions for starting a private practice are identified. Chapter 1 will also help you determine whether the private sector is indeed right for *you* at this time. Special skills and personality traits need to be evaluated and you need to assess your financial and social situations honestly prior to making the leap into private practice. Fifteen personal as well as practice goals are reviewed.

Chapter 2, "Selecting Options in Private Practice," helps you identify the many options you have when deciding to enter private practice. The pros and cons of a group versus solo practice, going full or part time, having a specialized versus generalized practice, buying versus starting a new practice, and selecting the form of organization to use all are addressed.

Chapter 3, "Setting Up Your Business," includes everything about setting up the business. There is nothing small about a small business, and everything you need to consider prior to starting out is detailed for you. This includes information on credentialing and selecting the office location. The chapter addresses making the decision to sublease, have a home office, or construct a new office. Facts on selecting a name for your practice as well as picking stationery, business cards, and furniture are examined. Insurance to obtain prior to beginning your practice also is itemized. A brief list of professionals with whom you need to consult is examined.

Chapter 4, "Clinical Record Keeping and Paperwork," addresses the importance of managing your appointment book and telephone book and ensuring confidentiality for your clinical files. Suggestions are offered on what to include in intake forms. An excellent form to use to obtain verification of benefits is examined. Maintaining a professional method of dictating therapy notes so your client as well as you are protected is included in this chapter. Last, dealing with terminate clinical notes and sending the termination letter are addressed.

Chapter 5, "Taxes," reviews the choices available when selecting a business entity. It also directs attention to your business taxes, your client's taxes, and how to ensure the greatest bookkeeping protection for the business.

Chapter 6, "Fee Setting, Collections, and Bookkeeping," considers the importance of the financial records. This chapter focuses on fair collecting so the client as well as the therapist is well served. Handling missed appointments, identifying delinquent accounts and collecting bad debts, working with insurance companies, third-party reimbursements, and developing a reliable bookkeeping system are detailed. The proper way to handle bank accounts, check writing and bill paying, and petty cash are discussed. The materials and system you will need to implement to ensure a dependable, effortless bookkeeping system are described.

Chapter 7, "Legal Aspects of a Private Practice," looks at legal issues with respect to malpractice, privileged communication, selecting an attorney, subpoenas, depositions, and court appearances and fees. The primary causes for malpractice actions are detailed and examined.

Chapter 8, "Safety Issues," examines the risks that exist for the therapist, personally and professionally, as well as for the client. Protocols to follow when working with a suicidal, battered, violent, or child-abusing client are detailed. Learning how to screen the potentially litigious client also is discussed.

Chapter 9, "Marketing," is lengthy as it includes marketing and the development of referrals. It contains information on identifying target markets, advertising, maintaining credibility, and making a successful marketing call. The use of setting goals and learning how to evaluate your success are included. The chapter also identifies other systems that may help your marketing efforts, such as psychiatric hospitals, other mental-health-care providers, and managed care.

Chapter 10, "Ethical Aspects of a Private Practice," considers the impact of value differences, confidentiality, informed consent, privileged communication, premature termination, abandonment, and emergencies on the ethical aspect of your private practice.

Chapter 11, "Retirement Planning," looks at retirement plans that each therapist must consider, especially those plans without any other type of retirement. Saving for the future is the focus of this chapter.

Chapter 12, "Employees: Hiring, Managing, Firing," observes considerations in hiring staff, both from an efficiency standpoint as well as tax consideration. This chapter includes how to hire well, handle personnel records, delineate secretarial tasks, manage good staff, and improve staff performance. How and when to fire an employee also are discussed.

Chapter 13, "Additional Avenues in Private Practice," addresses additional avenues of earning a living in private practice. Many psychotherapists are content with sticking to conventional hourly sessions in their offices. Others desire diversity in their work. Opportunities for the newly independent psychotherapist as well as the seasoned practitioner are explored.

Finally, in Chapter 14, "Taking Care of Yourself," I address the need to have emotional as well as financial staying power, especially when first starting out.

Having a private practice is not for everyone. And that is okay. I hope this book will help you to make that decision, and offer "hands-on" guidance. In a field where success tips often are kept secret, I hope to demystify the unknown. Ultimately, I hope to be able to smooth out the rough spots for others and make their beginnings in private practice less scary, and less trial and error, than was my own.

I wish you the best in your career, and hope that you will feel comfortable individualizing what I present. What is offered is my knowledge and experience. Take from the book what works for you, and develop your own style.

ONE

Attraction of a Private Practice

Is It Right for You?

Attraction of a Private Practice

Ask a number of psychotherapists why they went into private practice and you will be certain to get a multitude of reasons. The motivations for entering private practice are individual and multifaceted. Typically, therapists who decide to enter private practice have a long history of extensive therapeutic experience and are highly educated, well-established professionals. Let us look at the varied reasons for entering private practice.

■ Autonomy

Some therapists decide to establish a private practice because of a desire for autonomy. After a therapist has spent years working for an agency, her or his desire to become more independent becomes more prominent. The restrictions of agencies often inhibit independent decision making and discourage healthy risk taking. Private practice offers the vehicle for this autonomy. You are in charge of all aspects of your practice. You are totally responsible for your success or failure. And you cannot be fired!

When a therapist is employed by others, many decisions are the domain of the agency, not the therapist. For example, some agency policies require that a substantial minimum fee be collected from patients. Practitioners in private practice may decide to assume minimum payment or gratis from clients. Therapists in private practice also decide which professional meetings

1

to attend, selecting conferences that advance professional interests rather than those that simply serve agency needs.

■ Freedom From Routine

Private practice allows freedom not typically available in an agency setting. Therapists in agencies are generally limited in the length and timing of vacations. In private practice, you determine when and how often to vacation. Of course, you need to consider cross coverage and the resultant loss of income. (However, the newly establishing therapist can expect to be working long days, evenings, and weekends during the start-up years.) The pace of work is determined by the therapist, not an agency. Unconventional hours can be arranged, allowing for golf on Friday afternoons and clients on Saturday or Sunday afternoons.

The freedom also may include the ability to express oneself through self-selected office design and decorations that reflect the therapist's—not the agency's—tastes.

■ Challenge

Private practice is much more than performing psychotherapy in your own office. It is the opportunity to use specialized skills one otherwise would have been unable to develop. Managerial skills include hiring and maintaining a staff. Business skills include pinpointing the best geographical location for an office and setting and collecting fees. The success of your marketing skills will determine, to a large extent, how large your practice will become. Creative skills are called upon all the time in a private practice. The more versatile you are, the more enjoyable and personally rewarding the practice can become.

■ Financial Compensation

The desire or need to make more money is a valid and significant motive for seeking private practice. Therapists can earn considerably more in the private sector than as employees.

With job security becoming less and less certain due to present economic conditions, it is nice knowing that you need not worry about being laid off. Of course, there are financial drawbacks to having your own practice: You must meet your overhead every week, and you will encounter economic changes that are out of your control.

▪ Juggle Demands of Parenthood

A flexible time schedule can be beneficial to the client as well as the therapist. A therapist who is frustrated at not being able to juggle the demands of parenthood and profession comfortably can reduce her or his stress by arranging less traditional office hours. The hours may be reduced or split, with morning and evening office hours and afternoons at home with the children. Also, the office may be set up at home or nearby, thereby minimizing the lengthy daily commute.

▪ Select the Type of Client Population

Another significant advantage of private practice is the ability to select the type of client population you wish to work with. In an agency, opportunities to specialize or to work with a specific population often are not possible. In private practice you could elect to work solely with substance abusers, codependents, or children. Alternatively, you could have the freedom to have a varied practice.

▪ Reduction in Available Jobs

A change in society's values also has influenced the movement into private practice. The movement away from social reform has resulted in reduced funding for mental-health-related services at the local and national levels. Governmental funding has been reduced, and private agencies are working with smaller budgets. The result is a loss of jobs for therapists in more traditional settings. Qualified therapists may be looking into the private sector at a quickened pace.

▪ Latitude From Bureaucracy

Movement away from the bureaucracy of an agency, with its slow changes, politics, and frustrating paperwork, is another motivator for becoming a private practitioner. A healthy private practice will not be encumbered with forms that serve little purpose. The flexibility to make professional judgments will exist. The therapist will be able to make independent decisions and change will be possible quickly and with little effort.

▪ Level of Integrity

After continued exposure to unrealistic pressure and rigidity, the therapist may develop a low sense of self-worth. A private practice typically enables the therapist to convert his or her values and philosophies of life into a harmonious outcome, and one in which the therapist can develop and maintain an increased sense of integrity.

■ Personal Satisfaction

In a private practice you are able to enjoy the independence of being an entrepreneur. You are able to evade the routine and boredom that can develop when working for others. By assuming the leadership and responsibility for your practice, and being able to plot out where you want to go, you—not someone else—will be directing your own work. This will increase your motivation, which in turn will enhance your self-esteem and work productivity. Because you are able to use your skills as and when you wish, you are likely to become more satisfied with your professional life. Financial rewards also are bound to result.

But Is Private Practice Right for You?

The decision to go into private practice is deeply personal. It is imperative that you make an honest self-appraisal of your personal, professional, and financial needs. Listed below are 15 categories that are important for a clinician to evaluate prior to making the decision to combine business with psychotherapy.

■ Belief in Yourself

At the time when your colleagues may become your competitors, when your work is done in isolation, when you are handling all the unknowns, and when the rewards are slow in coming, it is essential that you maintain the belief that you will be successful. Success will begin in your psyche and will influence your competence and outcome. Remember, self-confidence will be necessary during the slow times. You have to believe in yourself, have a mission, and know in your heart of hearts that you can be successful. When you find yourself getting discouraged, remember that Babe Ruth struck out 1,330 times in his career. Develop a singleness of purpose and never, never give up.

■ Professional Presentation

First impressions are lasting impressions. You only have one opportunity to make a first impression. In the competitive business of private practice, a bad first impression can shut doors on considerable amounts of business. People want to go to a therapist who looks successful. Tidy attire, conservative style, organized office space, and proper preparation for presentations are important for confidence building in others. Know the population you are serving and dress with them in mind. For instance, I dress casually for my adolescent therapy group, conservatively for a court testimony, and boldly if I am giving a presentation.

Perhaps the issues of appearance and behavior were best expressed by a Stanford University faculty member (Kriss, 1975), a physician, who was commenting on his view of how other physicians should dress: "The physician's dress should convey to even his most anxious patient a sense of seriousness of purpose that helps to provide reassurance and confidence that his or her complaints will be dealt with competently" (p. 1024).

■ Good Communication Skills

To help build a practice, you will probably find that there is a need to give public presentations. If you are not a good speaker, consider getting help by attending Toastmasters, a national public speaking group that helps people improve their presentation skills for a nominal fee.

Good communication pertains to written, verbal, and nonverbal skills. Written communication such as letters to prospective referral sources and handouts with your name on them convey much about you. The ability to be tactful in handling difficult people projects much about your verbal communication skills. Are you able to convey your concepts in a manner that is received positively? Are you able to handle conflict successfully? The nonverbal communication you exemplify on marketing calls reflects on your capabilities as a psychotherapist.

■ Personal Qualifications

To go into private practice you must have intangible qualities such as leadership, creativity, a desire to learn, impatience with routine, flexibility, innovativeness, an ability to deal with the unknown, and a positive outlook on life. Your physical and mental health have to be good. Ideally, your social life should be stable so as to allow you to focus on your practice. You also need to be able to handle stress in a healthy manner.

■ Entrepreneurial Style

You must be a self-starter with abundant energy who enjoys the roller-coaster ride of the unknowns and risks that private practice can bring. You must have vision, enthusiasm, determination, persistence, chutzpah, and a desire to succeed. You must be able to establish and reach for new goals. You must be able to assume responsibility for taking risks, have a low frustration tolerance level, and be a natural leader. You must have had sufficient clinical expertise.

Many an entrepreneur has begun late in life. Ray Krock began McDonald's in late middle age. Colonel Sanders began Kentucky Fried Chicken in his 60s. Do not let age be a deterrent.

■ Good Organizational Skills

You need to be able to organize yourself efficiently to complete all your responsibilities. No one will be telling you what to do. No one will be reminding you to pay your income taxes, call an insurance company, or dictate a clinical note. If you are disorganized, you will become overwhelmed—a death sentence to a businessperson. When chaos occurs, you will need the ability to sort through and focus on what is important and disregard the rest. You need to be able to create your own work structure, and be able to adapt to changes that impact it.

I have learned to take 15 minutes at the end of each day to review my responsibilities and obligations for the next day and to scan the week ahead. This assures that I am prepared and prevents unfortunate errors from occurring. Those who cannot plan for the future end up spending most of their time fighting off the crises of today. No matter how competent the support staff, the therapist is still accountable. Good organizational skills include prioritizing tasks and being able to delegate responsibility rather than getting overwhelmed by the details.

■ Enjoy Working

To have a successful private practice you need to enjoy hard work. There have to be inner drive, strength, and courage that will help you when the days and weeks become long. Some of the work will be monotonous, boring, or downright dislikable, but will need to be done by you. If you are able to hold on to the passion for enjoying hard work, you will be able to manage the difficult tasks.

The number of clients you see each week will never reflect the number of hours you work. You can only charge clients for direct therapy services. You will have hours of downtime for administrative activities such as talking with insurance companies, hiring, managing staff complaints, buying supplies, attending staffings at hospitals or staff meetings in your office, or marketing.

■ Ability to Defer Gratification

The rewards will be delayed. There will be hours of marketing before clients begin to call. Even when you market successfully, it may be weeks before a client is referred to you. Financial rewards are uncertain at best during the early months. You will have to spend money before you earn any. Insurance companies are slow to pay. Can you wait? Be prepared.

■ Capacity for Creative and Analytical Thinking

Creative skills will keep your practice active and alive. Good analytical thinking will help you stay committed and focused on budgetary constraints and results, setting objectives, exploring advertising options, supervising any employees, and projecting for the future. In other words, most successful clinicians in private practice need to have a good balance between left- and right-brain abilities. Be willing to seek creative or analytical help when necessary.

■ Good Physical and Mental Health

Physical and emotional stability are necessary when building your private practice. The long hours, the unknowns, and the frustrations can exacerbate problems you may already have. If you are coping with medical or psychological problems at this time, it may be advisable to consider delaying the opening of your practice.

Coping with stress will be critical to the well-being of your physical and mental health. As there are always numerous problems that may arise from managing a private practice, including worry about referrals, clinical judgment, payment of taxes and overhead, running an office, and conflicting personal commitments, it is necessary to have the ability to set boundaries on your work day so you do not become overly stressed and experience burnout. Manage your business; do not let your business manage you.

■ Clinical Skills

Expertise in your clinical skills is essential, as these skills not only will help the client but also will enable you to avoid lawsuits, improve the referral base, and offer a therapeutically sound environment in the office.

■ Family Needs

Establishing a private practice cannot occur in a vacuum. Consider the amount of time required for family needs, and what the impact of your absence will be. How will your practice affect your family vacations, educational needs, or decision to start a family? How will your use of family money to start the business and initial loss of income after leaving your agency job affect the family? Do you have a back-up plan in the event that your practice progresses too slowly? Starting a business affects the family and should be discussed with each member beforehand. It probably should not be initiated unless there is strong family support, as you will be working long hours at first, which will result in less time with your family.

■ Independence

Emotional isolation can occur, even when therapists are practicing in the same office together. Busy therapists often find it difficult to find the time to talk to each other, as they are seeing clients. You need to determine whether you can work in professional solitude. Therapists who cannot may be at risk for burnout from the pressures. A caution is to be wary of a tendency not to obtain supervision, when out on your own. Whether individual or peer, supervision keeps clinicians from becoming stagnant.

■ Financial

Can you afford to begin a private practice? You will have no steady income. You will have good income potential but initially will find your financial situation to be strained due to start-up costs and a limited number of clients in treatment. Even when you are bringing in a "good" income, you will experience peaks and valleys. In addition, you are not paid when you are sick, disabled, at conferences, or on vacation. Your income will be affected by bad weather, recessions, and other circumstances over which you have no control.

Your income will be unpredictable. You will never realize how many holidays there are each year until you count up how many days you are not getting paid. And yet your overhead, office staff salaries, rent, and advertising continue whether you work or not.

Make a budget and adhere to it. Be prepared to pay for consultations with other professionals and conference fees. If a malpractice litigation results, you will not have emotional or financial support from an agency.

Certain segments of the population may find difficulty in securing start-up financing from banks. This includes women, minorities, and retirees. Women may experience gender discrimination at banks as they typically have less credit history and fewer networking contacts to use as referrals. Minorities may experience discrimination in a similar manner. If retirees entering a private practice have any health problems, they may discover difficulty in securing financing from lenders.

■ Flexibility

You must be flexible enough to accommodate unpredictable changes. I liken my practice to an accordion. Sometimes it expands, and I am terribly busy. My pager is going off all weekend and all hours of the day and night. I am forced to make more hospital visits and to work later evening hours and weekends. At these times my personal life suffers. At other times, somewhat seasonally, my practice decreases. I am then allowed to catch up on paperwork, enjoy lunch with a colleague, or get out of town for a long weekend with my husband. I realize that I have little influence over these peaks and valleys, and have long since stopped trying to exert control over them.

As a therapist in private practice you will be on call 24 hours a day, seven days a week, for your clients, unless you make cross-coverage arrangements. Client needs do not always coincide with your needs. Working out a flexible balance between your work and personal life will require creativity. You will then have to set very clear boundaries.

Developing a private practice can give you the best of all worlds: career, independence, and the indescribable pleasure of self-fulfillment. Yet, businesses fail because of lack of knowledge, money, and support. If you remember to think of yourself as a businessperson and not just a psychotherapist, you will be better prepared to face the world that few clinicians were trained to expect.

TWO

Selecting Options in Private Practice

"As one door closes, another opens." This is true for those who enter private practice, but with one exception: not one, but a whole array of doors open. The opportunity to get involved in a group or solo practice, to work full or part time, to specialize, and to select a form of business are decisions each practitioner needs to consider. Your decisions will determine the type of practice you have.

Group Versus Solo

Although private practice may imply a solo practice, a common occurrence is for several therapists to form a group practice. The purpose may be to establish a comprehensive, multidisciplinary team, balancing strengths and weaknesses, or to reduce overhead. Sharing a lease, secretary, copy machine, telephones, utility bills, office supplies, reception-room furniture, and marketing expenses can result in a significant monthly reduction in bills. A group also may be able to save financially on insurance.

A group practice enables you to work with a selected client population and refer the clients with a different spectrum of problems to other group members. Although you can always "refer out" a client you wish not to work with, you are more likely to be assured of a reciprocal referral in the near future from another group member than from another therapist in the community. Your colleague is reminded on a daily basis of your referral simply by having daily contact with you. Other community therapists may forget. If the referred client is a member of a family with whom a therapist is already working, it is much easier to collaborate or to have joint sessions when both therapists are at the same location.

A group practice also lends itself to more accessible cross-coverage. The client's files are readily available in the office for the cross-covering therapist, providing better continuity of care. Of course, authorization for release of information must be obtained prior to sharing a client's file with a colleague. For the client, being able to be seen by a group practice therapist in the same suite already familiar to the client is less stressful than having to locate a therapist in a different office.

In terms of advertising and marketing, a group name will be better recognized in the community than the name of an individual practitioner. In presenting issues to be addressed in the community the group will carry more political clout. Expensive forms of advertising, such as television and radio, may be prohibitively high priced for the individual practitioner. Yet, this same advertising may be affordable when group practice members are contributing proportionately to the marketing investment. Members also can share attendance at hospital staffings and conferences as well as marketing calls, thereby allowing more time for therapy sessions. Regularly held group staff meetings can assure dissemination of information.

A group practice, with its many different personalities and motivations, often becomes a practice with extended hours. This can be quite advantageous for the group as it will be recognized in the community as a flexible, available practice, able to meet the needs of a wide variety of clients.

Ideally, group members should be able to divide responsibilities so a comprehensive practice can be developed with limited overlapping. For instance, if an ideas-oriented or right-brained person, connects with a business-oriented or left-brained person, the group practice can be complimented by the joining of creative and business orientations. If, however, each member views himself or herself as an "ideas" person, the individual who reluctantly assumes the administrative responsibilities probably will feel resentful about this burden. As a result, the business may be highly creative but financially unsound.

If you are to have a partner or partners, I recommend that each partner write personal expectations in detail, and then discuss them with each other. This will enable each of you to recognize potential difficulties prior to making the investment. The demise of many partnerships often is lack of planning. Differences can be worked out, but it is critical that your partner be someone who is cooperative, has the same amount of commitment to the group practice as you do, and shares mutual dreams. All partners should establish a method for settling conflicts as well as agreed-upon means of changing and ending the partnership.

Therapy is tiring, and at times it can feel lonely and isolating. A group practice can offer you the opportunity to seek out emotional support, professional consultation, brainstorming, and friendship with esteemed colleagues, in between sessions. Therapists need to be able to take care of themselves while also caring for their clients.

One difficulty that may arise in a group practice is the arrangement in which the partner signs contracts with a "noncompete" clause, stipulating that a departing therapist cannot establish a practice within a specified number of miles of the existing practice, for a certain time period. Or, the contract may read that the clients belong to the practice and cannot be treated by the departing therapist. This creates a hardship for these clients, who already have established a trusting relationship with the therapist and must now either terminate with her or him or travel to another geographical area. Any group contract should consider the clients' interests as well as the clinicians'. An option may be that the therapist continues treating her or his clients but pays a percentage of the billings for these clients to the former practice for a predetermined period of time.

Another difficulty that arises when belonging to a group is the risk of being held legally responsible for the actions of another group member. It is possible that partners will be presented with a malpractice lawsuit if a client's attorney is looking for a "deep pocket." Most attorneys will go after as many individuals as legally possible. To avoid the costly process of extricating oneself from such a lawsuit should a partner sue, it is best to confer with your attorney and develop a "hold-harmless" agreement. Such agreements will not be as helpful if a partner's client is suing.

A final caution for wariness in forming a group practice is to consider carefully value, ethical, and lifestyle differences that may make such a venture impractical. If group members' morals, tidiness, clinical, or business standards vary significantly, conflict likely will arise, and hence should be addressed candidly in early discussions. For some, it may be better to have a solo practice and to maintain one's independence than to have to balance with others.

Some practitioners go into a group practice because they think it will be less intimidating than going it alone. This is poor rationale for selecting a group practice. If this is your hidden agenda, then resolve your anxiety in a more appropriate manner.

A solo practice means total freedom and independence. It means accounting to no other professionals. Whereas group practitioners tend to associate more and more with each other over time, solo practitioners do not develop this "isolating" characteristic. Solo practitioners do need to exercise caution against stagnation. Supervision and networking with colleagues can prevent this from occurring. This broader networking of solo practitioners can result in more professional contacts, which lead to more referrals, more personal growth, and an increased awareness of issues in the community.

Full Versus Part Time

A traditional manner of entering private practice is to begin on a part-time basis, while still working at your full-time job. This approach offers comfort to those who cannot afford to take the risk of living without a paycheck, or those who are squeamish about potentially draining their financial reserves.

There are serious drawbacks to the part-time practice while still employed. It will be very taxing to divide your energy between two jobs. You are likely to feel frustrated and drained. You may begin to neglect yourself and family responsibilities. You will not have time to market your services adequately if some of your energy is directed toward a full-time job. When you are ready to market, other professionals have already gone home for the day. As a result your private practice will not grow quickly, but your frustration will.

Part-time private practice office needs will differ from a full-time practice. Rather than make the financial commitment to an office you will use infrequently, consider subletting a block of time from another professional's office, perhaps another psychotherapist. Evening hours are considered "prime time" for therapy, and are likely to be unavailable. If these are the hours you are wanting to work, you may discover an attorney, physician, or dentist who would be receptive to subletting you space for the times you request. This type of arrangement also could help lead to referrals.

You also may wish to limit your overhead by not hiring a secretary. Either handle your own typing or contract with another therapist's secretary to do your typing and filing of insurance in the evenings or on Saturdays.

You will need to be accessible to your clients and will want to obtain either an answering service or an answering machine. The answering machine can give instructions on how to page you. You will probably need to have a pager in either case, depending on how available you want to be to your clients. You can contract with your clients to be available only during certain hours or at all hours. Be clear about when you are and are not available.

Benefits of starting out part time in a private practice while still holding onto your full-time position include the ability to receive benefits from your employer, such as health insurance, vacation, and sick leave. Depending on your full-time job, you may be able to establish a referral and marketing base. It also gives you the opportunity to "test the waters" to determine whether the private sector appeals to you.

In addition, some therapists may desire only a part-time practice in order to fulfill other roles, such as parenting or other academic or professional interests. If your intention is to keep your practice part time, you will have to struggle at times with the dilemma of turning referrals away. After all, many therapy hours are unavailable due to your full-time practice. Although this will allow you to be more selective about whom you choose as clients, it will be difficult to turn away potential income. Keeping your agenda in focus as to why you selected a part-time practice will decrease the possibility of compromising yourself.

Specialized Versus Generalized Practice

Ours has become a world of specialization. Physicians, attorneys, and dentists specialize. Often, therapists specialize because it allows them to work exclusively with the population they want. In addition, specializing can be a good marketing tool.

The problem with specializing is that it limits the number of potential clients you can acquire. Especially at the beginning of your career, drawing in referrals will consume much of your time. If you choose to begin as a specialist, many, many potential referrals will not be made because you are not viewed as able or willing to work with populations outside your area of specialization.

A therapist needs to be able to deal with a variety of issues, and a general practice helps to develop skill in several areas (as well as to get your practice off the ground a little faster). For instance, although you may be a specialist with sexual abuse, it would be negligent to identify only abuse issues when marital discord, chemical dependency, or codependency issues are also clinically present in your clients. If you are a specialist and identify issues you do not work with, you will need to refer the client to another therapist for work in the identified areas of concern. Some therapists discover that a specialized practice becomes boring and prohibits growth. Others feel that working with the same population and issues continuously provides greater satisfaction.

Buying Versus Starting a New Practice

Selling a psychotherapy practice is uncommon today but does occasionally occur. If a practice is for sale, find out why it is being sold. Be certain to identify what is for sale. This includes two types of assets: tangible and intangible. The tangible assets are those that are easily measurable. Generally, the purchase of someone's practice will include the furniture, equipment, office lease, supplies, mailing lists, marketing files, and any tests the practice owns.

The intangible assets are the goodwill aspects of the practice that are impossible to measure. This includes the practice owner's reputation in the community, how many clients will continue to work with the practice purchaser, how many referral sources will remain loyal to the practice, and any expectations that a percentage of clients will remain with the practice. Be aware that the practice of "buying patients" is neither acceptable to professional organizations nor congruent with professional ethics. Only the goodwill can be sold.

The seller should help the purchaser through introductions to referral sources, other professionals, and local institutions. The seller should keep a copy of all client records, as tax and legal issues could arise years later. Copies of records may be made for the purchaser, if written consent is provided by the seller's clients.

Make sure the selling therapist pays off all debts prior to your purchasing the business. Study the business records for the past several years so you can determine its profitability as well as liabilities. Income tax returns of the principals will also help you to develop an appropriate purchase price. Make certain that all past taxes have been paid.

Consider using an attorney to help develop a contract that will serve your interests. Take nothing for granted. An accountant can go over the records of the practice to determine the value. When offering a contract, you must set a limit and be willing to walk away. If you make an emotional purchase decision, it could be very costly.

It can cost less to purchase someone else's practice than it would cost to start up your own. It will also save you time and effort in starting up, as all or most of the supplies and equipment may already be available. When starting a new practice there is a period of downtime between the time you open your office and the time you bring in clients. Purchasing a practice enables you to have immediate revenue.

Disadvantages of purchasing a practice include the risk of paying too much for unnecessary or dated equipment and furniture in a poor location. Or, if the former therapist had a poor reputation, you run the risk of inheriting it. Finally, the purchasing therapist should have a personal style similar to the seller's (Weitz & Samuels, 1990, p. 389). This will be necessary for client transference.

Most therapists will not buy a practice but will slowly develop their own. The opportunity to acquire another person's practice is rarely available.

When the opportunity to sell does arise, often the seller has difficulty assigning an appropriate price to the practice. The therapist will often set an exhorbitant price due to the emotional attachment that evolved from having put so much energy into developing and maintaining the practice. The price has to be based on objective, rather than subjective, facts. Too often therapists want to charge large amounts for their practices because they see this being done by physicians, dentists, and attorneys.

Therapy differs from other professional practices. Therapists do not have the equipment that medical practices carry. Also, transference issues are a greater issue in psychotherapy. Clients will experience grief, anger, denial, and resistance due to the perceived abandonment from their prior therapist. Therefore, it is likely that the shift of a client from one therapist to another will be more tenuous. Selecting a therapist's practice to purchase whose personality and theoretical style are similar to yours will decrease the likelihood of premature termination from treatment.

Because it is usually salaried individuals who are interested in purchasing a practice, they generally do not have large amounts of cash available. For this reason it may be beneficial to negotiate purchasing a practice through a less conventional payment schedule.

I sold my practice in 1992 when my husband's corporate relocation required us to move from Houston to the Washington, DC area. Realizing that my practice would present too heavy a caseload for an established practitioner, and that a beginning or relocating therapist might lack the funds for such an investment, I sold my practice to a psychiatrist who had a large practice and several therapists working with him.

It is unethical to request a percentage of payment from clients seen by the buyer. No money should be exchanged unless the client experiences some benefit. With this in mind, I designed a contract that included the following elements:

Buyer:

1. Agreed to Seller's fee for the practice. Paid initial part of the fee upon signing the contract. The balance of the fee was to be paid in 10 monthly installments. The amount decided upon was based on reasonable compensation for Seller's reputation in the community, Yellow Pages advertising, telephone number, community knowledge of Seller's telephone number from billboard and other previous marketing, and community referrals.

2. Maintained in strict confidence all files, names, phone numbers, general information, etcetera, provided by Seller's clients or Seller.

Seller:

1. Allowed main business phone line to be taken over by Buyer.
2. Wrote a letter to former clients, seen in the past 12 months, informing them of move and recommending that consideration be given to the Buyer for future therapy. Advised them at the same time that other choices were available should they wish to have information of such options.
3. Introduced Buyer to Seller's current clients.
4. Provided Buyer with names and addresses of current and prior clients.
5. Provided Buyer with a brief summary of current clients, after obtaining a written consent for release of information from the clients.
6. Spent one-half day with Buyer discussing marketing strategies and techniques.
7. Introduced Seller's referral sources to Buyer.
8. Shared Seller's list of managed care contracts with Buyer.
9. Wrote letter to managed care companies explaining that the Buyer and his group practice would be seeing Seller's clients.
10. Provided Buyer with copies of presentations to the community Seller had made.

I held my last session in the buyer's office to ease the transition for my clients going to a new location for therapy. Both the buyer and I found this contract to be reasonable and fair. I chose not to incur legal fees by having the contract drawn up legally. Instead, I knowingly selected an individual with high ethics and whom I felt confident would be consistent and fair with maintaining the contract.

Type of Business Organization

Your practice can take a variety of forms, based on size and your goals. Each offers different benefits to the psychotherapist.

■ Sole Proprietorship

A sole proprietorship is the simplest form of business. One person, or one couple, has exclusive ownership and exercises all control over legal, financial, and organizational decisions. Many therapists like this arrangement because it allows them to be free from regulation and to receive all the business profits.

Drawbacks include having unlimited exposure of loss to creditors for both your business and personal assets. A sole proprietorship also can be a lonely and isolated method of practice. You may not have access to other individuals' input and experience in making business decisions.

■ General Partnership

A partnership is comprised of two or more therapists who come together and divide responsibility for the business. Partnerships offer each partner lower start-up costs, additional sources of revenue, and more ideas than does a sole practitioner form. It is relatively simple to form, only requiring a registration. It offers possible tax advantages and limited outside regulation. A partnership can enable people of various skills and strengths to pull together and compliment each other's strengths.

It is important to have a written partnership agreement spelling out the following:

- Who are the partners?
- What are the objectives of the partnership?
- What will the draw and expense accounts be?
- Who can sign checks?
- Who is responsible for the books and records?
- Will the partnership buy insurance (discussed in Chapter 3)?
- How much money will each partner contribute?
- How much time will each partner contribute?
- How will profits be distributed?
- What are procedures for adding a new partner?
- What are procedures for terminating a partner?
- What are procedures for handling the business in the event a partner becomes ill, unable to practice, or dies?
- What are procedures for changing the agreement and settling arguments?

One limitation of a partnership is that each partner is personally responsible for the other's business liabilities. One person no longer has total control over the business, but must share responsibility for decision making with others. You need to have the interpersonal skills to relate and work through conflicts with a partner. Finally, it can be hard to find partners with whom you are comfortable. There is a potential for time-consuming decision-making processes, should partners not share similar goals and expectations for the business.

All income is taxable. One's income is taxed as personal income of the partners. You must pay employment and local taxes, even though the partnership itself will not be paying income taxes.

Partnerships are terminated when an additional partner is brought in or when a partner withdraws or dies. Your attorney should draw up a contract identifying what to do in the event that partners choose to terminate their partnership due to disagreements, sale of practice, or death of a partner.

■ Professional Corporation

Corporations come in two forms: C corporations and S corporations. Unlike the sole proprietorship and general partnership, the professional corporation (PC) has a legal existence of its own, separate from its owners. It may sell stock, borrow money, and lend money. Ownership is transferable. Professional corporations are closely regulated and must follow rigid rules in terms of charter restrictions, broad record keeping, day-to-day operations, bookkeeping, paperwork, and clinical time.

Benefits of being incorporated include owners being able to be hired as employees, thereby reducing the corporate income taxes. Except in an S corporation, medical and dental expenses can be deducted. Life and disability insurance premiums can be disbursed by the corporation with pretax dollars for the therapist. If you are considering significant expansion and needing financing from banks, it may be easier to obtain loans if you are incorporated.

Despite wild claims made by some individuals, creating a professional corporation does not mean extravagant purchases, such as vacations and artwork, can be made without adequate justification for your practice. Nor does getting incorporated automatically offer tax advantages. The tax rate is higher than for other forms of organization, and without good planning, the earnings may be taxed twice. Tax savings may not be sufficient to warrant the numerous organizational costs of legal incorporation and filing fees together with annual franchise taxes in most jurisdictions.

One's personal assets are protected from general creditors of the corporation but not from professional liability claims. Malpractice suits can be filed against the owner and the corporation.

Corporations typically take only a few weeks to establish. You will need to fill the positions of company officers, such as chairman of the board, vice president, secretary, and treasurer. But you can elect yourself to fill all of these positions.

To help advise you in selecting the best form of professional organization for yourself, be sure to consult with a certified public accountant and an attorney who is familiar with the field of psychotherapy. You can also become more familiar with corporations by obtaining the free booklet from the IRS, *Tax Information on S Corporations,* booklet #589.

THREE

Setting Up Your Business

A business is like an intricate recipe: Leave out one ingredient and the end product is negatively affected. Consider the ingredients carefully and learn how they are necessary parts to the whole product. There is nothing small about setting up a small business. The amount of consideration you give to the many details required for establishing your practice will be directly correlated with future success or failure.

Credentials

A variety of advanced training programs offer the education and credentials necessary to enter a private practice. There usually is a requirement that the graduate pass a professional certifying examination(s) before putting up a "shingle" to practice independently. In addition, most states require either licensing or credentialing, documented professional activities, or demonstrable skills prior to recognizing an individual's right to practice independent of an agency. Licensing requirements, reflecting minimum standards a practitioner must meet to enter private practice, vary from state to state. Typically, one is required to have a specific education, degree, practice experience, and pass state competency exams to qualify for a license. States that do not offer licensing often have certification requirements similar to licensing. (For a list of certifying state offices for counselors, marriage and family therapists, psychologists, and social workers, see Figure 3.1.) Opening a private practice prior to meeting these requirements, which often takes a couple of years after graduation, can result in either an inability to receive third-party payments

(text continued on page 28)

Below is a list of telephone numbers of certifying bodies in each state for professional counselors, marriage and family therapists, psychologists, and social workers.

PROFESSIONAL COUNSELORS

Alabama Board of Examiners in
Counseling
(205) 934-0498

Committee of the Arizona Board
Behavioral Health Examiners
(602) 542-1882

Arkansas Board of Examiners in
Counseling
(501) 235-4057

California Board of Behavioral
Science Examiners
(916) 455-4933

Colorado State Board of Licensed
Professional Counselor Examiners
(303) 894-7766

Delaware Board of Professional
Counselors
(302) 739-4522

Florida Department of Professional
Regulation Mental Health
Counselors
(904) 487-2520

Georgia Composite Board of
Professional Counselors, Social
Workers, and Marriage and Family
Therapists
(404) 656-3989

Idaho Bureau of Occupational
Licensure
(208) 334-3233

Kansas Behavioral Sciences
Regulatory Board
(913) 296-3240

Louisiana Board of Examiners
(504) 922-1499

Maine Board of Counseling
Professionals
(207) 582-8723

Maryland Department of Mental
Health/Hygiene Professional
Counselors
(301) 764-4732

Massachusetts MACD Licensure/
Government Relations
(617) 338-1053

Michigan Office of Health Services
(517) 373-1870

Mississippi State Board of
Examiners for Licensed
Professional Counselors
(601) 325-8182

Missouri Committee for Professional
Counselors
(314) 751-0018

Montana Board of Social Work
Examiners and Professional
Counselors
(406) 444-4285

Nebraska Bureau of Examining
Boards
(402) 471-2115

North Carolina Registered Practicing
Counselors
(919) 737-2244

North Dakota Board of Counselor
Examiners
(701) 235-5891

Ohio Counselor and Social Worker
Board
(614) 466-6463

Oklahoma Licensed Professional
Counselors Committee
(405) 271-6030

Oregon Board of Licensed Professional Counselors and Therapists
(503) 378-5499

Figure 3.1. Certified Bodies

Rhode Island Division of
Professional Regulation
(401) 277-2827

South Carolina Board of Examiners
in Counseling
(803) 734-1765

South Dakota Board of Counselor
Examiners
(605) 224-7172

Tennessee State Board of
Professional Counselors and
Marital and Family Therapists
(615) 367-6207

Texas State Board of Examiners for
Professional Counselors
(512) 459-2900

Vermont CCMHC Advisory Board
1-800-439-8683; (802) 838-2390
(callers in Vermont)

Virginia Board of Professional
Counselors
(804) 662-9912

Washington Department of Health/
Professional Licensing Services
(206) 753-1761

West Virginia Board of Examiners
in Counseling
(304) 345-3852

Wyoming Mental Health Professions
Licensure Board
(307) 777-6529

*MARRIAGE AND FAMILY
THERAPISTS*

Arizona Board of Behavioral Health
Examiners
(602) 542-1882

California Board of Behavioral
Science Examiners
(916) 445-4933

Colorado Board of Marriage and
Family Therapy Examiners
(303) 894-7766

Connecticut Marriage and Family
Therapy Certification
(203) 566-1039

Florida Board of Clinical Social Work,
Marriage and Family Therapy, and
Mental Health Counseling
(904) 487-2520

Georgia Board of Professional
Counselors, Social Workers, and
Marriage and Family Therapists
(404) 656-3989

Indiana Health Professions Bureau
(317) 232-2960

Iowa Public Health Department
(515) 281-3231

Kansas Behavioral Sciences
Regulatory Board
(913) 296-3240

Maine Professional and Financial
Regulation Department
(207) 582-8700

Massachusetts Board of Allied
Mental Health
(617) 727-1716

Michigan Marriage Counseling
Board Department of Licensing
and Regulation
(517) 373-1699

Minnesota Board of Marriage and
Family Therapy
(612) 643-2580

Nevada Board of Marriage and
Family Therapist Examiners
(702) 486-7388

New Hampshire Board of Psychology and Mental Health Practice
(603) 226-2599

New Jersey Board of Marriage
Counselor Examiners
(201) 648-2534   *New mexico*

North Carolina Marriage and Family
Therapy Certification Board
(919) 760-4536

Figure 3.1. (Continued)

Oklahoma Marriage and Family
Therapy Licensing Department
of Health
(405) 271-5585

Oregon Board of Professional
Counselors and Therapists
(503) 378-5499

Rhode Island Board of Marriage
and Family Therapists Division
of Professional Regulation
(401) 277-2827

South Carolina Board of Examiners
for Counselors and Therapists
(803) 734-1765

Tennessee Board of Certification
for Professional Counselors
and Marriage and Family
Therapists
(615) 367-620

Texas Health Department Licensing
and Certification Bureau
(512) 834-6657

Utah Division of Occupational and
Professional Licensing
(801) 530-6628

Washington Professional Licensing
Services
(206) 753-6936

Wisconsin Association for Marriage
and Family Therapy
(414) 784-6858

Wyoming Professional Licensing
Board
(307) 777-6529

PSYCHOLOGISTS

Alabama Board of Examiners in
Psychology
(205) 242-4127

Alaska Department of Commerce
and Economic Development
(907) 465-2551

Arizona Board of Psychology
Examiners
(602) 542-3095

Arkansas Department of Professional
Regulation Board of Examiners in
Psychology
(501) 682-6167

California Board of Psychology
(916) 920-6383

Colorado Board of Psychologists
Examiners
(303) 894-7766

Connecticut Department of Health
Services
(203) 566-1039

Delaware Board of Examiners of
Psychologists
(302) 739-4796

District of Columbia Board of
Psychologist Examiners
(202) 727-7823/24

Florida Board of Psychological
Examiners
(904) 922-6728

Georgia Board of Examiners of Psychologists State Examining Board
(404) 656-3933

Hawaii Department of Commerce
and Consumer Affairs
(808) 586-2702

Idaho Bureau of Occupational
Licenses
(208) 334-3233

Illinois Clinical Psychologists
Licensing and Disciplinary
Committee
(217) 785-0872

Indiana State Psychology Board
(317) 232-2960

Iowa Board of Psychology Examiners Professional Licensure
(515) 281-4401

Figure 3.1. (Continued)

Kansas Behavioral Science Regulatory Board
(913) 296-3240

Kentucky State Board of Psychology
(502) 564-3296

Louisiana Board of Examiners of Psychologists
(504) 293-2238

Maine Department of Business, Occupational, and Professional Regulation
(207) 582-8723

Maryland Board of Examiners of Psychologists
(410) 764-4787

Massachusetts Board of Registration of Psychologists
(617) 727-9925

Michigan Board of Psychology Department of Licensing and Regulation
(517) 373-3596

Minnesota Board of Psychology
(612) 642-0587

Mississippi Board of Psychological Examiners
(601) 353-8871

Missouri State Committee of Psychologists
(314) 751-0099

Montana Board of Psychologists
(406) 444-5436

Nebraska Board of Examining Psychologists
(402) 471-2115

Nevada Board of Psychological Examiners
(702) 688-1268

New Hampshire Board of Examiners of Psychology
(603) 226-2599

New Jersey Board of Psychological Examiners
(201) 504-6470

New Mexico Board of Psychologists Examiners
(505) 827-7163

New York Board for Psychology
(518) 474-3866

North Carolina State Board of Examiners of Practicing Psychologists
(704) 262-2258

North Dakota Board of Psychologist Examiners
(701) 663-2321 ext. 202

Ohio State Board of Psychology
(614) 466-8808

Oklahoma Board of Examiners of Psychologists
(405) 271-6118

Oregon Board of Psychologist Examiners
(503) 378-4154

Pennsylvania State Board of Psychology
(717) 783-7155

Rhode Island Board of Psychology
(401) 277-2827

South Carolina Board of Examiners in Psychology
(803) 253-6313

South Dakota Board of Examiners of Psychologists
(605) 642-1600

Tennessee Board of Examiners in Psychology
(615) 367-6291

Texas Board of Examiners of Psychologists
(512) 835-2036

Utah Psychology Examining Committee
(801) 530-6628

Figure 3.1. (Continued)

Vermont Board of Psychological
  Examiners
  (802) 828-2373

Virginia Board of Psychology
  (804) 662-9913

Washington Examining Board of
  Psychology
  (206) 753-3095

West Virginia Board of Examiners of
  Psychologists
  (304) 366-5170

Wisconsin Psychology Examining
  Board
  (608) 266-0257

Wyoming Board of Psychologist
  Examiners
  (307) 777-6529

SOCIAL WORKERS

Alabama State Board of Social Work
  Examiners
  (205) 242-5860

Alaska Board of Clinical Social
  Work Examiners
  (907) 465-2551

Arizona Board of Behavioral Health
  Examiners
  (602) 542-1882

Arkansas Social Work Licensing
  Board
  (501) 372-5071

California Board of Behavioral
  Science Examiners
  (916) 445-4933

Colorado State Board of Social Work
  Examiners
  (303) 894-7766

Connecticut Department of Health
  Services
  (203) 566-1039

Delaware Board of Social Work
  Examiners
  (302) 739-4522

District of Columbia Board of Social
  Work
  (202) 727-7454

Florida Board of Clinical Social Work,
  Marriage and Family Therapy, and
  Mental Health Counseling
  (904) 487-2520

Georgia Composite Board of Professional Counselors, Social Workers,
  and Marriage and Family
  Therapists
  (404) 656-3989

Hawaii Department of Commerce and
  Consumer Affairs
  200 N. Vineyard Street,
  Honolulu, HI 96817

Idaho Bureau of Occupational
  Licensing
  (208) 334-3233

Illinois Social Workers Examining
  and Disciplinary Board
  (217) 785-0877

Indiana Social Work Certification
  and Marriage and Family
  Therapist Credentialing Board
  (317) 232-2960

Iowa Board of Social Work Examiners
  (515) 242-5937

Kansas Behavioral Sciences Regulatory Board
  (913) 296-3240

Kentucky State Board of Examiners
  of Social Work
  (502) 564-3296

Louisiana State Board of Certified
  Social Work Examiners
  (504) 673-3010

Maine State Board of Social Work
  Licensing
  (207) 582-8723

Maryland State Board of Social Work
  Examiners
  (410) 764-4788

Figure 3.1. (Continued)

Massachusetts Board of Registration
of Social Workers
(617) 727-3074

Michigan Board of Examiners of
Social Workers
(517) 373-1653

Minnesota Board of Social Work
(612) 643-2580

Mississippi State Board of Health
(601) 987-4154

Missouri Advisory Committee for
Licensed Clinical Social Workers
(314) 751-0018

Montana Board of Social Work
Examiners and Professional
Counselors
(406) 444-4285

Nebraska Board of Examiners in
Social Work
(402) 471-2115

Nevada Board of Examiners of
Social Workers
(702) 784-1555

New Hampshire Board of Examiners
of Psychologists
(603) 226-2599

New Mexico Board of Social Work
Examiners
(505) 827-7167

New York State Board for Social
Work
1-800-342-3729

North Carolina Certification Board
for Social Work
(919) 625-1679

North Dakota Board of Social Work
Examiners
(701) 222-0255

Ohio Counselor and Social Worker
Board
(614) 466-0912

Oklahoma State Board of Licensed
Social Workers
(405) 946-7230

Oregon State Board of Clinical
Social Workers
(503) 378-5735

Pennsylvania State Board of Social
Work Examiners
(717) 783-1389

Rhode Island Department of Human
Services
(410) 464-2121

South Carolina Board of Social Work
Examiners
(803) 765-2214

South Dakota Department of Commerce and Consumer Affairs
(605) 642-1600

Tennessee Board of Social Worker
Certification and Licensing
(615) 367-6207

Texas Council for Social Work
Certification W-403
(512) 450-3255

Utah Division of Occupational and
Professional Licensing
(801) 530-6628

State of Vermont
Secretary of State
(802) 828-2363

Virginia Board of Social Work
(804) 662-9914

Washington Social Work
Certification Advisory Committee
(206) 753-1761

West Virginia Board of Social Work
Examiners
(304) 348-8816

Wyoming Mental Health Professions
Licensing Board
(307) 777-6529

Figure 3.1. (Continued)

from clients' insurance companies or censorship from one's professional organization.

Financial Status

The first step is to make an honest appraisal of your current financial situation. Many people who leave their jobs and set up their own businesses make a mistake when analyzing what they will need to earn. You will need to be able to live at least 6 months without drawing a salary. In addition, you will need to set aside money for your start-up costs.

To calculate start-up costs, consider your monthly operating expenses: rent, heat/electricity, legal and accounting services, supplies, advertising, telephone, insurance, salaries, and quarterly taxes. One-time expenses will include security deposits for the telephone, gas, electric, and rent. Depending where you rent office space, you may need to figure in renovation costs.

Office supplies need to be anticipated. These include stationery, business cards, appointment cards, postage, pens, and so on, along with a minimum amount of equipment needed to run an effective office. This may include a computer (with accompanying software and printer), a typewriter, telephones, a photocopier, a filing cabinet with a lock for client records, a dictaphone for transcriptions, a tape recorder, and a pager. Either you will need to contract with an answering service or have an answering machine. You also will need to have a reserve fund for unexpected situations and emergencies.

Consider the season in which you plan to start up. Traditionally, summer and the period between Thanksgiving and Christmas are slow for therapists. You can anticipate needing more money during those periods to carry you. Also, you will not be paid for vacations, holidays, or sick days.

If you are borrowing money from family and friends to start your new business, write up a loan agreement with them specifying the plans for a fair repayment schedule. A written contract gets you accustomed to managing your business in a professional manner. Be explicit about the conditions of the agreement. Although some relatives may not charge you interest, be aware that the IRS may consider that loaning money below the prevailing interest rate constitutes a gift. The lender may then have to pay a gift tax. Some people may consider turning to their parents for a loan. Borrowing money from family can be emotionally traumatic if certain issues are not addressed.

First, realize that loans with family will always have strings attached. Unlike the emotionally unattached investment of a bank, parents may give overt or covert advice, judgment, and monitoring. They will see the purchases you make or the vacations you go on and challenge them more diligently than would the bank. After all, the bank does not walk through your home and see the new wall-to-wall carpeting or your holiday plans for Bermuda . . . with what they may consider "their money" (Hyatt, 1990).

No matter how well intentioned, parents cannot be emotionally detached from their loan. You are their child, regardless of your age, and they will view you as a child rather than a professional psychotherapist. Dependencies on parents that were broken long ago may be reestablished. You may begin to feel responsible for your parents' livelihood. You may experience guilt about taking from your parents' nest egg. Families have ended up forever fractured by such loans (Hyatt, 1990). You may want to rethink the cost of dealing with bank interest rates or save up the necessary money yourself rather than borrow from family. Remember, bank loans may be less than they appear because the interest may be a tax-deductible expense.

The "cleanest" method of starting a private practice is to use your own funds. This can be accomplished by careful budgeting and saving earnings from your previous, salaried position.

Policy and Procedure Manual

A policy and procedure manual will provide you with guidance in working consistently and effectively with partner or employee situations that typically occur in a private practice. Policies reflect your general plans on meeting your goals. They will help you in making decisions about situations that have no clear procedures. Policies help reduce frustrations and promote consistency in the day-to-day basic business functions. Procedures are the specific day-to-day rules. The manual should be written in simple, concise language so it is easily understood and not likely to be misinterpreted by different readers.

As time progresses, amendments to the original policies and procedures will need to be written. Be certain that everyone in the office is aware of the revisions. In many states therapists can be held liable for the actions of their employees if policies and procedures for handling clients and their material—bills or appointments or records—are not spelled out in writing.

Two main areas should be incorporated in the policy and procedure manual: employee and partner. The employee section will include the following areas.

Equal opportunity employment practices—Guidelines pertaining to affirmative action, fair employment, and policy not to discriminate in recruitment, hiring, compensation, or promotion.

Probationary period—Purpose, length of time, and what if any benefits will be accrued.

Attendance—Working hours, breaks, absenteeism, tardiness, notification of illness.

Benefits—Sick leave, paid holidays, annual leave, personal leave days, bereavement leave, group insurance, jury duty, maternity or paternity leave.

Withholdings and deductions—Including withholding taxes, Social Security taxes, and insurances.

Disciplinary action—Description of course of action to be taken. This may include a verbal warning, written admonishment, suspension, final written warning, and termination.

Resignation/termination—How much notice is expected for the employee to give the employer in the event of a resignation. How much notice the employer is to give the employee in the event of a termination. Identify the causes for immediate termination.

Overtime—How it will be calculated.

The handling of clients and their materials—The fact that a client is seeing a therapist is in and of itself confidential in a number of states. How and to whom any information about a client's relationship to the practice is given must be spelled out in writing.

The partner section will include the following items:

Cross-coverage—Describe the expectations of each therapist in terms of covering another therapist's clients. Detail how payment is dispersed.

Assignment of referrals made to the practice—May be made on a rotating basis among therapists.

Emergencies—Detailed plan for handling emergencies with clients.

Financial—How income and office expenses will be divided.

Selecting an Office Location

Regardless of what type of office you establish, consider selecting a location convenient to your clients. Decide whom your clients will be. If you plan to obtain clients from managed care contracts, consult the managed care companies to determine what geographical areas need to be served. If you plan to market yourself heavily to professionals, consider locating your office near their offices, perhaps in the same building. If you plan to work primarily with families, consider locating an office near residential or neighborhood shopping areas. Safety concerns for the therapist, staff, and clients need to be assessed. Consider the lighting, security, availability of other people, access to parking, and the time of day you will be practicing when selecting a location.

Subleasing

For those who want to establish a private practice on a slower, more cautious path, subleasing already existing office space may be an attractive option. There are three ways to pay for sublet space. The first is to pay a set amount each month. A second method is to pay per session, which is particularly attractive for small or beginning practices. Finally, one may pay a percentage of the gross income. Under this structure, consider a floating percentage that decreases as your gross increases. The percentage payment can become expensive, and may even be considered by some to be fee-splitting. It needs to be closely evaluated for its potential ethicalness and financial outlay. Do consider, however, the attractiveness of not being charged for periods of absence, such as vacations.

Office location decisions must be made with great consideration, as it is expensive and embarrassing to move too frequently. If you plan to sublease an office you will need to ask the following questions: What are the charges? Are secretarial services included? If not, are they available, and at what cost? What hours are available for subleasing? What if there is an emergency and you need to use the office during "off" hours? Who else might be using the office that you or your clients will have contact with? Is parking available? Is the environment safe? Be cautious of selecting an office location simply because the rent is cheap! It may cost you more in the long run.

Home Office

To be conservative about spending money or to be able to postpone renting an office until your needs are better established, you may wish to consider a home office. An office in your home offers a variety of unique problems and bonuses. In the comfort of a familiar setting, you can slowly become versed in business practices and test your business skills.

If you plan to use your home, first check into the zoning laws in your community. Whereas some states permit a professional to practice anywhere without regard to regulations, violation of zoning laws can result in your business being shut down quickly and you desperately casting about for a new location. Contact your city hall or county offices for specific zoning regulations.

Set aside a room in your home to use exclusively for your practice. This may enable you the option of declaring a tax deduction for the room and a proportionate amount from your telephone, gas, electric, and other expenses related to your business. Preferably the room should be close to the entry door with a bathroom nearby. Bedrooms should not be in proximity as they may create sexual confusion for certain patients.

In using your home you need to consider the patient population and potential risk to you both in the loss of privacy and possible safety. A therapist loses his or her privacy when clients can assess the value of household items and declare that they must be paying the therapist too much, or intrude into areas of the house that are personal. Angry clients can also go into the bathroom and use items in the medicine cabinet to harm themselves as an expression of anger at the therapist. Acting-out borderlines, enraged spouses, or addicted clients will know where you live. The screening of clients is critical if you have an office in your home.

Recognize that it may be stressful for your family to have you home more often. It may be distracting for you to have the doorbell ring during a session because a delivery is being made, or to hear the children bickering upstairs. Invest in good soundproofing, or consider converting your garage into an office. This enables you to avoid some of these problems and secure a more private environment for your practice. It also will separate your business from your home somewhat, affording a more professional presentation. A home office also may reduce your family stress. If you have an elderly family member or child at home who requires intermittent attention, having a home office could be an attractive alternative.

Some clients and colleagues will view your home office as less professional. If you use your home as your office, consider using a P.O. box for an address. A separate business telephone line will help to provide a boundary between your personal and professional life and will prevent confusion on your part as to how to answer the telephone after work hours. In addition, a business listing will permit you to have a listing in the Yellow Pages. It will also provide you with a listing with the directory assistance operator, further professionalizing your practice.

Be considerate of your neighbors. This includes assuring that your clients do not habitually park in front of their homes and do not leave trash on their lawns. If you are generating too much traffic your neighbors are likely to complain.

Check with your insurance company before opening a private practice in your home. If you submit a claim based on your business and they were not aware of your practice, they may disallow the claim. Often, business pursuits endorsements are available for your homeowner's insurance at a reasonable cost (Richards, 1990, p. 63).

Before deducting expenses and depreciation on part of your home for income tax purposes, assess the real estate market in which you live. If your office is in your home and your home appreciates in value, you will need to pay capital gains tax on the percentage of the house that you were deducting for your office. It will be well worth your time to discuss this matter with an accountant before making expensive mistakes. The accountant may even advise you not to declare the home office deduction on your income tax.

Negotiating a Lease

Once you have found an office that appears suitable to your needs, it is advisable to have an attorney review the lease. Specific questions you may need to address include: Is this rent reasonable for the area? Is there adequate parking for you and your clients and staff? What restrictions exist in the lease that could impact on your practice? Do you have the freedom to sublease or take in additional therapists? What are the options for renewing the lease? What services are included in the lease for office and building cleaning? What provisions are made for security, both during normal working hours and in the evenings and on weekends? Who are your neighbors, what are their businesses, and will their noise level or clients affect you? What are the building hours, and how will that affect you in the event you wish to have early morning, late evening, or weekend appointments? Will electricity, air conditioning, and heat be available after hours? What soundproofing has been installed and is it adequate? If changes to the office space are made, who pays for them? What flexibility do you have to change the interior of your office? What additional expenses can be passed through to you and is there a cap on such charges?

If the space is too big for your purposes but you like it otherwise, ask the landlord to close off offices you will not be using and for which you will not be paying. If your landlord refuses to do this, consider converting the spare office into a play area for children, and fill it with children's toys.

If you are acquiring someone else's office, make sure the lease is transferable. Once again, have an attorney review the lease to "judgment proof" your decision.

■ Leasing Office Space

When shopping for an office, consider selecting an office building with other professionals. You may develop referrals from other sources in the building and it provides a better environment for your clients.

Security is of utmost importance, too, especially because many "off" hours are used to see clients. Good security consists of adequate lighting, having other people around, and locked building doors at night. Security is likely to be provided for in an office building with other professionals. If your office is not on the ground floor, make sure the building has an elevator suitable for wheelchair accessibility.

Once you have selected potential office space to lease, spend time watching traffic walking and driving by at different times of the day. Does it get too congested? Is it isolated? What is the parking availability? How well lit is it at night? How accessible is the office during peak traffic hours? How easy is it to find?

Assess the office based on your immediate as well as future needs. You might want to change the adjoining wall separating two offices at a later date so one office may be enlarged to function better as a group room and the smaller office to serve as a play room or storage room. You might want to improve the soundproofing, carpeting, or wallpaper or add plumbing for a bathroom. If so, negotiate the cost for these improvements, and spread the cost throughout the term of the lease.

If you already own office furniture, draw a diagram of the office and fill it in with your furniture. A spectacular office may be wrong for you if your furniture does not properly fit, or if it does not accommodate the colors. It may end up costing you considerable amounts of money in replacement furniture or may compromise the effect you are attempting to create in the office.

■ Leasing a Second Office

If you are considering leasing a second office, it is probably because you have been successful and wish to expand. Or, because you are in a small, perhaps rural, community and feel the need to have two offices located miles apart. Or, you want to practice in a geographical area that will bring in managed care referrals.

Take into consideration advertising costs when selecting a second location. If the second office is in a significantly different location, any of the advertising you do—newspaper, direct mail, billboards, etcetra.—will need to be duplicated.

Investigate the competition prior to committing yourself to the second office. Be realistic about the work you need to commit in marketing. Remember, your reputation probably will not carry over to the new location.

Office Construction

Carefully review plans for any modifications to the office space. Be sure to emphasize the need for adequate soundproofing because this need differs from many other types of offices. I know of one therapist who felt so confident with her contractor that she did not review the construction plans carefully. As a result, she ended up with offices that had walls that stopped approximately 5 inches from the ceiling. The contractor had done this to improve air circulation (a very common practice), but it proved to be a disaster for conducting therapy sessions. The result was hard feelings between the psychotherapist and the contractor and construction costs that greatly exceeded her initial contract.

Most therapists would not wish to consider exploring the possibility of building or buying an office building until they are very well established. Owning your office can prove to be economical over the long run, once tax benefits are factored in. Should you wish to consider such an option, be careful to select a good location, and one that will help the building hold its value over the years and continue to present a professional image. Get recommendations on which professionals to contract with from other therapists who have had their offices built. Be sure to have an attorney involved with reviewing the contract.

Soundproofing

Soundproofing is essential for a professional practice. Not only is it uncomfortable for people in the waiting room to be able to hear others in their sessions, but it is a breach of confidentiality not to protect your client's privacy.

Central air conditioning conflicts with soundproofing. You can either opt for the wall unit air conditioner or put extra soundproofing in the walls between interviewing and waiting rooms to compensate for the sound that will travel with central air conditioning. A radio playing at a low volume in the waiting room will help drown out voices by providing "white noise." Carpeting will absorb noises better than hardwood or tile floors. Select solid doors for maximum sound insulation and install dusters on the bottom of the doors to aid in soundproofing.

Furnishings and Equipment

The way you furnish an office defines the type of practice you have. The office demeanor begins in the parking lot. The therapist's counseling organization's name, therapist's name and credentials, and suite number should be listed in the directory provided by management at the entry of the building. The front door of the office should list the name and credentials of each therapist practicing in the office.

■ Waiting Room

Clients and referral sources will develop further impressions based on what they see when walking into your waiting room. Above all, it should be tidy, bright, and inviting. A cleaning service is necessary as a busy therapist, despite best intentions, will not keep an office clean and neat. Have magazines that reflect your patient population.

Because I treat men, women, and adolescents, I have a variety of magazines that will appeal to each group. I like human interest magazines, which are calming for "borderlines." Have soft, nonoffensive, relaxing music playing from a radio. Offer complimentary coffee and soft drinks.

Business cards, brochures, and fliers announcing activities of the therapists in the office should be neatly displayed in the waiting room. Easy access to these enhances the likelihood of clients picking one up to take to a friend. Clients are not the only people who have access to your waiting room. Salespeople as well as delivery and repair people will walk into your waiting room. Having catchy, colorful fliers in the waiting room helped me one day when a repairman picked up a flier about my women's therapy group. He took it home to his wife, who later called me for an appointment. His wife joined my group and later told me that she had not known whom to call for help. Hang your diplomas, or framed articles you have written, in the lobby to further establish your credibility. These will provide comfort to your clients that you have the credentials to help them with their problems.

Have two signs made that state "Make checks payable to [your name or name of your agency]," and "Payments due when services are rendered. Thank you." Place one on the secretary's desk and attach the other to the wall. Not having ashtrays will help deter unwanted smoking, but if desired, add a third sign, "Thank you for not smoking."

I have a strong nonsmoking policy in my office. I find smoking to be offensive and a fire hazard. Clinically, I would rather see the patient deal with stress more appropriately in treatment. I have never lost a client due to my nonsmoking policy.

■ Furniture

The secretarial area requires a large desk with locks on all drawers. Locks are particularly important as this desk is often exposed to clients. Checks and confidential papers are usually kept in the secretary's desk and need protection. The desk needs to be arranged so papers and the computer screen cannot be read by a client entering, waiting in, or leaving the office. Your secretary will need a desk long and wide enough to accommodate a typewriter and/or computer, dictaphone, calculator, telephones, message holder, and other miscellaneous items. A calculator needs to have a printout tape, should calculations require attachment to a receipt or records. Sometimes the photocopier is located near the secretary's desk. You may wish to have a file cabinet behind this desk to accommodate easy access to frequently used files and supplies. Storing supplies out of view creates a neater and more organized appearance than if they are kept in the secretarial area. When selecting a file cabinet, purchase for your long-term needs. Anticipate that your files will increase in number. It will prove to be more economical than adding a second file cabinet later on. Be certain to select locking file cabinets for security.

If the waiting-room size permits, purchase a cabinet upon which your business cards can be displayed. Ideally, this piece of furniture will have sliding doors to a bottom cabinet, which you can fill with children's toys. These are good stress reducers for children.

If you are inexperienced in furnishing an office, consult an interior decorator. Select furniture that will feel comfortable to the client population with whom you will be working. For example, a therapist working solely with adults may include antiques, oriental rugs, and ornate furniture that would be uncomfortable to children. A therapist working solely with women may use pastels in decorating that may feel uncomfortable to some men.

Only use quality furniture. It will look more professional and hold up over time. If start-up funds are restricted, consider renting furniture with an option to buy. A nice feature with rental is that as you change your likes and dislikes or needs, a rental company will be able to accommodate you. Another option is to purchase used furniture, often obtainable from other professionals.

The clinical offices should include a small desk or table for writing notes at the end of the session. The chairs should be far enough apart to avoid physical contact, and at a right angle to each other so clients do not have to have eye contact with one another. The therapist's chair should be the one closest to the door to allow for quick exit, if ever needed. Any therapist who has had a raging, potentially violent client standing between himself or herself and the door will appreciate the dangerous and powerless position a therapist can be in. Also, having the therapist's chair by the door allows the therapist to open the door easily for the client at the end of the interview. Clients will perceive this as caring and protective. Just be careful not to block a client's path to the door. A sofa also should be included, which will allow for couples to sit closely. Endtables offer a place for a client to put a drink or for you to leave brochures of events you will be presenting (Figure 3.2).

Identify the largest number of clients you would likely have at one time and prepare seating for that number. If space is at a premium, consider purchasing comfortable folding chairs, which can be stored away until needed.

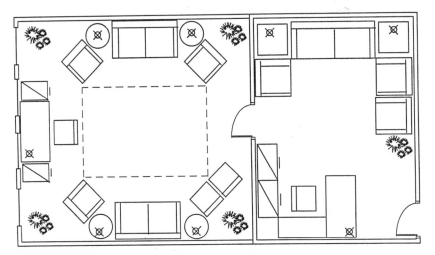

Figure 3.2. Professional Office and Reception Area
SCALE: 1/4" = 1.0'
DRAWN BY: DDD

I have an adolescent therapy group that usually numbers around 7 or 8 teenagers. This is comfortable for my office, which holds 9 people. At one time the size of my group grew to 15 teenagers. I realized that I would have as much success at getting them into my office as squeezing them into a telephone booth. Finally, I realized that because the group was held in the evening, I could send my secretary home a little early and hold the group in the office waiting room. It worked beautifully. We had the necessary privacy and the teens each had a chair and enough space between them. Sometimes you have to use creative problem solving!

Periodically step back and look at your office to assure yourself that it is projecting the general appearance you want. If it appears messy, it will convey a message about your therapy. If it is overcrowded, it will communicate a message of you being overwhelmed.

■ Professional Materials

Depending on your selected professional area, you may need professional materials. These may include toys, testing equipment, or psychological tests. Store toys out of view of small children, as they may prove to be a distraction. If you are a psychologist providing psychological testing, you will need to consider what tests you will want to purchase.

■ Lighting

Lighting should be comfortably bright. Some people are very uncomfortable and feel exposed in overly bright lighting. Low light may be interpreted as seductive or impair some people's vision. Because you will be spending much of your day in the office, select lighting that is comfortable for you. Some people get headaches from fluorescent lighting, which is used by most offices. Having alternative lighting, such as lamps, may be preferable.

■ Cleaning Service

Most buildings include cleaning services in the contract for office space. It is important to have clean offices, as your clients will interpret sloppy offices to mean sloppy work. If you contract with a cleaning service, they will come in nightly to vacuum, dust, and empty trash cans. Set up the hours when your office will be cleaned. Janitors and cleaning crews are very jarring if they arrive during a late evening or Saturday session.

■ Telephone System

When selecting a telephone system choose one that is user friendly with features that will make your business day a little easier and more comfortable. Get a telephone with features for last number dialed (LND) and automatic redial of busy numbers. This is important for calling insurance companies, which often are busy, busy, busy. Develop a sensitivity for your future needs so as to avoid purchasing items that will serve you for only a short time. Consider purchasing a telephone that has options for more lines than you currently need. The secretary may need to keep one line on hold with an insurance company but be able to answer other lines. Therapists and clients are rarely at a loss for words on the telephone and may tie up lines for periods of time.

You do not want your clients or potential clients to experience a busy signal or a continuously ringing telephone, especially if they are in acute stress. Potential clients faced with a busy signal will probably call another therapist. A busy signal to a client in acute stress is like calling 911 in an emergency and being put on hold. All told, it is bad business. Providing Muzak when someone is on hold may prove reassuring to clients that they have not been abandoned as they hold. Develop a policy of never allowing the telephone to ring more than three times or allowing someone to be on hold more than 1 minute. This will avert the possibility of your new referral developing a negative opinion and calling another therapist.

3 Rings max

on hold only 1 min

Do not get call waiting. It is too tempting to continually put a caller on hold so you can respond to the second caller. This conveys a message of unimportance to the initial caller and will hurt your business.

■ **Answering Machine Versus
Answering Service**

Unless you have a practice with clearly boundaried time, you must be available for crises 24 hours per day. As you cannot always be immediately available by telephone, you need to consider the pros and cons of an answering machine versus an answering service.

Those with a limited practice and budget may opt for using an answering machine. If this is your choice, invest in a reliable machine that will offer you good sound quality in the taped message. Select one that offers unlimited response time so your clients will be certain to communicate all that they need. A machine that will record the time of the call is also important. Make certain the machine offers remote message retrieval so you can call in to it frequently. Frequently calling in ensures your being available on a timely basis for someone in crisis as well as ensuring that you do not lose a new referral.

Anyone with an answering machine can attest to the number of "hang-ups" they receive. Some clients are too self-conscious to leave a message or they find it too impersonal. Likewise, some practitioners feel the machines do not present a professional image or do not provide for immediate communication with a client in a crisis. For these psychotherapists, an answering service is a more desirable option. Select an answering service that is familiar with the mental health profession. As you are dealing with human beings and not machines, you can communicate some of your own needs to the service.

I do not want my telephone calls held by my service. I want to be paged even if the purpose of the call is only to cancel an appointment or even if the client tells the answering service that it is not important. I ask the answering service not to "save" me by holding onto my "insignificant" calls. I realize that clients may minimize their serious concerns to the answering service; therefore, I would like to be able to talk with them as soon as possible. I feel it communicates a message of caring to my clients. The answering service I use will also "red flag" crisis calls on my pager. They know I will call back immediately for such emergency calls.

As the answering service consists of people, not things, it is important to consider their feelings and needs as well as your own and your clients'. Be reliable about calling in for messages. Remember them over the holidays with a card or a holiday gift, delivered by you. Use that opportunity to redevelop the relationship with each operator. Develop a friendly relationship and maintain it throughout the year by visiting at Christmas, Valentine's Day, and July 4th (or at another point during the summer). Of course, it is their job to communicate messages, but it is human nature to go that extra mile for those we like.

This has served my clients and me well time and time again. As the answering service knows I will call in within an hour (unless it is an emergency, and then I will call immediately), they will page me again if they have not heard from me. Once, the answering service operator took it upon herself to call an upset client back to tell her that I would be delayed a few minutes in calling her because I was on the telephone with another client.

Do not accept an answering service that is so busy that they continually place your callers on hold. Periodically monitor the service by having a friend call you when the answering service is picking up your calls. If the caller is not treated well, if it takes too long for you to be called by your service, or if the service is losing messages, address this with the owner or manager of the company. If they do not make the necessary changes, change companies.

Technological changes are resulting in some therapists selecting voice mail, a service offered through telephone companies. With this service a caller hears your greeting and leaves a message. You hold a private pass code ensuring confidentiality in retrieving messages. Messages can be retrieved from any location. Some voice-mail systems will call your pager if you have a message. This is particularly attractive to those who do not have a secretary and want to be notified of urgent calls.

■ Pager

I believe pagers simplify one's life. When first starting out in my private practice I did not carry a pager and called in to my office regularly for messages. Now, with my pager, I feel less encumbered, knowing I can be contacted when necessary.

Technology keeps changing, but there are primarily two types of pagers. All pagers have a tone as well as a silent, vibrating announcement that a message has arrived. The less expensive model displays a telephone number to call to get your message. A limitation is that you have to call the number to determine who is calling you. The memory bank is limited in the number of telephone numbers it will hold.

The second style is more expensive. It prints out a written message. The memory bank holds more messages and you can lock in specific telephone numbers for future reference. This model is desirable for the very busy professional who benefits from not having to call the secretary or answering service for each message.

note

I never give out my pager number to other professionals or clients. I fear that they will misuse it or dial incorrectly, thereby believing they have called me when in fact I never receive the page. Having all calls going through my answering service provides for reliable transmission of communication.

■ Computer

A computer can save considerable time for administrative functions. It can allow you to do the bookkeeping (accounts receivable, accounts payable, billing, reports on unpaid accounts, insurance forms, and payroll) and appointment scheduling, retain marketing and mailing lists, handle correspondence, and store handouts or talks you prepare for community presentations, among other things.

You will have to be somewhat knowledgeable about computers, although you do not need to be a computer whiz to benefit from owning one. Taking a basic course, purchasing the correct software programs, and having a computer book as a reference should establish your skills sufficiently so you will have enough knowledge to use your computer with ease and confidence. You will need to spend some time coordinating the records you wish to transfer to the computer to assure that the computer is able to work effectively for you. The better organized your practice is, the fewer problems you will have with integrating your computer. Use of computer passwords can provide protection for the confidentiality of information stored on the computer. Be certain that office staff regularly "backs up," or copies your files onto disks—at least weekly—in the event your machine breaks or you inadvertently erase files.

■ Miscellaneous Office Supplies

For telephone messages, use the kind of message book that allows for duplicate message sets. This way, if your secretary gives you a message with an important telephone number that you later misplace, it is retrievable in the carbon copy. I have come to rely on the duplicate message book to jot down communications with my secretary or to log temporarily a name or telephone number I might later misplace.

Have a business card holder as well as a card file in which you can type in the information on each card. Because many people will give you business cards, it is more time efficient simply to slip the card into the plastic holder in the card holder than to spend the time to transfer the information. In addition, you may have notes on the back side of the business card that you have made to remind yourself about that individual.

Develop "pending files" to which any communication between you and the secretary or other office staff can be shared. Develop the habit of checking the pending file daily. Pending files promote tidiness of the office as they are kept in the secretary's drawer.

Naming Your Practice

The name of your psychotherapy practice should convey what you do. This enables your practice name to do some ongoing marketing. It will prove more effective than naming your practice after yourself. For example, naming my practice Counseling Associates of Houston provided more information and conveyed more credibility than would have Eileen Lenson, ACSW, CSW/ ACP, BCD. Linking the geographical location of your office with what you do can be helpful for the public. Select a name that will be listed in the first third of the telephone book. This ensures a greater likelihood that "cold referrals" will have a good probability of calling you as opposed to the competition. Pick a name that will not confine you in the future. Do not select a name that specifies a certain type of clientele and restricts another.

Select a solid name that a person of any professional or socioeconomic background would feel comfortable associating with. Steer clear of cute or artsy names. To protect your name, consider registering it and getting a trademark (TM). To apply for federal registration of a trademark, you must obtain a written application from the Department of Commerce Patent and Trademark Office, submit a drawing of what you wish to have trademarked, pay a $200 filing fee, and provide three examples of how the mark has been used if it has had previous usage. For further information, contact The Commissioner of Patents and Trademarks, Washington, DC 20231, or call (703) 305-HELP (Manbeck & Samuels, 1992, pp. 3-5).

Familiarize yourself with names by going to the telephone book and looking under the categories of "counselors," "psychotherapists," "drug and alcohol," and "psychologists." Out-of-state telephone books can also be helpful. If you will be practicing very close to another state, it will be valuable to look at the neighboring state's telephone books as well as yours to assure that the business name you wish to select is not presently being used. In addition, your county office may be able to supply you with names that have been registered in your county. You will not want the confusion that could result from duplication.

Stationery

At times your stationery will offer people the first impression of you and your practice. It may be in a letter, a mailing, or a business card passed from one person to another. For this reason, your stationery must be selected carefully. Many states will require you to have specific information such as your license number and degree on stationery and business cards. Check with your regulatory agency before printing any advertising or stationery.

■ Letterhead

The stationery should contain the following: your company name, what you do, the address, and the telephone number. A logo is not important. If you do want a logo, do not spend a lot of money having one developed for you. Save your marketing dollars for other realms. The quality of the paper is important. Do not attempt to save money here. When you write to businesses or insurance companies, the stationery will be delivering a message of how you view yourself (Figure 3.3).

Rather than using black ink, consider selecting a color. Use white, or off-white, paper for a dignified presentation. Always use the same logo, print, colors, style, and format in any stationery, business cards, brochures, or promotional material you have made up.

Tell the printer you want to proofread the stationery before you accept it. Trust your own judgment—not the printers'—when making the selection. Obtain samples of other therapists' stationery and study them to determine what you like and what looks professional.

■ Business Cards

I love collecting business cards. Other therapists' business cards will help you learn what styles and formats you do and do not like. Some are so plain I am left perplexed as to what exactly they do. Others distract me because they are so crowded.

Keep your business cards simple and clean looking. Only print on one side. You do not need to have all of your information with regard to various groups led, expertise, and so on, on your business card. People will call for more information. Do, however, help people understand why they should come to you or refer others to you, by offering a benefit. For example, include a short phrase such as "Short-Term Therapy for Long-Term Results" or "Emergencies Seen Immediately" (*Practice Builder,* 1989b).

Use embossed cards (Figure 3.4). Listing what you do on the business card will help sell you, but do not state the obvious. Initially, order 500. After they are used up you may want to make changes. If the cost difference is minimal, however, order 1,000.

Aim to get rid of your business cards. Leave them in the waiting room. Give them out freely at talks and conferences. Include them in corre-

EILEEN S. LENSON, ACSW, CSW-ACP
PSYCHOTHERAPIST, DIPLOMATE

17101 MAIN STREET, STE. 100
HOUSTON, TEXAS 77068
TELEPHONE: (713) 548-1898

Figure 3.3. Letterhead

spondence. Use them at retail stores when asked for your address or phone number.

I once was called for an appointment by a sales clerk because I left my business card with her to contact me the following day regarding a skirt I was looking for. I could have written my telephone number on a slip of paper, but a business card served a dual purpose: providing my telephone number and subtly marketing myself as well.

> **COUNSELING ASSOCIATES** *Of* **HOUSTON**
>
> **Eileen Lenson, ACSW, CSW-ACP, BCD**
> **Psychotherapist**
>
> Short Term Therapy - Long Term Results
>
> 17101 MAIN STREET, STE. 100 HOUSTON, TX 77068
> (713) 548-1898

Figure 3.4. Business Card

■ Appointment Cards

A good appointment card will help avoid missed appointments. For years I used the type of appointment card that included the client's name, my name, and date and time of next appointment. Because some people organize themselves more to the day of the week than to the date, I have amended my appointment cards to include the day of the week (Figure 3.5).

Like business cards, appointment cards should be kept simple. They should include the address of your practice and telephone number. I also had my cancellation policy of calling at least 24 hours prior to the appointment printed on the card to help remind clients that they will be billed if they fail to show without giving me proper notice.

As seeing a therapist is a private matter, clients often do not carry their therapist's business card on their person, for fear of loss of confidentiality. Being able to carry an appointment card, which carries less identifying information of my being a therapist, is more comfortable to many clients.

Insurance for Your Practice

According to the United States Chamber of Commerce, the value of employee benefits such as vacation and holiday pay and health and life insurance is equal to approximately a third of one's salary—a sizable chunk of money! Now that you are a private practitioner, you can expect to pay for all of those benefits previously afforded you. You also will need to consider protection for your business, which previously was not a concern. The necessary insurance will need to be acquired prior to beginning your practice.

Your accountant or attorney may be able to recommend a good insurance agent or broker. It is a good idea to get several recommended independent agents and shop comparatively for the best coverage. The coverages, premi-

COUNSELING ASSOCIATES *Of* HOUSTON
17101 MAIN STREET, STE. 100, HOUSTON, TX 77068

An appointment has been scheduled for:

_____
With

_____

Day_____ Date___/___/___ Time_____

If unable to keep appointment, please give 24 hours notice or be
billed at regular rate. Office: (713) 548-1898

Figure 3.5. Appointment Card

ums, and service can vary greatly. Be sure to understand what the coverage is, and do not simply assume that because you purchased a policy it will provide you with adequate protection. Develop a trusting relationship with an insurance agent so you can get professional advice that is individualized for your particular needs. To do so can protect you from unnecessary insurance traps later on.

Locate an insurance representative who is familiar with psychotherapy practices. Rather than becoming fragmented, try to select only one agent or broker to handle your insurance coverage, except for malpractice insurance. This should prevent the likelihood of developing duplication or gaps in coverage. Also, in the event of claims, you will be able to have one agent fighting for you with the insurance companies. Below is a brief description of the types of insurance coverage you need to consider when setting up your business.

■ General Liability

Liability insurance protects business owners and their employees from financial loss due to covered claims of bodily injury, property damage, personal injury, or advertising injury and resulting medical expenses in connection with business operations. This is important as some personal insurance does not protect you in the unfortunate event that someone is injured arising out of your business operations. Liability judgments are often high. A single judgment could possibly bankrupt you.

■ Property Insurance

Although often called a "fire" policy, this commercial property policy can be purchased as a package to include several aspects of coverage for your business. Some are as follows:

- Protection against loss from any damage caused by fire, lightning, explosion, hurricane, tornado, hail, smoke, riot, aircraft, vehicles, or sprinkler leakage to the premises, equipment, and furniture.
- Protection against loss from vandalism and malicious mischief.
- Protection against loss from crime. This insurance provides reimbursement for losses due to robbery, burglary, or vandalism. Depending on your jurisdiction, crime insurance may cost less if you install an alarm system.
- Protection against loss of papers and records. This coverage can help to pay for reconstruction of paper and records if destroyed by a covered peril, such as fire, windstorm, vandalism, and so on.
- Protection against loss from business interruption. This is a property and casualty coverage that can encompass the loss of earnings resulting from your practice closing down due to a covered disaster. The loss must be due to property damage, as opposed to illness or injury. "Extra expense" coverage will cover your extra expenses due to relocating your office location "temporarily" during repair of your permanent office, if it cannot be occupied.
- Protection against loss from electronic equipment damage. Computer policies are valuable in today's business world to protect both hardware and software. If you have computers and/or important data on a computer an electronic equipment protection policy would warrant your investigation.

■ Employee Dishonesty Coverage

This deals with protecting against loss due to dishonest employees with access to cash receipts or other company assets. This may involve cash, such as keeping a client's cash payment rather than depositing it in the bank; depositing checks to a "dummy" account; or stealing equipment and supplies.

Employee dishonesty coverage can be purchased separately. It is a Fidelity Bond. It can be separate from crime insurance.

Once it has been learned that an employee is dishonest, the insurance company will not cover losses for subsequent dishonest actions by that employee. If the employer does not fire the employee, the employer then assumes the entire risk should the employee continue to steal (Smith, 1990, p. 169).

■ Workers' Compensation

Depending upon the state you live in, workers' compensation may be required by law if you have any employees. It will provide compensation to employees who are injured or become ill due to their employment. If an employee suffers a job-related illness or injury, the employer can be held responsible. The employer will then be required to pay for the cost of medical care, a part of lost wages, and possibly other benefits. If you have workers' compensation for employees, you may also include yourself in the coverage.

Each state has a law specifying what amount must be paid by the employer. So employers can meet their legal obligation in paying the amount required by law to injured employees, most employers are required to purchase workers' compensation insurance.

Workers' compensation insurance can be purchased from a private insurance company in most states. In some states workers' compensation can be purchased from private insurance companies as well as from the state. And in a few states workers' compensation can be purchased only from the state (Smith, 1990, p. 162).

■ Professional Liability or Malpractice Insurance

This is mandatory, especially in our litigious environment. Although an independent agent may offer this insurance, your professional organization is often the best place to obtain good coverage at affordable rates. Some insurance companies are changing their policies from an "occurrence" to a "claims made" form. This means you are protected by the coverage only if the policy is in effect at the time of the occurrence and when the claim is reported. The implication here is for psychotherapists to have coverage from the very beginning of their practice to years after retirement from the practice. However, this market is becoming increasingly competitive, and more insurance companies are offering professional liability coverage at competitive prices.

■ Major Medical Health Insurance

Many therapists have spouses who are employed in jobs that offer family health insurance. Typically, this will be the most cost-effective option to select for those who can take advantage of this opportunity. Others need to seek health insurance on an individual basis, which can be confusing, costly, and widely variable in terms of coverage. If you are associated with any group, try to obtain your medical insurance though them, as group rates are considerably less expensive than are individual.

If you have just left your full-time employment, consider continuing with your present medical insurance by obtaining the Consolidated Omnibus Budget Reconciliation Act (COBRA) coverage. This is a conversion policy that allows you to continue with the same insurance plan you currently are enrolled in at your job, although now you will also pay the portion that had been partially paid by your employer. In the event you resign from your job for the purpose of going into private practice, your employer is obligated by law to offer you the COBRA plan. Although coverable periods for COBRA will differ based on the reason for discontinuing employment, as long as you have not been charged with gross misconduct, you may be covered for up to 18 months after resignation. Because this is a group plan, your rates will probably be less expensive and the coverage more comprehensive than you would have been able to obtain as a private practitioner.

■ Disability and/or Business Overhead Expense

This policy is costly but worth considering if you are the sole source of income for your family. Should you incur a physical disability due to accident or sickness, this insurance coverage will assure you a guaranteed monthly income for a prespecified period of time. It provides reimbursement for actual expenses incurred, subject to maximum benefits, if you become disabled due to a covered accident or sickness. It is designed to help a business survive the interruption by providing money to make up for "what would have been."

Either of these types of plans will normally have a waiting period (30, 60, or 90 days or longer) before benefits begin. They also will have a maximum monthly benefit, length of time benefit is payable, or maximum total benefit payable restriction. Benefits are provided only for covered disabilities as defined in the policies. Make certain that "covered disabilities" is defined broadly enough for the policy to be worthwhile. Emotional disability would only be covered if provided for by the policy.

■ Long-Term Disability

If you are disabled and unable to work for a prolonged period of time, long-term disability insurance will provide you with an ongoing, monthly income. You select the amount of income you want to receive. Rule of thumb is to look to replace 60% of your income. The amount you will need depends on your expenses as well as how much you are willing to pay for the insurance. The length of time you receive the benefit can vary. You may wish to select benefits to last 2 years, until 65 years old, or even your entire lifetime. Again, the length of time selected will affect how much you pay for the insurance. When inquiring about long-term disability insurance, inquire about the companies' interpretation of "disabled," whether sickness as well as accidental injury are covered, whether the disability premiums and payouts are tax deductible, and whether more than one disability can be covered in a lifetime (*Psychotherapy Finances,* 1992b).

■ Life Insurance

Life insurance provides continuing financial security to your beneficiaries in the event that you die. There are two major types of life insurance: term life and permanent life.

Term life carries the lowest premiums, as it offers no cash value, just protection. It protects the insured for a specified period of time, at rates less expensive than permanent life insurance, although the rates increase as you grow older. It can provide good protection when one's children are small. Consider using it for temporary coverage. Permanent life insurance, sometimes called equity insurance, allows you to establish equity. The premiums are based on your age at the time of purchase. This equity can be used to borrow against at rates specified in the policy.

If you have employees, you may wish to make insurance a part of your employee benefit package. This is a matter of choice on your part. Your agent or broker can provide you with enough information to make that decision.

As the needs of your practice will change from year to year, select a time to do an annual review of your insurance needs to determine whether your needs have changed. In particular, look for gaps in coverage that may have arisen as your assets have grown. Once your financial situation stabilizes, consider umbrella policies, which offer significantly more coverage for liability at a nominal fee.

Consultants

Establishing a private practice is a personal matter, but one that should not be made without consulting with other professionals. Specifically, you will need to work closely with an accountant and an attorney.

■ Accountants

Accountants are valuable in helping you set up your accounting and bookkeeping systems and helping develop a system of financial control. You, your bookkeeper, or your secretary can do the posting and recording of the daily transactions of your business. Your accountant, on a monthly or quarterly basis, reviews your books to make sure the system is properly implemented and advises you on your financial progress and areas where you might improve your financial performance.

An accountant will organize your payroll system and prepare periodic financial statements. An accountant also can help you establish tax policies, reduce your tax liabilities, prepare your annual income tax returns, identify acceptable income tax deductions, and audit your books. If you have a computer, he or she can set up computerized systems for your business. If you need to get additional financing through a bank, your accountant can help you prepare a loan application. She or he can do cost analyses and profit and loss statements, help prepare budgets, and do forecasts for your business plan. If you are considering a major purchase, an accountant can help advise you. Finally, an accountant can help you select among a variety of plans for your retirement.

As taxes and accounting are areas of ever changing specifications, it is recommended that you work closely with your accountant to keep abreast of the most recent rulings. Generally, word-of-mouth referrals from other therapists can help you in selecting a certified public accountant (CPA). This will enable you to choose someone who is familiar with psychotherapy practices as well as small businesses. As with an attorney, discuss the accountant's fees prior to employing or engaging her or him, and have a clear understanding of what services she or he will be offering you.

A good CPA can help free you to do more therapy. As with attorneys, accountants do not come without a cost, so the more responsibility you assume in learning about and controlling your financial situation, the less likely you are to spend unnecessary money on accountants.

■ Attorneys

A wise psychotherapist recognizes the limits of his or her expertise. This is why he or she learns to value the skills of an attorney as a business advisor. To not do so could be disastrous to his or her practice.

An experienced generalist who has dealt with mental health professions before, and who is not a family friend, should be able to help by offering useful suggestions. These include the intricate system of rules, regulations, and constraints involved with beginning new enterprises, buying or leasing office space, hiring employees, incorporating, and expanding your practice. You can be helped with preparation of documents you may need or how to obtain delinquent payments from clients. The attorney can help with objective negotiation, as you may be too subjective to be able to negotiate well. This can help with liability and libel problems. The attorney can help determine how to collect debts owed you or offer advice about handling a disgruntled employee or angry client. The attorney should be able to show you how to take advantage of tax laws and guide you with estate planning.

The attorney can review professional liability policies you are considering to determine coverage and identify ways to reduce costs. As psychotherapists often are naive about how to write clinical notes for legal acceptability, an attorney can impart helpful suggestions on appropriate documentation. In the event that you are subpoenaed to testify in court, an attorney can help clarify for you whether you are entitled to privileged information. In some cases, the judge may rule differently. In short, an attorney can help delineate what type of legal shape your business will take and will identify the advantages and disadvantages of these decisions.

To keep legal costs down, spend time educating yourself on the issues you plan to discuss so the attorney is not spending time educating you. They typically charge by the hour, so do not waste time! They also may offer to provide services on a retainer. This consists of legal council for a flat monthly fee. Discuss fees before retaining an attorney. Put the fee structure in writing. Ask for regular billings so the expenses do not increase beyond what you can afford. Do not be afraid to ask for a detailed billing. Remember, attorneys charge differently than do psychotherapists. Most charge for telephone discussions as well as for the time spent preparing the invoices.

Ask for copies of any written communication that comes out of their office that pertains to you. This will provide you with a history of how different situations were handled.

Just as we would caution a parent to bring his or her adolescent into therapy at the first signs of unmanageable behavior, so should we, as therapists, turn to attorneys at the beginning of our practice, and not only when a problem has arisen. More is discussed about working with an attorney in Chapter 7.

There are so many decisions to make when setting up a business. Keep the decisions in perspective. Do not waste time obsessing over the small decisions, as they will distract you from moving ahead. If you have given serious consideration to all of the above categories and have been able to resolve most of the problems that naturally develop, you are ready to open your doors for your private practice.

FOUR

Clinical Record Keeping
and Paperwork

Private practice is not an escape from clinical record keeping and paperwork. Record keeping requires self-discipline and good habits. To understand the many uses and potential abuses of clients' records is to appreciate the importance of this task. Perhaps some of the resistance to paperwork can be worked through if you understand the value and necessity of maintaining good records.

Appointment Book

Record keeping begins with your appointment book. You will use an appointment book to document how you are spending your day: clients seen, marketing contacts made, miles driven, telephone calls, and so on. It can also be used as a method of verifying whether or not a client came to see you should your billing get confused, or serve as a reminder to write a note for the clinical records if the tape recorder malfunctions. This has helped me on several occasions. I tape-record my notes and my secretary transcribes them for the clinical records. I have had the horrible experience of a tape tearing. As I need to have a clinical entry for each session with a client, I am able to use my appointment book to re-create history and identify which dates are missing documentation.

Write appointments in pencil to allow for the inevitable changes you need to make during the week. Several times when the secretary has erred by not billing for a session, both the written note and my appointment book have served to confirm that I did indeed see the client on a given date. Keep one appointment book so as to keep the process simple.

As you will probably be working in the evenings, it will be necessary to have the after-five-o'clock hours listed. I have found the type that lays out the week at a glance works best for me. It enables me to scan the week easily without turning many pages, and allows me sufficient space to write notes. In addition to documenting your appointments, the appointment book also can be used to log frequently called telephone numbers. It serves to double as a telephone book, then, without any additional burden.

Do not discard your appointment book at the end of the year. Preserve it as you would your clinical records. In the event of a legal matter, the appointment book would provide additional documentation about how you spent your day and what clients were seen. Do not let clients see your appointment book, as they will be able to see other client's names, which would be a breach of confidentiality.

Telephone Book

Many times you will find yourself away from the office and needing to call a client. Your secretary may be out, with no one available at the office to look up the telephone number. For these infrequent yet critical times, I carry a compact telephone book listing my client's telephone numbers.

Confidentiality

Before discussing clinical records, it is critical to discuss confidentiality. Any inadvertent disclosure of clinical records would jeopardize the therapist-client relationship. Therefore, all efforts must be made to guard records from the public. A policy of not allowing records to leave the office without a signed consent form from the client is necessary. If someone calls and inquires whether or not the client is in therapy, a response such as, "We cannot confirm nor deny anyone's treatment in our office without a written consent for release of information," is appropriate. If a client's confidentiality is breached the client may be able to successfully sue the therapist, either civilly or criminally.

Clients need to understand the limits and exceptions to confidentiality when they enter therapy. Records can be subpoenaed by the court in lawsuits. Most therapists do not enjoy "privileged communication" in court and, therefore, must testify about their clients and allow their records to be reviewed. More is addressed on confidentiality in Chapter 7.

Legal Requests
for Clinical Notes

In the course of your career you may be ordered by the court, in the form of a subpoena, to provide privileged or confidential information regarding one of your clients. The subpoena will instruct you to hand over all documents, reports, and notes concerning the case.

The first thing you will want to do is contact an attorney to help determine whether you are required to surrender any or all of this information. You may be reluctant to do so because it results in the breaching of a client's confidentiality. If, on the other hand, you do not release the information, you can be held in contempt of court and subject to fines or jail.

Mark each paper relinquished to the courts as "confidential." Send only copies, keeping the original for your own records. Notify your client of what has transpired.

Client Requests
for Clinical Notes

It is generally accepted that other than in some special circumstances, clients do have the right to have access to their records. It is helpful to gain an understanding of why the client is interested in reviewing the records. Always review the records with the client so jargon and any concerns may be addressed and the client can be supported. This offers the client an opportunity to refute anything he or she feels is inaccurate in the records. It promotes openness between the therapist and the client. It is good to always keep in mind that notes may be read by the client at some point.

If more than one member of the family is being treated, maintain separate records for each person. This protects the confidentiality of each family member, should records be requested (Woody, 1988, p. 139).

Intake Forms

Client records begin with intake forms. Every office should develop a set of forms that suits their needs. Intake forms enable you to obtain information in a reliable, consistent manner. These forms become the contract between the therapist and the client, and establish expectations each have of the other. After the client has signed all forms, it is important to spend a couple of minutes confirming the client's expectations of treatment.

■ Verification of Insurance Benefits

The initial form needed is called the Verification of Insurance Benefits form (Figure 4.1). This form is used by the secretary (or the therapist if there is no secretary) to gather information from the client prior to setting up the appointment.

The tentative diagnosis is particularly important as policies often vary greatly for psychiatric versus chemical dependency diagnoses. It will help identify the client's deductible, and the dollar maximum allowed from the insurance company per visit, per year, and per policy. This information is given to clients before the initial visit so they know what the out-of-pocket cost will be for them to pursue therapy.

As each insurance company has different expectations with regard to filings, the Verification of Insurance Benefits form helps with this process by having a section for the secretary to inquire as to whether the Health Care Financing Administration (HCFA) 1500 claim form is to be used, and whether an original needs to be kept on file.

When inquiring about reimbursement schedules, the statement that the insurance company pays for "reasonable and customary" charges is not sufficient. Use the Current Procedural Terminology (CPT) code list and ask whether these codes are covered. Although the CPT code list is written for physicians, it is accepted that nonphysicians also provide these services. Finally, if a precertification number is issued, it is documented on this form along with the name of the person spoken with at the insurance company in the event further clarification is needed.

Although the form may sound tedious, it is comforting because it offers structure and a script from which the secretary can gather information. Future therapy sessions run more smoothly and payment is more likely assured as a result. On several occasions my office has been able to resolve conflicts with regard to payment from insurance companies because of the detailed information obtained on the Verification of Insurance Benefits form.

Because I often do not know prior to seeing a client what his or her needs will be, I automatically have my secretary examine outpatient as well as inpatient benefits. This has helped me tremendously over the years. Sometimes I will be seeing an outpatient in my office after 5:00 P.M. and suddenly have a need to explore hospitalization. Insurance companies are closed at that hour and I need to make decisions that could have substantial financial implications for the client. It is best to know ahead of time whether the insurance company uses specific hospitals as preferred providers, thereby reducing the cost to the client. It allows me to know what their inpatient deductible is as well as the maximum allowed. It also puts the client at a greater comfort level, knowing the inpatient hospitalization costs.

COUNSELING ASSOCIATES *Of* HOUSTON

VERIFICATION OF INSURANCE BENEFITS

Patient Name: _____

Date of Birth: _____
Address: _____
Social Security Number: _____
Telephone: Home: _____ Work: _____
Insured's Name: _____
Social Security Number: _____
Employer: _____
Group Name: _____
Group Number: _____
Insur. / Managed Care Co.: _____
(Primary/Secondary) _____
Ins. Co. Phone Number: _____
Ins. Co. Address: _____
Other Ins. Co.: _____
Any Pre-existing Clauses? _____
Diagnosis: _____
Precertification Required? _____
Precert. Approval Number: _____

	Outpatient Benefits		Inpatient Benefits	
	Mental & Nervous	Alcohol/ Substance Abuse	Mental & Nervous	Alcohol/ Substance Abuse
Deductible				
Amount Satisfied				
Percentage				
Dollar Max. / Visit				
Dollar Max. / Year				
Dollar Max. / Policy				
Visits per Week				
Visits per Year				
Effective Date				

1500 Claim Form: Yes / No
Original on File: Yes / No
Acceptable Providers: LPC, CSW-ACP, supervised by M.D.: _____
Acceptable Treatment: Individual____ Marital_____ Family____ Group____
Self-Insured: Yes / No

Date: ___/___/___   Person Contacted: _____

Info. Obtained By: _____   Therapist: _____

Figure 4.1. Verification of Insurance Benefits Form

You should advise your client about insurance company requirements. You will be providing the insurance company with a diagnosis, number of times and dates client has been seen for treatment, and what type of service was provided. This information will be stored on a computer with the insurance company. For individuals who are in sensitive jobs or are uncomfortable with the loss of control over who has access to personal information about them, payment in full to the therapist and bypassing use of the insurance company may be a more desired option.

■ New Client Packet

The second in the set of intake forms is called the New Patient Information Packet. This is a set of six pages. Specific information elicited on the first page includes identifying information about the client and the client's insurance company (Figure 4.2).

The second and third pages describe the fees and policies of the office, including the 24-hour cancellation policy. The client is to sign at the bottom of this page, acknowledging an understanding of this policy (Figure 4.3).

The fourth page, on informed consent, is an acknowledgment that the client is coming for therapy voluntarily and can terminate at any time she or he wishes. This will help protect you in the future from an angry client suing you for malpractice for holding him against his will. Again, the client is to sign this page (Figure 4.4).

The fifth page of the packet assigns benefits from insurance to be paid directly to your office. Of special importance, it outlines the client's financial responsibility for all charges not paid by the insurance. The client also signs this page (Figure 4.5).

Last, a consent for release of information form is included in each packet. It is only signed by the client if a specific name is written in with whom the information is to be shared (Figure 4.6). When the client signs this form, talk over with your client what information will be shared, what gains are anticipated, and what possible adverse effects could result from this disclosure. If written material is to be released, discuss it first with the client.

A large part of my practice is with adolescents, and I want to be able to discuss a client with the school counselor. However, for a while I was experiencing difficulty because the school counselor did not have a consent for release of information to me. Obtaining that release often took up to 2 weeks—precious time to lose. So I developed a reciprocal release of information form that enables me to release information to a source and that source to release information to me. This has been a wonderful modification. I can get the information more quickly because the school counselor is no longer bound by confidentiality while waiting for a consent to be signed. My client benefits

COUNSELING ASSOCIATES *Of* HOUSTON

17101 MAIN STREET, STE. 100
HOUSTON, TEXAS 77068
TELEPHONE: (713) 548-1898

Date:_____

Referred by: _____

Therapist:_____

NEW CLIENT INFORMATION
Please Print & Complete in Full:

Client's Full Name: _____
                First   M.I.   Last

Mailing Address: _____
                Street   Apartment Number

_____
        City   State   Zip

Telephone: _____
            Home   Work

Date of Birth: __/__/__ Age:_____ Social Security Number:_____-_____-_____

Employer of Client:_____Occupation:_____

Address of Employer: _____
                Street   City   State   Zip

SPOUSE INFORMATION
Name:_____Social Security Number:_____-_____-_____ DOB:___/___/___

Mailing Address: _____
(if different from client)
Telephone:_____
                Home   Work
Employer:_____Phone:_____

CHILDREN INFORMATION (List siblings if client is child.)
Name: Date of Birth: Age:
_____   ___/___/___   ____
_____   ___/___/___   ____
                                   ___/___/___

PLEASE FILL IN THIS SECTION IF CLIENT IS UNDER 18 YEARS OF AGE
Parent/Guardian:_____Phone:_____
Address: _____
        Street   City   State   Zip Code
Employer:_____Phone:_____

IN CASE OF EMERGENCY, PLEASE NOTIFY
Name:_____Phone: _____
Address: _____
        Street   City   State   Zip Code

Previous/Present Therapist/Psychiatrist (If applicable): _____

> **Note:** Payment is due when services are rendered. Checks are payable to Counseling Associates of Houston. Please submit an insurance card for copying.

Figure 4.2. Intake Packet, Client Information Form

COUNSELING ASSOCIATES *Of* HOUSTON

17101 MAIN STREET, STE. 100
HOUSTON, TEXAS 77068
TELEPHONE: (713) 548-1898

PATIENT INFORMATION

FOR YOUR INFORMATION

At the time of your initial visit you will be asked to complete some routine forms. These forms consist of a patient history form, consent to treatment form, an assessment of benefits form (if applicable), and a release of information form. The release of information form should be discussed with your therapist before completing. If you are in an adolescent therapy group, we need a release of information form filled out for your school counselor.

In general, the number of visits you will require will depend on the type of problem(s) that exist, the recommendations made by your therapist, and the effort you put into working on the problem(s) in following through with the recommendations.

APPOINTMENTS

Appointments will be scheduled at a time mutually acceptable to both the patient and the therapist. We require 24-hour advanced notice of cancellations except in an extreme emergency.

Appointments missed or canceled with less than 24 hours notice will be charged at the usual rate.

FEES

Our fee is $100.00 per 50 minute session. This includes individual psychotherapy and family (conjoint) psychotherapy. If you are involved in your psychotherapy, your fee will be determined by your therapist.

It must be clearly understood that payment of fees for office services is required at the time of service.

You are required to pay in full for the first visit. This is our office policy, and many times it takes care of your yearly deductible on your insurance (if applicable).

Upon return visits, you will be held responsible for paying what your insurance does not cover (i.e., if your insurance covers 50%, they will pay $50.00 and you will pay $50.00). Your portion is due when services are rendered.

Figure 4.3. Intake Packet, Practice Policies

because the systems are communicating with each other. My secretary automatically sends a copy of the release to the school counselors for their own records. Now some school counselors are so familiar with my form that they will talk to me about a client before actually receiving the release of infor-

COUNSELING ASSOCIATES *Of* HOUSTON

17101 MAIN STREET, STE. 100
HOUSTON, TEXAS 77068
TELEPHONE: (713) 548-1898

REGARDING HEALTH INSURANCE

Patients who carry health insurance must remember that professional services are rendered and charged to the patient. Our office will provide the courtesy of filing your insurance but cannot accept responsibility for collecting or for negotiating a settlement of a disputed claim. You are responsible for any balance left on your account that your insurance carrier does not pay.

All health insurance policies are not the same. The amount of reimbursement you receive depends on the type and amount of coverage your policy provides. Verification of benefits is not a guarantee of payment, and may be subject to denial upon review.

If we are filing your insurance for you, we may need you to provide us with an original insurance claim form. You may obtain an original claim form from your employer or your insurance company. Please make sure the claim form is signed by the insured in the place marked for assignment of benefits, and all other required places on the form.

If you have an insurance card, please allow us to make a copy of it for our files.

CONFIDENTIALITY

Your therapist needs to know a lot about you in order to effectively help you with your problem(s). You can rest assured that we keep all information about our clients STRICTLY CONFIDENTIAL. Absolutely NO information about you or your case will be released to anyone without your written authorization and consent.

In order to effectively serve you and your needs, we want you to feel comfortable with the Counseling Associates of Houston and your therapist. If you have any questions or concerns that you feel will help us better serve you, please bring them to our attention. Thank you.

I HAVE READ THIS PATIENT INFORMATION PACKET, I UNDERSTAND THE REQUIREMENTS AND RULES OF THIS OFFICE, AND I AGREE TO THE TERMS THEREIN.

Signature: _____

Date: _____/_____/_____

Therapist: _____

Figure 4.3. (Continued)

mation form because they trust it will be coming along shortly in the mail. Another way to expedite the process is to have the student hand carry the release of information form to the school counselor the following school day.

COUNSELING ASSOCIATES *Of* HOUSTON

17101 MAIN STREET, STE. 100
HOUSTON, TEXAS 77068
TELEPHONE: (713) 548-1898

INFORMED CONSENT

I consent to the evaluation/treatment process with Eileen S. Lenson of the Counseling Associates of Houston and I understand that this process may include myself, my child, and/or other family members.

The procedures of this office have been explained and I understand them.

I understand that I have the right to withdraw from treatment at any time.

_____
Signature of Patient; if Child, Parent or Legal Guardian

_____
Signature of Child or Adolescent

Date_____/_____/_____

Figure 4.4. Intake Packet, Informed Consent Form

Sometimes clients will be overwhelmed when they are handed this intake packet. However, it only takes 5 to 7 minutes to fill out. Clients are asked to arrive 15 minutes prior to their first session so they will have time to orient themselves to the office procedures and complete the paperwork. If a client so desires, I provide her or him with a copy of the packet to take home for future reference. Once these documents are signed, they become a permanent part of the client's clinical records.

Clinical Notes

You must retain clinical notes. They will be necessary as proof that you saw the client and what services were provided. They also provide readily available information you may need to share with other professionals, furnish information that will assist in recall of previous sessions, and provide documentation you will need in the event of a legal situation.

COUNSELING ASSOCIATES *Of* HOUSTON
_____

17101 MAIN STREET, STE. 100
HOUSTON, TEXAS 77068
TELEPHONE: (713) 548-1898

ASSIGNMENT OF BENEFITS

I hereby assign payment of authorized benefits to which I am entitled to be made directly to Counseling Associates of Houston for services performed at the center. I authorize any holder of medical information about me to release any information needed to determine these benefits payable for related services.

This assignment will remain in effect until revoked by me in writing. A photocopy of this assignment is to be considered as valid as an original. I understand that I am financially responsible for all charges not paid by said insurance. I hereby authorize said assignee to release all information necessary to secure payment.

Signature: _____

Date: _____/_____/_____

Figure 4.5. Intake Packet, Assignment of Benefits Form

Not to keep clinical records puts you at risk for malpractice. To others, your charts will reflect the quality of care you provide. Undocumented records reflect inefficiency and negligence. Unfortunately, many clinicians put much more thought and work into their therapy sessions than is recorded in the clinical notes. Notes are often sparse, incomplete, or nonexistent. Develop the habit of treating your clinical records as you would your clients.

Writing or dictating your therapy notes on a daily basis is important. Sometimes it is resistance to maintaining clinical records that results in therapists delaying in documenting sessions. This can be due to concern about increased access to records by insurance companies as well as by clients, or due to time restraints that prevent timely documentation. If your practice is busy, your time will be torn between seeing clients and taking care of their immediate needs, returning telephone calls, and responding to office responsibilities. Maintaining notes can easily slip into a lower priority.

It is perfectly acceptable to have handwritten notes, assuming they are legible. My experience is that the process of handwriting notes is too time-

COUNSELING ASSOCIATES *Of* HOUSTON

17101 MAIN STREET, STE. 100
HOUSTON, TEXAS 77068
TELEPHONE: (713) 548-1898

RELEASE OF INFORMATION

I,_____, give Eileen S. Lenson permission to release and receive information

regarding my treatment, with Mr./Ms./Dr._____, for the

period beginning ___/___/___ and ending ___/___/___ .

Signature:_____
        Patient

Date: ____/____/____

Signature:_____
        Eileen S. Lenson, ACSW, CSW/ACP, BCD
        Psychotherapist

Date: ____/____/____

Figure 4.6. Intake Packet, Release of Information Form

consuming. I take brief notes during the session. I then dictate full progress notes into a portable tape recorder, often while in my car on the way from the office, to the hospital, or home. The next day my secretary transcribes these tapes for the clinical records. I have found this to be a great use of downtime, and am more tolerant of long drives and traffic jams. Do not worry if your notes are not perfect. The sooner you record your notes, the more likely you are to include the pertinent data. Too long a lapse in time from session to documentation can result in you forgetting the content of the session or key information you want to capture.

Records should not be damaging to your client. They should be factual and thorough. Write them with thoughts of litigation and jury interpretation. It is permissible to modify your records, but once they are requested by the court, you are ordered to leave them unaltered.

If your client is going to have access to your records, arrange to review the records together. Because the notes are written for the mental health provider and not for the client, they often are filled with jargon, impressions, and diagnoses. This can prove to be confusing and overwhelming to a client, who has little understanding of the written content. Therefore, it will be more beneficial for the client to review the records together, and be able to process the information and his or her feelings as the information is received. Charging the client for this review is acceptable if a lengthy period of time is required. Or, you may wish to incorporate the record review into a regularly scheduled session.

Your notes should be able to speak for themselves without you having to justify them. A malpractice case in which you were unable to provide documentation of what you did would reflect poorly on you, and offer you little defense. Likewise, should your client have to go to court on a matter that has clinical relevance and your notes do not adequately reflect the content of your sessions, your client could end up compromised. If you think of litigation when writing your notes, you will have good clinical records.

Your initial notes should include how both you and the client view the problem, as well as why the client is coming to see you. The initial notes should reflect who referred the client to you and the presenting problem. Document all relevant historical and development of complaint information necessary for forming a tentative diagnosis and an initial treatment plan. Identify previous treatments the patient has been involved with (Schrier, 1980).

When documenting after each session, keep notes factual, as that is more professional. They may be brief. Only put in subjective information when it can be supported by clinical observations. Date each entry. Include the content of the session, and the status of the symptoms. Note behavior, especially noncompliant behavior. Put a description of how the client subjectively feels. Use quotes when relevant. In addition to making notes after each session, enter notes on significant telephone conversations, such as a telephone call to Child Protective Services, and any recommendations. Document any recommendations or referrals to specialists or adjunctive therapy that you made and whether or not these recommendations were followed up by your client. Do not collude with your client to treat certain issues but not document them in your records.

When a client ends therapy, include a termination note covering the reason for termination; how the client was doing, feeling, and interacting with others at the time of termination; and how he or she had improved. Detail a recapitulation of the course of treatment; progress made; client's attitude toward the therapist, as well as himself or herself, at time of termination; recommendations; final diagnosis; and prognosis.

Paying for the insurance or copayment for the session does not entitle the payor access to another person's records. Sometimes you may encounter a situation where a husband demands the right to read his wife's records because the insurance is in his name. Only in cases where the adult client is determined to be incompetent, or the client is a child, can another person have access to a client's records. Even these situations should be approached cautiously, because it is important to maintain trust with your client. If someone wants access to a client's records, it is worthwhile to inquire what the person is hoping to learn by having access to the records.

I cannot overemphasize the need to keep organized, consistent, and legible records. Some mental health professionals write sloppy or infrequent notes, hoping it will offer them some protection if their notes cannot be read in court. Remember two sentences: "Sloppy writing reflects sloppy work," and, "If it is not documented, it is not done."

Maintain your clinical notes in a file folder with the client's name typed on the outside for identification. Have two files for each client: one for the clinical records and an identical one for intake and insurance forms. This will simplify your or your secretary's search for documents.

Do not keep two sets of records, one for your office and one for court, designed to prevent disclosure of information. Document honestly. Failure to do so could seriously jeopardize you professionally or your client personally. Remember, respectable recording is conducive to good psychotherapy. Maintain clinical records that are correct, precise, objective, and up to date.

Termination Letter

When terminating with a client, send a letter formalizing the termination (Figures 4.7 and 4.8). I send a form letter, which I may modify, to inform them that they are now on my inactive file because they have not indicated a desire to continue with treatment. A copy of the termination letter is placed in the client's file. You are then protected legally should something happen to the client after you have stopped treating her or him.

A surprising benefit I have had from the termination letter is that some clients will be reminded that they have unresolved issues to explore and will call and request that they not be put in my inactive file, and instead schedule an appointment.

Old Files

Keep old files. My recommendation is to keep them long beyond IRS and legal stipulations. Records do not take up enough space to warrant disposing of them, considering that a legal case might evolve. They could provide a

COUNSELING ASSOCIATES *Of* HOUSTON
_____

17101 MAIN STREET, STE. 100
HOUSTON, TEXAS 77068
TELEPHONE: (713) 548-1898

September 3, 1992

Ms. Jane Doe
12234 Gravel Street
Houston, TX 77090

Dear Ms. Doe:

This is to inform you that we will soon be placing your records in our inactive file.

If you wish to continue therapy, or would like to in the future, please notify me at this office at 548-1898. I hope you are doing well.

Sincerely,

Eileen S. Lenson, ACSW, CSW/ACP, BCD
Psychotherapist

ESL/ky

Figure 4.7. Individual Termination Letter

significant amount of information at a later time. You may remain liable for cases involving a child until the child reaches 18 years of age. This may exceed state laws. When you do decide to discard old records, shred them to ensure confidentiality. Keep your closed files apart from your current files in a secure, locked cabinet.

If you sell your practice, you will give your records to the new owner only if your clients sign consent forms. In this situation, make a copy of the records for yourself, should a need for them arise in the coming years.

Correspondence

Correspondence provides a historical record of your practice. It reflects communication with marketing contacts, insurance companies, clients, hos-

COUNSELING ASSOCIATES *Of* HOUSTON

17101 MAIN STREET, STE. 100
HOUSTON, TEXAS 77068
TELEPHONE: (713) 548-1898

September 3, 1992

Mr. and Mrs. John Doe
555 Smith Drive
Houston, TX 77000

Dear Mr. and Mrs. Doe:

As you have not indicated that you would like to remain in therapy, we soon will be placing your records in our inactive files.

If you would like to continue therapy in the future, please contact me at 548-1898. I hope you are doing well.

Sincerely,

Eileen S. Lenson, ACSW, CSW/ACP, BCD
Psychotherapist

ESL/ky

Figure 4.8. Couple Termination Letter

pitals, landlords, office supply companies, and so on. Such documents can be helpful in the event you are entangled in a lawsuit and need proof of your communication and involvement.

Make a copy of all correspondence that leaves your office. If it pertains to a specific client, insert a copy in the client's file. For all other correspondence make separate files and label them appropriately.

Forms

Your practice will use a variety of forms. They may include intake, insurance, referral acknowledgments, patient verification, and patient-seen forms. Keep each packet of forms in its own file. Store the files in a drawer or cabinet that is readily accessible.

Resource File

From time to time you will want to refer your clients to community support or self-help groups. To do so you will find it helpful to obtain lists of groups, 12-step meetings, as well as other information for you to use for referral. Having photocopies of community resources available in the area will enable you to have ready access to a handout referral sheet.

FIVE

Taxes

Do not open your doors for business until you have a clear understanding of your tax responsibilities. Taxes are uninteresting and complex, but essential to understand. You must know what taxes you are responsible for, how to fill out the forms, when to withhold tax money from your employees, and how to develop a reliable record-keeping system. To ignore taxes is to risk the consequences of the IRS closing your business for lack of payment, while continuing to hold you personally responsible for trust fund withholding taxes.

An accountant can deal with the complicated, confusing record keeping and reporting and can explain to you precisely what you are required to do. By setting up a good system for doing this at the beginning of your career, you will have an organized method for managing and controlling your taxes from the beginning. The IRS offers, free of charge, Publication #334, *Tax Guide for Small Business,* which discusses the maintenance of business books and records, and Publication #583, *Taxpayers Starting a Business.*

Select Business Entity

First you will need to select what type of business entity fits your practice best. Each type—sole practitioner, partnership, and corporation—has different tax concerns that you will need to consider.

■ Sole Proprietorship

As discussed in Chapter 2, if you create a sole proprietorship, the business will be seen as your personal business extension. You will be responsible for estimating and remitting both self-employment (the equivalent of Social Security) and income tax on a quarterly basis. You will report any profit or loss from your business on a Schedule C (Form 1040), Profit or Loss From Business.

■ Partnership

If you have selected a partnership (which requires two or more people), you will need to report any profit or loss from your business on Form 1065, U.S. Partnership Return of Income. A balance sheet and schedule of partners' capital also may be required. For more information obtain IRS Publication #541, *Tax Information on Partnerships.*

■ Corporation

Corporations do not necessarily save tax money. The profits are sometimes taxed twice: once as corporate income and again when distributed to the shareholders (which most likely is you) as dividends. The corporation does, however, get special deductions that the sole proprietor and partnership entities do not get. Most corporations use Form 1120, U.S. Corporation Income Tax Return, or Form 1120-A, U.S. Corporation Short-Form Income Tax Return, for filing. To help you understand what is expected of corporations, get Publication #542, *Tax Information on Corporations,* from the IRS.

Due to decreasing tax benefits for corporations, fewer therapists are using this form of structuring. According to *Psychotherapy Finances,* the usage dropped from 11% to 8% from 1988 to 1990 (*Psychotherapy Finances,* 1991a, p. 5).

■ S Corporation

An attraction of electing to be treated as an S corporation is the opportunity to avoid double taxation. Those who qualify for an S corporation will be exempt from paying the federal income tax at the corporate level. To qualify for S corporation status, you must have a domestic corporation; only one class of stock; no more than 35 shareholders; the shareholders can only be individuals, estates, and certain trusts; and the shareholders must be citizens or residents of the United States. Income tax returns are filed on Form 1120S, U.S. Income Tax Return for an S Corporation. If you plan to organize under an S corporation, obtain Publication #589 from the IRS, *Tax Information on "S" Corporations.*

Taxpayer Identification Number

You will need to use an identification number when filing your income tax return forms. If you have a solo proprietorship, you may use your Social Security number, unless you have employees. If you have a sole proprietorship with employees, a partnership, or a corporation, you will have to obtain an employer identification number (EIN) to use on your tax forms. You can obtain it by completing Form SS-4, Application for Employer Identification Number, obtainable at IRS and Social Security Administration offices. It will take approximately a month for your EIN to be processed, so be certain to apply for it long before you need to use it. It is currently possible to have an EIN issued by phone with a simultaneous filing of Form SS-4.

You may need to obtain a new EIN if you change from a sole proprietorship to a partnership or a corporation. Also, a new EIN will be required if you have a partnership that incorporates or becomes a sole proprietorship.

Maintain Records

Develop a simple, workable system from the beginning for maintaining all bookkeeping and business records that will play a role in preparing your reporting of income tax. Set the books up to work around your tax year, be it a calendar or a fiscal year. The annual accounting period will depend on the type of business entity you have.

Regardless of type of business entity, you will need to maintain the following books and records for bookkeeping purposes:

1. Business checkbook and savings accounts. Your books should clearly reflect your income as well as your disbursements. Your business bank accounts should be kept separate from your personal accounts. Any deposits or withdrawals from your bank account should have clear notations indicating what the purpose was so that you can understand whether it represents taxable income or qualifies as a tax-deductible business expense.
2. Cash receipt log. This includes the petty cash fund, which is used to pay for small purchases, as well as cash deposited from payments on accounts.
3. File containing employee compensation records. Include a checklist for when you are to pay income, self-employment, or estimated taxes, as well as Social Security (FICA), federal and state unemployment tax,

and excise taxes. These may vary by location of your practice and choice of entity, but reports must be filed and taxes paid on time or you will suffer serious financial penalties.

Part of the key to assuring acceptable bookkeeping and business records is to be certain to maintain complete records. In the event of an audit your records will provide the documentation required to substantiate your claims on your tax returns.

Maintain the following records for business purposes:

1. All documents that describe your business
2. Names, addresses, and Social Security numbers of all therapists who have worked at your office
3. Names, addresses, Social Security numbers, dates hired, wages, and raises of all employees who have worked in your office
4. Leases
5. Insurance policies
6. Bank statements
7. Ledger and journals
8. Bank deposits and business receipts
9. Tax returns for all previous years

Business Deductions

You will pay taxes on all profit realized from your practice. Therefore, you will want to keep a record of all deductions (expenses) recognized by the IRS.

Although practitioners are busy people who prefer to focus on their clients versus record keeping, it is necessary to develop good, routine habits of documenting your expenses. If you are sloppy you are likely to forget an expense and will inadvertently pay more on your income taxes than necessary. Try to conduct your business as though you will be audited. If you are audited, the IRS will want to verify your income, deductions, and any other information claimed on your return. Keep all receipts and canceled checks to justify the expenses declared as deductions.

Credit cards can provide an easy way of paying for purchases and also developing an accessible tracking system for business expenses. Have deliveries made to your office, not your home. It more clearly identifies the purchase as being a business expense. Out-of-pocket expenses under $25 do not require a receipt, although I recommend you obtain a receipt if possible.

Maintain a log of all travel expenses, mileage, meal expenses, and any other business-related expense you incur during the day. Keep the log in a convenient area. Otherwise you are likely to procrastinate entering the expense and forget it entirely. I use the free Hallmark pocketbook-size calendars to jot down mileage and expenses. Keep your log in your purse, Day-Timer, or car.

You will want to deduct all legitimate business expenses. The IRS makes changes from year to year as to what is an acceptable deduction. You will always need to consult your accountant as to whether or not your deductions are allowed. However, a couple of rules of thumb do apply here. First, to claim an expenditure as a business concern, it must have been incurred in connection with your business. Second, it must be ordinary (common and accepted in your business) and necessary (helpful and appropriate for your business) (Department of Treasury, 1990, p. 1). For example, a desk would be an appropriate purchase that is tax deductible; however, a desk from the Ming dynasty with ivory and pearl engravings costing $12,000 may not be an appropriate deduction. It may not be considered ordinary or necessary for one's practice and most likely would be viewed as a nondepreciable investment.

Typical items that are tax deductible include rent (computed by square foot); home office (must be used exclusively for practice); contracted services such as secretarial, accounting, and legal; advertising; bank service charges; out-of-town business travel; conventions; books and professional journals; magazines for the waiting room; professional entertaining (such as for marketing); telephone, pager, and answering service; burglar alarm; business cards; office supplies; professional gifts; postage; utilities; insurances; licenses, certifications, and dues; play therapy supplies; office secretarial service; office furnishings; payroll and payroll taxes; safe-deposit box; depreciation of furniture and fixtures; and improvements (Department of Treasury, 1990, p. 9).

You may also deduct expenses on your car. This is done in one of two ways: take a standard mileage allowance, or maintain records on expenses incurred. The latter will allow you to depreciate your car. Use trip sheets, logs, or similar records to list the expenses properly. Obtain IRS Publication #917, *Business Use of Your Car,* free of charge if you have more questions.

Education can be tax deductible as well, assuming you use it to maintain or improve your skills. This can include tuition, books, fees, photocopying, and transportation. For further information obtain the free Publication #535, entitled *Business Expenses,* from the IRS.

Bonuses to employees may be acceptable deductions so long as they are not considered to be gifts. Gifts are deductible, but will have an annual limit as to how much you may deduct for each individual.

If you are planning to take a deduction for depreciation, such as on computer equipment or your car, request Publication #5343, entitled *Depreciation,* from the IRS.

Every therapist has experienced not being able to collect a fee for sessions provided to clients. However, these bad debts can only be used as a tax deduction if you use the accrual method of accounting. You may deduct any actual costs paid in an effort to collect fees.

Self-Employment Taxes

Self-employment tax is the Social Security tax for self-employed individuals. The Federal Insurance Contributions Act (FICA) uses Social Security taxes to provide finances for the federal program for old age, survivor's, disability, and hospital insurance. When you were employed by someone else, your federal withholding and your FICA were deducted before you ever saw it. In addition, your employer paid half your FICA. If you are incorporated you must pay the whole FICA for yourself and half that of your employees. If you are self-employed you pay self-employment tax rather than FICA.

When you work for someone else and get paid a salary, your federal withholding is deducted from your salary. You never see the money and the pain is lessened. However, when you are a self-employed clinician, you must learn how to estimate how much you will earn, calculate your tax liability, and remit your taxes quarterly. You will either estimate your taxes based on last year's taxes or estimate your quarterly liability based on the current year's income. Estimated taxes are considered the "pay-as-you-go" plan. You will need to complete Form #1040-ES, Estimated Tax for Individuals. IRS Publication #505, *Tax Withholding and Estimated Taxes,* will provide more information. Estimate your taxes cautiously: The IRS charges an interest penalty for underpayment. The payments are due April 15, June 15, September 15, and January 15 of the following year.

Sole proprietors and partners must pay the self-employed Social Security tax. If you are incorporated and are an employee of the corporation, you do not have to file a formal declaration of estimated taxes. If you are an owner of a sole proprietorship or a partner in a partnership, the amounts you withdraw from the business are not subject to payroll withholding taxes. Instead, you will pay a self-employment tax (instead of Social Security tax), with your estimated income tax, based on your business net profit.

Some deductions that are used to reduce income tax cannot be used to reduce the self-employment tax. These include your personal retirement deductions and health insurance. You will use federal income tax Form #1040-SE to file the self-employment tax. For more information obtain IRS Publication #553, *Information on Self-Employment Tax.*

Employment Taxes

You can expect to pay four kinds of payroll taxes as an employer: federal income tax withholding, Social Security, federal unemployment taxes, and state unemployment taxes. You will be expected to maintain employee records for the federal government. All employers are required to keep proof of employability recorded on an Employment Eligibility Verification Form #I-9 relating to your employees' nonresident alien status or residence in Puerto Rico or Virgin Islands. This reporting is due to the federal government's clampdown on the hiring of illegal aliens. The forms are available through the Immigration and Naturalization Service (INS).

Your role as a private practitioner has changed. Now, not only are you liable for paying taxes, but if you have employees you also will be responsible for collecting taxes through their wages. The federal government will require that you withhold income taxes in connection with your employees' salaries on all wages paid above a certain minimum. You have to withhold income taxes from your employees' wages and send these taxes to the IRS. The requirements for withholding, reporting, depositing, and paying income tax are determined from the tables in Circular E, *Employer's Tax Guide.* This publication is available free from the IRS.

Federal Payroll Tax Returns (Form #941) are due quarterly on April 30, July 31, October 31, and January 31. The income tax and Social Security taxes, along with the employer's portion of the Social Security tax, will be documented on these returns.

Federal Income Tax Withholding

You will be responsible for withholding federal income tax from your employees' wages. You will need to keep the following records for filing your payroll tax reports:

1. Each employee's name, address, and Social Security number
2. The period covered for each payment and its amount
3. Amount of wages subject to withholding in each payment
4. Amount and dates of withholding tax

5. Reason that the taxable amount is less than the total payment, if applicable
6. Your employer identification number (also called an EIN)
7. Duplicate copies of returns filed
8. Dates and amounts of deposits made with government depositories
9. Period for which your employees are paid by you while they are absent because of sickness or personal injury, and the amount and weekly rates of the payments
10. Your employees' withholding exemption certificates
11. Any agreement between you and an employee for the withholding of an additional amount of tax
12. Copies of records of any nonresident aliens working for you
13. Amount of health and accident plan payments

The amount you withhold will be based on the number of exemptions the employee claims.

Social Security and Medicare Tax

You will have to withhold and match Social Security and Medicare taxes from your employees' salaries. These taxes must be remitted to the Internal Revenue Service together with the above federal income taxes withheld. The remittance is generally made at your local bank with a depository coupon form.

Social Security taxes apply to only the first $53,400 of wages paid an employee during a year. Medicare taxes apply to the first $125,000 of wages. For FICA and Medicare, maintain the following records:

1. Amount of wages that are subject to FICA and Medicare taxes
2. Amount and dates these taxes were collected and deposits made
3. Justification for any difference between the amount of wages earned and the amount of wages that were taxable, if applicable

Federal Unemployment Tax Act (FUTA)

These taxes are required of employers to supplement state unemployment funds. Businesses are taxed as a means of reimbursing the federal government for the funds it has provided for state unemployment. You will be taxed according to your state's ability to repay the federal government. You will pay if you had a payroll of at least $1,500 the previous calendar year, or if you have retained at least one employee at least part of each workday for 20 weeks. Your employees do not pay into these funds. You will need to maintain the following records:

1. Total amount you paid your employee during the calendar year
2. Amount of the wages subject to the unemployment tax and, if applicable, why this amount differs from the total compensation
3. Amount you paid into the state unemployment fund, showing the payments deducted or to be deducted, and the payments not deducted or to be deducted from your employees' wages

These annual returns are filed either on Form #940 or Form #940 EZ (for smaller businesses), the Employer's Annual Federal Unemployment Tax Return, due on or before January 31 of the following year.

State Unemployment Insurance

You, the employer, pay this in full. This provides financial compensation to employees who have been laid off due to no fault of their own. You will fill out quarterly forms providing your state with information regarding the number of employees and salaries paid that quarter. This will generally include the computation and payment of a tax based on a percentage experience rate determined by your state. This helps pay for those eligible to receive unemployment compensation.

State Income Taxes

Most states impose an income tax on their residents. You withhold taxes for the state in which your employees live. They are based on taxable wages or net income of a sole proprietor or partner. Most state income tax returns are due April 15, but several states have later dates. Corporate income tax laws and filing dates differ.

County, City, and Other Local Taxes

Counties may tax property, real estate, equipment, and furniture. These business taxes may be a deductible business expense.

Personal Property Taxes

You will receive a form entitled Personal Property Tax Return, in which you list all property that your business owns, its original cost, and depreciated value. Your city will then tax you on a percentage of the total value. Large cities are likely to have higher taxes. All jurisdictions tend to levy heavy penalties for late payment.

Workers' Compensation Insurance

You may have a choice as to the purchase of workers' compensation insurance, although some states require coverage for employees. Each state has its own laws. Usually, insurance agents provide this coverage. It provides for medical coverage if an employee is hurt, financial assistance if an employee is disabled, vocational rehabilitation, and survivor benefits to a family if an employee dies.

Filing Forms

Forms you will need to know about for payroll taxes include the W-4, W-2, and W-3 forms.

The W-4 is the Employees' Withholding Allowance certificate. As with all other jobs you have held, the W-4 form is filled out as soon as you begin working. Keep your number of dependents current. This will affect your federal withholding.

The W-2 is the Wage and Tax Statement. You will be filling out and distributing these by the end of January of each year to each employee. It is a five-part form, with copies for your employee, you, and the Social Security Administration. The IRS will send them to you complete with instructions.

The W-3 is the Transmittal of Income and Tax Statements (TIN). These forms are fairly self-explanatory. They ask for the totals of all wages paid last year and federal and FICA deductions. One copy of all W-2 forms will be stapled to the W-3 form. The W-3 form is then mailed to your local Social Security office. These forms, too, are available from the IRS.

Client Tax Deductions

Clients can deduct fees paid to most therapists as a medical expense if it can be demonstrated that the services rendered were primarily for the "diagnosis, cure, mitigation, treatment or prevention of a significant mental or emotional problem" (National Association of Social Workers, 1987, p. 12). The therapist should document how the problem is a "manifestation or a result of a mental or emotional condition requiring treatment; and how the services contribute to alleviating and mitigating the problem and underlying condition" (National Association of Social Workers, 1987, p. 12).

Audits

The IRS is not out to get the honest taxpayer, but only those who intentionally evade payment of their tax obligations. However, the number of tax returns being audited is increasing. The IRS generally looks for red flags that returns may be waving, such as a high number of deductions (almost equaling your income), and unreasonable expenses atypical to your work (such as large travel expenses for conventions). Maintaining good records will help you in the event that you are audited. Failure to keep good records, supported by invoices, canceled checks, bank deposit slips, cash receipts, and sales slips, could result in you having to pay more taxes than you should because of disallowed deductions.

Keep records longer than the statute of limitations requires. Your tax records provide a good history of your business as well as business decisions made. You may find that referring to old records is helpful in making ongoing decisions, and they also could be useful to the executor of your estate should you die.

SIX

Fee Setting, Collections, and Bookkeeping

No matter how good your clinical skills are, if you do not have the foggiest notion of how to cope with the financial side of your practice, your business is doomed to failure. It is each therapist's professional responsibility to keep accurate records. Do not deceive yourself and think that you can hire a secretary or bookkeeper to handle the books and divorce yourself from the function. To do so will only cost you money and headaches in the long run.

Fee Setting

The fees set for therapy reflect your education, training, experience, self-confidence, geographical location, and length of sessions. Money carries enormous emotional associations that can significantly influence a therapist's comfort with fee setting, ability to address and resolve payment disputes, and, ultimately, income. These issues need to be recognized prior to establishing a private practice, as they can affect the process of treatment via how professionally you are viewed in addition to transference and countertransference issues with your clients.

A therapist I once worked with consistently reduced her rate 35% for all patients, regardless of ability to pay. In response to my inquiry as to why she did this, she claimed to "have the values of a social worker." In actuality she was hiding behind her own lack of confidence as a therapist and worthiness to collect the designated fee. Charge what is reasonable and fair—to all parties.

Fees are a condition of therapy. Each therapist must assume an active role in setting the fees for each client. It is a part of the contract between therapist and patient. Often, therapists will avoid having such discussions with their clients for fear of appearing to be more interested in the income than their client's well-being.

Discussion of the fee should take place prior to the first session, when the therapist discusses the "housekeeping" issues, such as cancellation policy, cost and length of each session, payment schedule, and so on. The client has a right to know her or his financial responsibilities and your financial policies. The therapist must feel comfortable with collecting payment, as any ambivalence will be communicated to the client. Clients will need to be informed that regardless of your office's attempts to collect payment from an insurance company, that payment of fees is the client's basic financial obligation. This will protect you from nonpayment of therapy sessions should an insurance company refuse to pay. It also protects your new client with clear boundaries and containment.

Generally it is best to develop a rapport with the potential client prior to quoting a fee. This may be accomplished over the telephone. It is important for the therapist to always go over the fee, even if the secretary has, as well as other boundary issues. Such discussions ensure that agreements are clear and that clients' issues with them can be fairly addressed right at the beginning of therapy. This is one way to exhibit adult caring and fairness and to establish appropriate rapport.

Although clients expect to pay for professional services, they often are surprised by the fees. They may defer making an appointment unless they develop a sense of confidence and commitment in you or your office staff that you will be able to help them with their problem(s). They need to know that you will be honest and fair with them.

To determine at what rate to set your fees, either confer with colleagues or call therapists located within a 30-minute drive of your office, as clients will drive that distance for their therapy. Inquire about the therapist's fees as well as how they determine their sliding fee scale. Also, factor in your experience. A therapist with years of experience and perhaps an area of specialization should not be charging the same as a licensed clinician just obtaining vendorship.

Set one fee for an individual, couple, or family session, if they each take the same amount of time. Some therapists see couples and/or families for lengthier sessions than individual sessions and charge accordingly. For group therapy, therapists charge approximately 50% to 70% of the individual session fee. Some therapists charge more for initial evaluations, but I would only do so if it required a lengthier session. A new trend evolving for group therapy is to charge a flat fee for being in the group, but providing the members with 4 free weeks (because there are 4 months with 5 weeks). The members are then charged whether they attend the group or not.

Different clients may be charged "adjusted" fees. Some therapists develop a sliding fee scale for referred new clients with limited financial means. My experience has been that the predetermined sliding fee scale is meaningless as a measure of payment ability. For example, if two families of equal income wish to have a sliding fee for therapy, the therapist's fee-sliding decision will be based on the following criteria: (a) Who is the referring source? Is it someone I am wishing to cultivate? (b) Does this particular type of case interest me? Will it serve me in future referrals to work with this case? (c) In my judgment is the sliding fee justified?

Do not ask the client what he or she feels he or she can afford to pay. Therapy is a choice. Clients make the choice to come to therapy. There has to be a reasonable cost to it.

It also is expected that therapists accept some "pro bono" cases, which involve services rendered at no cost to the client (Canter & Freudenberger, 1990, p. 222). An opportune time to do this is when the insurance has been exhausted and the client can no longer afford your services. Accepting the client at a limited cost keeps the therapeutic relationship intact and prevents "dumping" the client onto community agencies. It is acceptable to see the client at a limited cost and to recontract with the client as to what the goals in treatment are. Minimally, the client must be out of a crisis. To work with clients when they have insurance but to terminate them when the insurance "runs dry" is to run the risk of developing a reputation in the community as being insensitive, unethical, and "money hungry."

A way to avoid this situation is to review with your client at the beginning of treatment what the insurance coverage is and how long it is likely to last. If it is a limited policy, share with your client what the out-of-pocket expenses would be. This will preempt feelings of abandonment that may arise later on if insurance runs out.

If your client was expecting to pay for the therapy when the insurance runs out but then finds himself unable to do so, it is fully acceptable to transfer him to a community agency. However, you must do so in a smooth manner and not when he is in a crisis.

Therapy is a choice, and the decision to choose therapy is based in large part on the client's value system. For example, if the family is struggling because they are paying for an elderly parent to live in a nursing home, I am more likely to want to accommodate that family than I am a family who has a cash flow problem because they just bought a vacation home. Asking clients for information about their financial situation is important. It provides realistic and objective information on which to base your decision of appropriateness for a sliding fee. It also provides you with information on the value the prospective client places on therapy.

I also am more inclined to reduce my hourly rate for a prospective client who was referred by a good or potentially good referral source than I am for a telephone book referral. I may also reduce my rate if the client agrees to be seen during my less frequently scheduled hours, which generally are noon to 3:00 P.M.

Never accept a client at a fee less than you are comfortable with, as you are likely to develop a negative countertransference with the client. An alternative consideration to sliding your fee is to offer shorter sessions, such as 30 minutes rather than the usual 45-, 50-, or 60-minute session. This arrangement enables you to continue seeing the client with shorter, more focused sessions and is less likely to compete for the limited number of billable hours you have to offer each day. Another option is to increase the period of time between sessions, assuming your client is sufficiently stable.

If a client is a professional, she or he may request a professional courtesy, which means to be treated at a reduced rate. Each therapist makes his or her own decisions regarding this policy. My experience is that developing a practice of professional clients can ensure less fee sliding in the long run, as they in turn will be in a position to refer many future clients. Therefore, offering a reduced rate to other professionals can be a wise investment. However, be aware that giving professional courtesy is against the law in some states. Also, you cannot "write off" the copayment. This is illegal. It can also contaminate the therapy, creating resentment on both sides about the client "owing" the therapist.

As you begin your practice you may wish to set a lower fee so you can develop more referrals. The decision to lower or raise rates is an individual one. Consider the possibility, though, that you may become known in your community as providing a lower level of service, and only receive sliding fee referrals. Also, although it is satisfying to fill your schedule with any paying client—even a poorly paying one—it may be shortsighted. Perhaps the time would have been better spent marketing for full-paying clients. Reduced-rate clients also may be in treatment for a long time, further inhibiting your opportunities to establish a well-paying clientele.

The decision to raise rates may come when your practice is stable enough to justify an increased compensation to you. Or you may come to learn that other therapists in the community are consistently charging more and you are lagging behind the reasonable and customary charge.

A natural time to raise fees is at the first of the calendar year. People tend to accept the new year as bringing in new rates. If a client is relatively new, however, do not raise her or his rate. If a previously terminated client comes back for additional therapy, it is acceptable to charge the new rate. Treat the new rate as a significant clinical issue, as some clients are likely to view the raising of fees as the therapist being more interested in money than the client, rather than as a benevolent healer (Canter & Freudenberger, 1990, p. 223). Allow your clients at least 3 weeks' notice so the issue can be processed in the sessions. As inflation affects psychotherapists just as it does the rest of the population, you are justified in raising your fees. However, keep the increases modest. You may also want to let clients know your fee-raising policy when they begin their therapy with you, particularly if they seem to be long-term clients, with a statement such as, "Traditionally, I raise my fees once a year at the beginning of the year by $_____."

Billing

The secret to successful billing is to keep it as simple as possible. You will need to maintain records on whom you saw, fee charged, and amount paid. This can be accomplished whether you are using the more time-consuming general ledger card system or have a sophisticated computerized system. Either will be acceptable with the Internal Revenue Service, as all cash transactions are posted.

You will need to develop a method of accurately tracking which clients you saw each week. There are two ways to accomplish this. The first method is to use your daily calendar in your appointment book to provide recall for identifying which clients were seen. The second method is to develop a Clients Seen List, and to document which patients were seen each week (Figure 6.1). I have found that this method reduces the amount of energy put into reconstructing previous days and is quite accurate. Your secretary may not be aware of some clients you see because therapy hours often extend into nontraditional work hours. The Clients Seen List is a weekly summary sheet listing each client by name, date seen, amount charged, amount adjusted, and amount paid. The therapist fills out the client's name, date seen, and the amount the client paid. It is important for the therapist to fill in the amount the clients paid so the therapist is aware whether the clients are keeping up. It is an important therapeutic issue. The secretary fills in the amount charged, because he or she has this information at his or her desk on the ledger cards. As all client payments have been deposited with the secretary during the course of the week, he or she also will know what amounts have been paid and will enter this on the form. This form is then used by the secretary for billing purposes. The Clients Seen List can periodically be matched against the ledger cards to check for accuracy in billing.

COUNSELING ASSOCIATES *Of* HOUSTON

CLIENTS SEEN THIS WEEK

Page ____ of ____

WEEK OF:___/___/___ THROUGH ___/___/___

THERAPIST: _____

Date Seen	Patient's Name	Amount Charged	Adjustment	Amount Paid
___/___		$	$	$
___/___		$	$	$
___/___		$	$	$
___/___		$	$	$
___/___		$	$	$
___/___		$	$	$
___/___		$	$	$
___/___		$	$	$
___/___		$	$	$
___/___		$	$	$
___/___		$	$	$
___/___		$	$	$
___/___		$	$	$
___/___		$	$	$
___/___		$	$	$
___/___		$	$	$
			TOTAL	$

Figure 6.1. Clients Seen List

Formulate a schedule by which bills are sent out to clients on a routine, predictable basis. It may be that they are sent out after each session, or perhaps twice a month. Timely billing is critical from a communication point of view. It lets your clients know you are setting boundaries and it makes the financial side of coming to therapy more predictable. Do not let clients run up debts. Discuss financial issues as soon as they arise. An easy, yet reliable method of billing clients is to photocopy the ledger card, which will indicate dates seen, payments made, and balance due. An individualized, typed note at the bottom can relate explicit expectations you have of the client in regard to payment.

If clients pay after a session in cash, give the client a written receipt that provides for a carbon to be left with the secretary. An office copy of the receipt can protect against an impulse to steal the money. Also, should a client allege at a later time that she or he paid for a session and neither the client nor your office has a receipt, you will know that it is probably not true that the payment was made. The receipt should reflect the following information: agency's name, address, and telephone number; client's name; date seen; amount paid; amount due; and balance. The superbill, which is a receipt and billing form for mental health providers, will suffice as a receipt as well as a bill to submit to some insurance companies (Figure 6.2).

An option I have not pursued is that of using credit cards for patients who would prefer to charge their payments. You may wish to look into this; however, it will be more costly for you. Also, using credit cards may be allowing and encouraging people to overextend their limited resources, and collude with the destructive practice of getting today and "taking care of it" somehow in the future. Check with the various financial institutions on the effort involved in application for credit card acceptance.

Be assertive and businesslike from the beginning with uncollected accounts. They will lose loyalty once they have received the service. Talk with the client to determine whether it is a therapeutic or a financial problem that is interfering with payment for sessions. Be friendly, work out payment plans, but keep the payments coming in. Unpaid accounts will hurt your business, as you cannot deduct them from your income.

Fee Collection

In 1913 Sigmund Freud noted that "Ordinary good sense cautions the analyst not to allow large sums of money to accumulate but to ask for payment at fairly short regular intervals—monthly, perhaps" (Freud, 1913). Freud's concept of not allowing debts to grow has not changed with time. The general practice currently is to collect after every session.

A decision has to be made whether the therapist or the receptionist collects the payments. As I often work 12-hour days, but my secretary only works 8 hours per day, I will, in the very early morning or late evening hours, be the only one available to collect payments. Some therapists view handling the money as an undesirable, even dirty, chore. As I said earlier, payment is a

PLEASE RETURN THIS FORM TO THE RECEPTIONIST			NAME:	
			Previous Balance:	
ATTENDING PROVIDER'S STATEMENT			Patient:	[ ] M or [ ] F
Code	Procedure	Amount	Address:	
90844	Individual Psychotherapy		City: State: Zip:	
9084_	Conjoint Psychotherapy		Relationship: Birthdate:	
90847	Family Psychotherapy		Subscriber or Policyholder:	
90853	Group Psychotherapy		Insurance Carrier:	[ ] Medicare
90831	Telephone Consultation		Number:	[ ] Medicaid
90801	Psychological Evaluation		Hospital:	
			[ ] In Patient [ ] Out Patient	
90899	Other:		Date Symptoms Appeared or Accident Occurred:	

1 — 4 — 5 — 6

AUTHORIZATION TO PAY BENEFITS TO PHYSICIAN: I hereby authorize payment directly to the undersigned Physician of the Surgical and/or Medical Benefits, if any, otherwise payable to me for his services as described below but not to exceed the reasonable and customary charge for these services.	Month: Day: Year:
	Disability Related To:
	[ ] Accident [ ] Industrial [ ] Pregnancy [ ] Other
Signed (Insured Person) Date	Dates: From _____ To _____
AUTHORIZATION TO RELEASE INFORMATION: I hereby authorize the undersigned Physician to release any information acquired in the course of my examination or treatment.	OK To Return To Work _____
Signed (Patient or Parent if minor) Date	
Place of service: [ ] Office [ ] Hospital [ ] Emergency Room [ ] Other	Eileen S. Lenson, ACSW, CSW-ACP
Diagnosis or Symptoms:	17101 Main Street, Suite 100
	Houston, Texas 77068
	(713) 648-1898
Referring Physician: Date of Referral:	
Provider's Signature:	

Figure 6.2. Superbill

part of the therapeutic process. The therapist needs to work through any ambivalence regarding money to prevent his or her own negative feelings interfering with treatment.

When is the proper time to collect payment? I believe the majority of people are most comfortable paying after they received the service, and not before. Yet, there are some who would rather not have to stop after an intense session and be pulled away from their introspections. They might prefer to pay prior to the session. My office policy is to have my secretary expect payment at the end of the session. As part of the contracting with a new client I will inquire about her or his preference for timing of payment for each session. If the client wishes to pay prior to the session she or he may, or she or he may pay at the conclusion of the session.

At times in the past I noticed that my clients would not pay at the end of a session. This allowed clients to develop relatively large debts—a debt some would not want to pay. Now, when clients start to leave my office, I simply inquire, "How would you like to pay for this, Mrs. Jones?" This approach is simple, clean, and effective. This prevents a client from seeing the treatment as "free" and getting overextended. If clinical issues arise regarding the payment for therapy, we process them in a session. Clients will either hand me the payment or hand it to my secretary when leaving the office. By my requesting payment, my secretary avoids becoming triangled in, and this also protects my clients' privacy and boundaries.

If you do not have a secretary, are responsible for fee collections, and are finding difficulty separating the termination of your session from the point when your client should be paying you, you may want to consider collecting the fee at the beginning of the session. You may present it as follows: "I like to take care of the business part at the beginning, so that we do not end on a financial note, unless it is therapeutically appropriate. I believe it to be more beneficial to allow you to process the session as opposed to having to think about the finances."

Decide in advance on an upper dollar limit that you will allow clients to become indebted to you. Remember, if clients are not paying you for the sessions, you are giving them interest-free loans, while your overhead and other expenses continue. Furthermore, they are probably repeating destructive old issues of guilt, resentment, indebtedness, overcommitment, or lack of responsibility or ability to come through. Only allow a certain limit on your credit.

In situations that differ from conventional therapy, payment may be more difficult to secure. In cases of child custody evaluations or expert testimony, consider requesting payment in advance (Meyer, Landis, & Hays, 1988, p. 38).

Should a client give you a bad check, contact the client immediately and request that another check be submitted or that cash be dropped off at the office. Pass on any expense incurred by the bank to your client. If the situation occurs a second time, urge the client to pay in cash only, and discuss what is behind the bounced check, such as overextension, unrealistic financial expectations, unexpected expenses, or limit testing.

Payment Sources

There are several payment sources, such as private pay (direct pay from the patient); traditional insurance, which will pay for part or all of the therapy; employee assistance programs; health maintenance organizations; preferred provider organizations; exclusive provider organizations; managed care; and psychiatric hospitals.

■ Private Pay

In some cases clients will have no or inadequate insurance benefits. Others will wish to pay out-of-pocket rather than file with their insurance. These individuals can be expected to pay in full after each session.

Some practitioners, especially new ones with limited secretarial support, deal with all clients as a private pay, even though they have insurance. The client pays in full for the session and is responsible for being reimbursed by the insurance company. The therapist helps fill out the insurance form and provides a diagnosis. To help ensure consistent payments from self-pay clients, you may wish to offer a 10% discount on advance monthly payments.

■ Insurance

Medical insurance affords many clients the opportunity to obtain counseling that might otherwise be financially prohibitive. It does alter the anonymous, confidential nature of treatment, however. This should be discussed with your clients; not to do so can result in the withholding of important information vital to a trusting relationship.

It helps to be familiar with insurance policies, including how they reimburse and what their rules are. For instance, there will be differences between how Medicare, managed care, and commercial insurances reimburse for therapy sessions. Develop a working "carrier sheet" in your office that notes up-to-date information on the insurances, to assure that you are not overlooking specific criteria and guidelines.

If you plan to bill the client's insurance company, it is necessary to contact the insurance company before the first office visit. Be careful to follow the rule of confidentiality here. In many states you need your client's consent in writing before you mention any information about them to an insurance company or anyone else. This will allow you to determine what information and documentation is required, percentage of fee covered, claim forms to be used, and their "reasonable and customary charges." Unfortunately, insurance companies are a lot like poker players: They won't tell you a lot until you lay down your cards.

Insurance companies usually mandate education and credentials requirements for the psychotherapist. They tend to be much more interested in credentials than academic training. If your state offers licensing, it will be imperative that you become licensed. If the insurance company refuses to recognize your credentials, send them a copy of your credentialing or licensing number and the section of vendorship law that is applicable to your specialization. Also inquire about diagnoses that will not be covered by the insurance. Typically, the "V" codes in the DSM-III-R are not covered. Finally, it also helps to ask the insurance company what the quickest way is to get a claim paid.

Not to obtain the proper information from an insurance company can result in headaches, confusion, and financial chaos later. Do not expect your secretary to be able to obtain the necessary information from the insurance company while answering the telephones. Instead, when he or she is verifying benefits and coverage, have your secretary put on the answering service.

My secretary and I devised a form to use when calling insurance companies, entitled the Verification of Insurance Benefits (discussed in Chapter 4; see Figure 4.1). Because a decision to hospitalize a patient often occurs after hours, I now have my secretary routinely inquire about inpatient psychiatric benefits, even if the patient is coming in for outpatient therapy. She also inquires about coverage for mental and nervous conditions as well as chemical dependency during her initial call to the insurance company. This is because she is calling for coverage based on what I believe the diagnosis will be even before I have assessed the client. Someone who presents as having one diagnosis on the telephone may have a different diagnosis after our first session.

Having the person's name that provided the information at the insurance company is important as well, as discrepancies do arise and you will want to be able to refer back to a specific individual. Keep these information sheets in the client's folder. You also will find it helpful to ask your client for his or her insurance booklet. Photocopy the mental illness section and retain this information for your files.

If the client's insurance company informs you that they will pay for a number of visits per year, or that they will pay for a number of visits at one rate and a number of visits at another rate, document this on the Verification of Insurance Benefits sheet as well as on the ledger card. Either you or your secretary will be viewing the ledger card regularly and will be able to keep on top of what your clients' insurance companies are paying.

The insurance company will also state what percentage of a maximum charge they will pay. This may be based on the "reasonable and customary" fees they recognize for each discipline in your geographical area. Because you are an independent practitioner, you are capable of setting your fee higher than that compensated by your client's insurance company, providing you do not have a contract to provide services at a fixed amount. This means you will then have to inform your client that he or she will be responsible for the difference between the insurance reimbursement and your fee.

It is important to make certain that all the necessary forms required by the insurance company are completed carefully and in full. Billing insurance companies is contingent upon your client bringing in a signed claim form. Failure to do so may result in either the delay or failure of the insurance company to pay. If your client is delinquent with bringing in the form, continue to have the client pay in full until the form is brought in. Use the *Diagnostic and Statistical Manual,* third edition revised (DSM-III-R), for the diagnosis and use the code number in the insurance form.

Probably you will be using the revised Health Care Financing Administration (HCFA) 1500 claim form to file your claims with the insurance company. These forms can be ordered from the Government Printing Office,

Superintendent of Documents, Washington, DC, (202) 783-3238. Often you can have your client sign an original form and then photocopy the signed form to be used for subsequent sessions. The original signature will often suffice, with the rest of the information typed in for each subsequent session. Do be certain that the insurance company will accept a copy and not require an original signature. Consider purchasing a stamp of your signature so it can be used on the claim forms rather than you having to sign each one.

Use the Physicians Current Procedural Terminology codes (CPT) on the claim forms. They are obtainable from the American Medical Association. These will help clarify the type of service you provided to the third-party payor. The most typical codes you will use are: 90841 Individual psychotherapy—specify number of minutes; 90843 Individual psychotherapy—approx. 20-30 minutes; 90844 Individual psychotherapy—approx. 45-60 minutes; and 90853 Group psychotherapy—specify minutes.

As with all paperwork that leaves the office, keep a copy for the client's file. If your client is going to be submitting her or his own claim form, write your provider number (Social Security number) on the form so it can expedite payment for her or him.

You will not be able to collect from an insurance company until the client's deductible has been met. Until then the client will need to pay you out of pocket for the therapy sessions. After the deductible has been met, the insurance will then reimburse at a predetermined percentage or set dollar amount for each therapy session. If reimbursement from the insurance company has not been made within 4 weeks, call to verify receipt of your submitted claim. Note on the client's ledger card whom you spoke with, whether the claim was received, when the claim will be processed, and when the payment will be sent. If the insurance coverage was denied or charges were reduced, note this on the ledger card.

Every time you receive the Explanation of Benefits (EOB) from the insurance company, be certain to compare it to the copy of the insurance form you sent and confirm it for correct payment. Note that the EOB may contain payment for multiple claims. If payment was reduced or denied, the reasons should be included. If you have any discrepancy, call the insurance company to clarify why there is a difference. At these times it will be helpful if you have, in your files, a photocopy of your client's insurance booklet's mental illness section to refer to. Determine whether you have any contractual adjustments that you failed to consider.

If the percentage is verified as being different from what you originally understood, change your records, and contact your client. Your client will need to be aware of how this change will affect his or her account. If, however, you believe that the reason for the denial or reduced charge is incorrect, ask to speak with a supervisor.

Errors do occur. It is not a rare occasion to receive a check from an insurance company for a client who is unknown to your practice. Do not deposit the check. Do not deposit it hoping to keep the interest until the insurance company asks for it back. This will make you look like a crook and may trigger an audit by the insurance company. Void it out on the face of the check and send it back with a cover letter explaining the error.

Insurance companies will typically take 6 to 8 weeks before they begin making their first payments. Afterward, payments will come more quickly and regularly, providing you are billing regularly. If I am seeing a client weekly, I always have my secretary place an inquiry call if a month passes without a payment. Despite having established a track record of payment to you, the insurance company may begin sending the checks to your client or put the case in review. If you or your secretary feel that you are not getting accurate information from the insurance company, ask to speak to the supervisor. Note on the ledger card with whom you spoke, whether the claim was received, when the claim will be processed, and when payment will be sent. Also note whether the insurance coverage was denied or payments were reduced.

Be aware of penalties your state allows against insurance companies that do not pay in a timely manner. In Texas, for example, Article 3.62, "Delay in Payment of Losses; Penalty For," allows the therapist to assess the insurance company 12% damage for claims that have not been either paid or denied within the statutory 30-day limit.

Sometimes the insurance company will not pay on a claim because it is in "audit." In that event inform them that you need to be paid, even during the audit. Simply—yet firmly—request that they pay a portion of the percentage due you, and state that you will refund the money if there is a discrepancy. A trend is for insurance companies to do audits on your outpatient client's treatment. Make sure you have treatment notes for each session.

Be aware of what an insurance company must do. They must first investigate a claim before it is denied. If they deny claims that you were verbally told would be paid, mail them a copy of the Verification of Insurance form (discussed below) by certified mail. Include a cover letter stating: "This is what we understand the benefits to be. If this is not correct, please respond within 10 working days." They are required to respond but the period of time may range from 30 to 60 days, depending on the state.

If the insurance company sends you a bulk check, which is a single check representing payment for several clients you are treating, write notes on the EOB as to which clients' accounts were paid, and how much.

You can only bill the insurance company the amount you have charged the patient. That is, if a sliding fee is used for the patient, this must be passed on to the insurance company. It will be considered fraud to accept insurance reimbursement only. The client must be expected to pay the copayment amount. If you are willing to write off the out-of-pocket difference between the insurance coverage and your charges, the insurance company will not consider them to be realistic charges.

Keep records of your collection efforts that have resulted in you waiving the patient's fees so the insurance company will not request a reimbursement of overpayment. The insurance companies will want to know that you have made an effort to collect the difference.

It is not unusual to have a client request that you falsify the insurance claim forms by submitting a different diagnosis or to document the beginning date of therapy or the charge for the sessions as being different than they were. Some therapists will agree to such illegal, fraudulent, unethical arrangements. Either they view their actions as helping the underdog out with the rigid insurance companies, or they are protecting their own incomes by not wanting to lose the client.

There are two problems with falsifying claim forms. First, you are developing an alliance with your client based on deceit. How do you encourage your client to be truthful if you are being a negative role model? Instead, you and your client join together in a contaminated relationship. There are numerous deeper issues as well. This arrangement also could conclude in a blackmailing situation should your client become angry with you and threaten to inform the insurance company of your actions. It always undermines a healthy therapeutic alliance. Second, it is fraudulent to misrepresent the facts on the insurance claim forms. To do so could result in costly legal consequences. Being convicted of insurance fraud will lead to the suspension of your license in many states and the loss of your malpractice coverage.

Being open and direct with your clients about how you will complete insurance claim forms will, in the long run, result in better relationships with clients, which will result in fewer premature terminations. It also will enhance your own self-respect as well as word being spread throughout the professional and lay communities about your ethical behavior.

If a client's status has changed, you may need to change the diagnosis as well. The insurance company should be notified of any such changes. If a client is using two insurance companies, you must notify each of the additional coverage. One company will generally function as the primary insurer with the other as secondary.

While I was writing this book a potential client called and asked what my rates were. I told him $100 per hour. He asked that I bill him at $125 an hour, because his insurance would pay 50% up to $125, which would be $75. He wanted to then pay me $25 per session rather than the $50 required if I billed his insurance honestly. I told him I could not do this for two reasons: legal and ethical. It would be fraudulent to do so. Also, it would be establishing our relationship on dishonest terms, colluding against the insurance company. The therapeutic trust we needed to establish would be undermined and therapy would be compromised. He informed me that other therapists would agree to this sort of arrangement, and that it is done as a matter of common practice. I suggested that he consider what he wanted out of treatment, and that the choice was his. I never heard from him again, so I suppose he found a therapist who would comply with his illegal request. He was no loss as a client. He was asking me to make his problem my problem, to misrepresent information intentionally to the insurance company.

You must indicate billings for missed appointments on the insurance claim form. There should be a specific code number for this purpose. You typically cannot bill for services that were not performed.

When billing insurance companies, keep in mind that a therapist can only bill under her or his own name. With the exception of Medicare, the provider of services and the signer need always be the same person on the claim form. (With Medicare, therapy provided by an employee may be included in the employer/supervisor's bill.) To bill through another professional because the client's insurance will not reimburse for the therapist providing the psychotherapy, or to pay a referral source part of the client's fee as a kickback, is unethical and fraudulent. The professional organizations do not condone either practice. Both are seen as practices that do not have the client's interest at heart. Typically, the client is unaware of what is occurring. He or she is not aware that hidden agendas may exist in a referral being made, which may run contrary to his or her interests.

If, however, a therapist is working under the supervision of a physician, it is acceptable to bill under one's own name but include a statement that a physician provides supervision. In many cases the insurance company will accept this. In the event that the insurance company refuses to reimburse for the therapist's credentials the therapist may either consider seeing the client at a reduced rate to compensate for the coverage they would have been receiving under a "covered" therapist, or refer the client to a "covered" therapist. The latter can serve to develop a supportive network of cross-referrals with other professionals.

Failure to file insurance forms accurately and honestly can result in criminal charges and license revocation. As a therapist you have the responsibility to assure that forms are not being filed fraudulently. Never forget that it is much more expensive to have to defend oneself against insurance fraud than to forgo a reimbursement. To assist in complying with insurance companies, and to keep up with changes that may affect your billing procedures, invite representatives from the various insurance companies in once a year to provide updates.

■ Expired or Nonreimbursing Insurance

You are likely to encounter clients who suffer financial difficulties or exhaust their outpatient mental health benefits. You may wish to defer payment, terminate, or refer to another therapist. Be cautious about deferring payment and allowing a patient to develop a large balance due. I never allow this to occur because I can see it interfering with treatment. Rather than terminating, you may wish to renegotiate the fee. You may ask the client what she or he feels she or he can afford to pay. Remember that you already have a good relationship with the client and that trust will ensure his or her being fair with you. Avoid the error of offering the client to pay whatever he or she can afford at each session. Although fees may be negotiated, you need to remain in control of and responsible for the therapy session. If the client's financial situation improves, you may again renegotiate higher charges.

At times you may find that despite verbal confirmation that the insurance company would reimburse for your services, the claim is rejected. This is frustrating and can interfere with the treatment. Do not lose control and become verbally abusive with the insurance company. Rather, follow these recommended steps:

1. Speak with a supervisor. Report the name of the person who had given you approval to treat the client. Review your credentials and treatment plan.
2. Resubmit the claim.
3. Consult with your professional organization.
4. Have your client call the insurance company, or have your client have his or her employer call the insurance company.

Third-Party Reimbursement

According to *Psychotherapy Finances,* therapists are becoming increasingly concerned about reimbursement by insurance companies (Rosenberg, Butzen, & Butzen, 1984, p. 8). The day of fee-for-service is gone. Third-party reimbursement factors into more and more of therapists' cases, rendering the private-pay client a relic from another era. Fees are having to be negotiated prior to seeing the client.

It is important that you be well informed about each reimbursing entity. Thus, you can determine whether you even want to become a provider, furnish the necessary information required to obtain reimbursement, and learn how to protect the integrity of your practice. Next we look at employee assistance programs, health maintenance organizations, preferred provider organizations, managed care, and psychiatric hospitals.

■ Employee Assistance Programs (EAPs)

EAPs may be formed either in-house or contracted outside of a company. Most EAPs evaluate clients and then, functioning as gatekeepers, refer them to private practitioners, with little or no involvement with the insurance carrier. Some, however, will contract with psychotherapists at a lower rate than the open market will bring. There are benefits in this type of referral for the therapist who is not as busy as he or she would like to be. It gives the therapist the opportunity to receive a volume of referrals, which may help compensate for the reduced payments. Payments are often guaranteed by the EAP, making collections easier.

Some EAPs will try to negotiate the lowest payment possible. Do not be afraid to request a higher fee, but justify it based on specific credentials or training you have.

■ Health Maintenance Organizations (HMOs)

HMOs offer their subscribers "prepaid or periodic charges paid on a patient capitation basis, both of which involve financial risk by the professional provider" (Rosenberg et al., 1984, p. 2). HMOs will likely be less flexible than EAPs regarding fees. Their rates will be considerably less than the open market but you will receive volume. You cannot charge the patient above and beyond what the HMO insurance has agreed upon. Contracting with HMOs will be attractive to the newly established practitioner. Typically, the HMO focuses on keeping the utilization of services and, therefore, the costs, down. The therapist will have to balance the potential conflicts between meeting the HMO's requirement to contain costs with the client's interests and professional standards. Those clinicians who work with brief interventions are most likely to be satisfied working with an HMO.

■ Preferred Provider Organizations (PPOs)

PPOs function as brokers or middlemen between the purchasers of health care and the providers of health care. The PPO will contract with the insurance company or corporation to obtain lower health-care costs by establishing a provider panel consisting of a limited number of providers, negotiating controlled and usually discounted fees, speedy reimbursement, and a utilization review that they themselves perform or contract out (Rosenberg et al., 1984, p. 12).

The PPO will negotiate and contract with psychotherapists to provide clinical services at a lower rate. Generally the rates are fixed for your geographical area, but you may be in a position to negotiate a slightly higher reimbursement rate if you try. The practitioners typically will be expected to consent to utilization reviews.

The insurance companies or corporations will then have two scales of payment: better coverage to health-care providers who are signed up in their PPO and lower coverage for those health-care providers who are not included. Although the insured has a choice, there is an economic disincentive if a non-PPO provider is selected.

If you have signed a contract with an insurance company to become a preferred provider, it is usually expected that the rates to the client will be increased to your higher rate once the contract expires. It is not acceptable—and is unethical—however, to bill the client at a higher rate as a means of recouping the losses incurred by being obligated to see a client at lesser fees.

When contracting with a PPO, cautiously assess their financial and administrative capacities. Watch for potential problems in the following areas:

1. Number of patients. If the PPO is unable to provide a significant number of patients who will be using the psychotherapist's services, there will be only limited benefit to the fee reduction.

2. "Buy-in" fees. Various PPOs require that therapists pay one-time charges to compensate for start-up costs. These charges are to be paid at the start. Be cautious that the fees are reasonable.

3. Payment of provider charges. Determine how compensation will be made and whether any administrative charges can be expected. Also, if a subscriber who was originally approved for therapy is later found to be ineligible, will the PPO assume responsibility for payment of the charges (Rosenberg et al., 1984, pp. 20-21)?

4. Utilization review (UR) composition. If the UR panel is not composed of mental health practitioners, then your work and recommendations will be reviewed by people who lack the training to make competent decisions. This will affect your treatment.

5. Treatment reports. Typically, reports will be required prior to approval of continued therapy sessions. Learn ahead of time what is expected with regard to frequency of submission and length.

6. Treatment concerns. Some PPOs do not permit long-term individual psychotherapy, but require instead short-term intervention. They may not allow for group, marital, or family therapy. They may not reimburse for certain diagnoses, may control the number of sessions a client can be seen, and may not allow the client to be seen by a non-PPO provider whom the PPO provider has selected for cross-coverage in the event of vacation or sickness.

7. Abandonment. As the PPO may limit the number of sessions the therapist can see the client, it is possible that the client will still require therapy even though the PPO is no longer reimbursing for treatment. Rather than abandon the client, attempt to have the client pay for the sessions, slide your fee, or refer the client to an agency that can slide their fee.

8. Liability. Prior to participating in a PPO, determine whether you are required to indemnify the PPO against liability; whether your personal liability insurance provides coverage for contractually assumed liabilities; whether the other contracting providers are of high quality, or whether they have been found to be negligent in malpractice cases (Hiratsuka, 1990, p. 3). The hold-harmless clauses mean that you will agree to assume the liability, or responsibility, and that the PPO will not suffer any financial loss or harm as a result. This means that if the PPO is sued, you will assume responsibility for any judgment against the PPO for acts committed by you, the provider.

9. Financial stability. Investigate the PPO to make certain it is financially sound. If not, you may have difficulty getting paid.

■ Exclusive Provider Organizations (EPOs)

Unlike PPOs, whereby the insured are offered the incentive of lowered deductibles or copayment to use a provider recommended by the insurance company, EPOs require their subscribers to use their providers exclusively. Claims from other providers will not be paid.

■ Managed Care

Managed health-care firms are the gatekeepers for insurance payment. They try to control mental health and substance abuse costs while guaranteeing quality of care. They offer a variety of services, will preauthorize care or admission into a hospital, offer both quality assurance and utilization review services, and provide discharge planning.

In 1989 only three or four managed care firms offering mental health and substance abuse services to insurance companies, HMOs, and employers existed. By 1991 this number had increased to more than 300 firms. By the mid-1990s it is estimated that 50% to 80% of all employees in the United States will receive managed care services (*Psychotherapy Finances,* 1992a, p. 1).

Psychotherapy Finances (1992) notes that the majority of therapists (66%) now have a relationship with managed health care. This is a 15% increase from the previous year (*Psychotherapy Finances,* 1992a, p. 5). In a 1991 survey they found that 39% of therapists work with employee assistance programs, 35% obtain referrals from preferred provider organizations, and 30% obtain referrals from health maintenance organizations. The effect has been a reduced income for 41%, a reduced patient load for 36%, more disallowed claims for 40%, and a shortened length of therapy for 42% (Beigel & Earle, 1990, pp. 141-142).

Before signing a contract with a managed care firm, carefully review it and consider consulting an attorney. The contracts are not written with the therapist's interests in mind. However, some managed care firms are flexible. Issues to examine in the contract are as follows:

1. Is there any variance between the quality of the program and the cost? Are they cost-saving by cutting authorization for necessary treatment, or are they able to set limits on unnecessary treatment?

2. Determine the time frames for submission and payment of claims. They may claim to give you a bonus at the end of the year but actually it may be part of the payment they had promised.

3. As there are often many forms to complete for the managed care firms, you will want to explore the option of charging for the length of time and inconvenience in completing the paperwork. Some companies will pay.

4. Appraise the quality of the managed care contracts before signing them. How often are you able to renegotiate your contract? Does the contract offer a reasonable termination clause?

5. Does the plan offer a fee-for-service payment plan or "capitation"? Capitation is the process of paying the provider a set amount each month per plan enrollee, regardless of whether the psychotherapy services were utilized. This means that as the number of services rendered increases, the therapist will be making less. Capitation serves to shift the risk from the third-party payor to the therapist.

6. Will you be able to get a sufficient number of referrals? Is a specific number of clients guaranteed? Talk with other clinicians who are providers and learn from them about the number of referrals they have received.

7. What is their utilization review program? Is it peer review, and is it concurrent or retrospective? What are the written guidelines?

8. Ask for a provider directory. Once you have contracted with a managed care firm it is important to determine that you are in the directory and listed in the correct sections. Also, check the directory to find out

what psychiatric hospitals they use. If you do not currently have privileges at these hospitals, get them.

9. What is their notification policy for discontinuation of services to
members? Could the managed care company change contracts and
require clients to change therapists suddenly, not allowing for a smooth
transition?

10. What is their expectation of how you will manage noncompliant clients? As a provider, can you terminate with such clients?

11. What about client confidentiality?

12. Ask whether the company carries malpractice insurance for the utilization review and case management activities and whether the contract includes an indemnification clause. If the utilization review errs,
attorneys will pursue the one with the most liability coverage—you.
You will have to consult your personal liability insurance to be sure
you are properly covered.

13. Finally, are you allowed to continue seeing clients after the contract
runs out? Who do the clients "belong to"?

To work with managed care you will need to understand their jargon as
well as share an interest in goal-oriented, short-term therapy. You also will
be expected to communicate regularly with them, both through reports and
telephone reviews authorizing blocks of approved sessions. Find out what is
involved in the treatment reports.

■ Psychiatric Hospitals

In some areas of the country psychiatric hospitals and psychotherapists
work together to make billing simpler. Therapists are able to invoice the
hospital for each hour of therapy the patient has been seen. The hospital
reimburses at a predetermined rate. The benefit in this arrangement, in some
cases, includes payment to the therapist by the hospital even if the insurance does not reimburse the therapist. Some insurances reimburse M.D.s and
Ph.D.s only.

In the event you have a hospitalized patient, you will want to review the
insurance coverage and compare direct reimbursement with the hospital's
offer. At times, billing the insurance directly will net a higher return. However, if the insurance coverage is anticipated to be insufficient for payments
to the psychiatrist, psychologist, and others, it would be prudent to invoice
the hospital than to risk being omitted in a first-come, first-paid, insurance
payment program.

It is acceptable to bill the hospital, which generally is at a lower reimbursement rate than your standard rate, and then to turn to the patient for the

difference in out-of-pocket payment. I only bill the patient for the difference between what the insurance would have paid and the total amount due per session. You cannot bill the hospital and then bill the insurance for the difference, as the hospital is already billing the insurance company.

Often managed care companies will reimburse only the psychiatrist or individual therapist for daily inpatient treatment. In such cases, consider treating the patient on different days or alternating with billing the managed care company and making payment arrangements with the client.

We have to come to terms with the continually changing marketplace in which we live. Third-party payors want treatment for the symptoms, not the underlying cause. Short-term, solution-oriented therapy is being increasingly expected by managed care companies. Hospitals will increasingly be used for stabilizing patients, not treating them. Speaking the language of the reimburser will be important. Changes are going to be economically driven. To be frustrated by the changes is to be unable to go forward and stay current with reimbursers.

Bartering

Bartering is the process of exchanging services or goods. In olden times it was not uncommon for people to pay for services with produce or poultry. Bartering is less common today, but does still occur. The IRS views bartering as a source of income, and expects such exchanges to be declared for tax purposes as you would other sources of income.

The problems with bartering do not end with the IRS. Dual relationships may evolve, especially when services are being exchanged for services. It is more difficult to establish and maintain professional boundaries when bartering. It also is difficult to assign a price or determine what services or goods to exchange for the therapy. Finally, bartering can interfere with transference issues (Richards, 1990, p. 190). It also can create countertransference issues.

There is obviously good reason to reevaluate a situation before readily agreeing to a bartering relationship. This is not to say that a blanket prohibition on bartering should be issued. In certain rural or cross-cultural situations bartering is an acceptable practice. However, keep in mind that it may just be simpler in the long run to offer a sliding fee scale or pro bono work.

Delinquent Accounts

Regardless of how conscientious you are, there will be situations in which clients fall behind in their payments and refuse to pay. This happens in every therapist's practice at one time or another. Recognize this resistance as being a therapeutic issue that can legitimately be discussed in treatment. Failure to confront these issues will result in an erosion of appropriate boundaries between the therapist and client, and depreciate your position as a professional. If you are no longer treating a client, she or he will have less of an incentive to pay you what is owed.

Conscientious review of your ledger cards will keep you abreast of delinquent payments from clients or insurances. Do not allow an unpaid bill to increase to an embarrassingly large overdue account. The client may experience guilt, shame, fear, or become overwhelmed about her outstanding debt. Richards notes that "when a patient or client incurs a large financial debt to the supplier of a service, that patient or client is more likely to question the quality of the service out of guilt, shame, or anger about his or her financial situation" (*National Association of Social Workers News,* 1991, p. 5).

It is both legal and ethical to pursue delinquent payments, as failure to pay for psychotherapy services represents a broken contract. Therefore, privileged information is not breached. Confidential information about the client must still be protected.

For small claims court, an attorney is not required. You will need to have all relevant documentation. The judge or arbitrator will make a decision on the case, either immediately or within a few days. If your decision is to pursue payment in small claims court, notify your client one last time in writing of the overdue bill and your conclusion that it has to be followed up in court.

If the client is found to be responsible for paying the bill, he or she may still refuse to pay. At this time you have the option of placing a lien against his or her home or car. However, it is more advisable to write off some bad debts than to pursue payments in a hostile manner. It is better to evaluate that account and determine what your office could have done differently to avoid such a difficulty. Your best course of action is not to allow unpaid bills to get out of hand. Keep open lines of communication with your clients, and if they stop paying for the sessions, immediately discuss the difficulty, renegotiate your charges if appropriate, develop a payment plan, and look for underlying issues of resistance or anger. Stop having sessions if you are not getting paid, and use the sessions you are having to discuss the therapeutic and financial issues underlying the unpaid bill.

I feel that you should not use a collection agency or sue for failure to pay. My concern with collection agencies is that you lose control of how the collections are managed once you include an outside agent. They may abuse some of their power, which will reflect negatively on you. Aggressive billing may agitate your clients, who may then feel a need to pursue legal action against you. Failure to receive payment is one disappointment and headache, but being challenged with a lawsuit and its resulting emotionally and financially costly legal battles is a serious possibility coming from an angry client. If, following all attempts to collect payment, the client still will not pay, I recommend writing it off.

To improve the likelihood of payment, I recommend this six-step process:

1. Send a copy of the ledger card out monthly with an updated note typed in at the bottom indicating the delinquency in the account (Figure 6.3). Double-check for accuracy.

2. Call the client at home or at work. You can only call once a day; otherwise, it is considered harassment, and it is likely to anger the client and put him or her on the offensive. Do not call the client before 8:00 A.M. or after 8:00 P.M. unless the client has agreed that this is an acceptable time to call. Do not call the client at work if he or she asks you not to. You must respect this. Inquire what the problem is and try to work out a concrete payment plan. Try to avoid shaming or blaming the client for nonpayment. Do not allow the client to stall for more time on payment of a long outstanding delinquent account by requesting another bill be sent.

3. Get a credit report on your client. Learn her or his credit history. This will also let you know whether the client has funds available on her or his credit card(s). You may be able to gently remind your client that she or he can access money for the overdue account through a charge card.

4. If you still receive no response, send a letter encouraging the client's commitment in a "payment contract." This functions as a promissory note, and includes the balance due, the sum your client commits to paying, the date of such payments, and his or her signature. Include a cover letter and a stamped, self-addressed envelope (Figures 6.4 and 6.5). Send only letters that are matter-of-fact, never intimidating or rude.

5. When the client continues to ignore your attempts at reconciling the overdue account, send a letter encouraging his or her feedback as to whether he or she feels he or she does owe the stated amount of money, and if not, why (Figure 6.6).

6. Finally, when all other efforts have failed, send a certified letter in a plain envelope with no return address. If you send one of your letterhead envelopes, the client is likely not to pick it up. This letter should be "stiffer" than the first one (Figure 6.7).

STATEMENT

Eileen S. Lenson, ACSW, CSW/ACP
Psychotherapist
17101 MAIN STREET, STE. 100
HOUSTON, TEXAS 77068
(713) 548-1898

Client: DOE, John
11341 Fairview Lakes
Houston, TX 77053

Terms: Payment Is Due Upon Receipt. Thank You.

Date	Family Member	Professional Service	Charge	Credits Paym'ts	Credits Adj.	Balance
1993				Balance Forward →		0
6/20	John	Individual Psychotherapy	100.00	100.00		0
6/27	John	Individual Psychotherapy	100.00	50.00		50.00
7/3	John	Individual Psychotherapy	100.00	50.00		100.00
7/15	John	Individual Psychotherapy	100.00	100.00		100.00
7/22	John	Individual Psychotherapy	100.00	100.00		100.00

Pay Last Amount In This Column ↑

NOTE: PAYMENT IS PAST DUE!

Figure 6.3. Ledger Card

COUNSELING ASSOCIATES *Of* HOUSTON

17101 MAIN STREET, STE. 100
HOUSTON, TEXAS 77068
TELEPHONE: (713) 548-1898

June 19, 1992

Mr. John Doe
17115 Red Acres
Houston, TX 77090

Dear Mr. Doe:

As you have not contacted this office with your plans for compensation, I am sending you this document to fill out and send back. I have supplied you with a self-addressed envelope for your convenience.

Please understand that you must give me some kind of commitment to resolve your outstanding balance of $_____. I will work with you in any way I can. Thank you.

Sincerely,

Eileen S. Lenson, ACSW, CSW/ACP, BCD
Psychotherapist

Figure 6.4. Cover Letter for Payment Contract

Whenever there is communication about the billing, have your secretary jot a short note on the back side of the office ledger card. This provides a record of what has been occurring with regard to collections.

If your client can no longer pay for your services, either reduce your charges or refer out to another therapist in the community. Be cautious not to terminate prematurely, as it would be considered to be abandonment.

Missed Appointments

Each therapist develops a last-minute or no-show cancellation policy. Although some professionals, such as physicians and dentists, may not charge if a patient does not show for appointments, psychotherapy often is viewed differently. Some therapists say nothing during their initial discussion about office procedures, feeling that to anticipate missed appointments is to predict resistance. These therapists have no policy. Some charge a reduced fee,

---

PAYMENT CONTRACT

Date:_____/_____/_____

I, _____, hereby commit to paying $_____ .

per month, on the _____ of each month. If I have any problem with my ability to pay, I will
contact the therapist immediately.

Signed:_____

Figure 6.5. Payment Contract

whereas others charge a normal fee. My policy is to charge the normal fee if
a cancellation is made within 24 hours of the appointment. My belief is that
last-minute cancellations tend to be more due to resistance to deal with a
difficult issue than to valid justification for missing an appointment. Often,
when clients are reminded of the financial consequences for the late cancellation, they will decide to keep their appointment.

The intake forms signed by the client at the beginning of therapy outline
this policy. My clients are offered a copy of this signed agreement to help
remind them of what they signed. I allow for emergencies such as serious
illness or a family death, but expect minor illnesses not to become a form of
resistance to therapy.

Develop a set policy for fee collection and share your policy in written
form with the clients. Clarify how payments and billing are handled and how
last-minute cancellations and missed appointments are treated. If delinquent
fees or interest on unpaid bills are to be charged, this also must be included
in writing.

Bookkeeping

Sometimes, less is more. This applies to bookkeeping in psychotherapy.
To have a successful system, you need to have something down to earth that
you can understand and manage with ease, and that is reliable and accurate.
Therapists typically dread all aspects of bookkeeping—the recording, sum-
marizing, and assessing of all of the financial activity in the office. There is
no escaping bookkeeping. It is an intragal part of your practice.

Just as you would not make clinical recommendations to the parents of an
8-year-old child with enuresis until you had made a thorough clinical assess-

COUNSELING ASSOCIATES *Of* HOUSTON
_____

17101 MAIN STREET, STE. 100
HOUSTON, TEXAS 77068
TELEPHONE: (713) 548-1898

September 17, 1992

Mr. John Doe
17115 Red Oak Drive
Houston, TX 77090

Dear Mr. Doe:

As you have not indicated how you would like to pay off the debt you owe, please check whichever is applicable, and return this form to my office:

(   ) I agree to pay $_____ every month for _____ months.

(   ) I do not feel I owe this money, and the following is an explanation for my decision:

_____
_____
_____
_____
_____

Please understand that you are held responsible for the balance on your account of $50.00, and we will continue billing. Thank you.

Sincerely,

Eileen S. Lenson, ACSW, CSW/ACP, BCD
Psychotherapist

Figure 6.6. Owe/Do Not Owe Debt Letter

ment, neither should you run a business without a thorough understanding of your financial records. Just as you require ongoing clinical data to determine your treatment interventions with the 8-year-old child, so will you need the bookkeeping activity to enable you to evaluate the progress in your business.

Every bookkeeping system should include the following: ledger cards; a daily summary of expenses and charges; an accounts payable ledger, which will register the amount of money that you owe others, such as rent and payroll; a record of all accounts receivable, which registers the amount of money that is owed to you by clients; and a record of the payroll, an employee

COUNSELING ASSOCIATES *Of* **HOUSTON**

17101 MAIN STREET, STE. 100
HOUSTON, TEXAS 77068
TELEPHONE: (713) 548-1898

June 1, 1992

Mr. Lloyd Green
555 Oak Street
Houston, TX 77000

Dear Mr. Green:

As you have not responded to my request for payment, I am sending this letter certified to ensure reception. The balance on your account is $_____, and is seriously PAST DUE.

Please be reminded that you signed a written consent to psychotherapy with me, which is also an agreement to compensate for the therapy.

Your prompt remittance is appreciated.

Sincerely,

Eileen S. Lenson, ACSW, CSW/ACP, BCD
Psychotherapist

Figure 6.7. Certified Payment Overdue Letter

compensation record including all hours, pay, and deductions withheld for part- and full-time workers. The bookkeeping records the number and type of sessions held, name of person seen, date, and what the charge was. It notes when the insurance and client were billed, what if any amount of the charge is adjusted out for nonpayment or sliding fee, the total amount due, and dates payments were made.

Do not discard old ledgers, even though the IRS may no longer require your maintaining them. Because problems may arise years later from former employees, it will be invaluable to have the memory and history provided by the ledgers. I recommend keeping the ledgers for the duration of your practice.

The ledger cards on each client will be permanent records of your office that reflect all personal information on your clients. As noted above, they can be used for simplified billing by photocopying them.

The daily summary of expenses can be recorded on a ledger. The ledger paper comes with punched holes to allow for easy transfer to a ledger pegboard. When a daily sheet is complete, it is stored in a ledger book.

Completely organized pegboard systems are available that will allow you to take the ledger card and the superbill (a receipt and billing form for mental health providers) and line both onto the ledger paper. This paper is placed onto little metal projections on the pegboard to keep the paper fixed and prevent slipping. The carbonless systems allow you to write just once, rather than having to duplicate your entries by transferring the amounts from the ledger card to the ledger book. The bottom of each pegboard sheet is the daily log of charges or receipts. This will hold the information on all accounts receivable, and help furnish you with information on profit and loss.

The information on the superbill can serve as a bill to be sent to the insurance company, and a copy can be retained by you and a copy made available to your client. The superbill also can be used as a receipt for your client after each session, which he or she can then submit to the insurance company.

If a client's check bounces, call the bank. The bank will be able to account for what occurred. Call your client if the check was returned due to insufficient funds or if the account is closed. Try to work out an immediate resolution with regard to a cash payment. Once payment has been made, return the original check to your client. If your client's check bounced due to insufficient funds but your client plans to deposit adequate funds into the account, send the check back to the bank. Specify that you want the check held for collection. Any charges incurred as a result of bounced checks should be passed on to your client.

Bookkeeping should also allow you to budget for city, state, and federal income taxes. If you have employees, you will need separate payroll records for each employee. At the conclusion of each pay period you will post the gross wages, date of paycheck, number of regular hours worked, number of overtime hours worked, Social Security deductions withheld, federal income tax withheld, health and insurance deductions, vacations, sick leave, and advances to the payroll journal. If you plan to enter a partnership, you will be required to document each partner's investments and withdrawals. The IRS provides a free publication entitled *Tax Information on Partnerships* for anyone interested in learning more about setting up the bookkeeping for partnerships. If you plan to enter into a corporation, the bookkeeping will be larger scale.

If you are able to afford a computer, accounting software is available. Rather than the laborious task of manually writing down numbers and filling out insurance forms, you can select from a variety of programs that can handle the following: general ledger, accounts payable and receivable, billing, HCFA 1500 billing, budgeting, auditing, check reconciliation, invoicing, purchase orders, payroll, depreciation, adjustment for budget control, holding and maintaining mailing lists, and printing business forms. Many programs are less than $100, although many also are available in the $500 to $700 range.

The next progressive step up is a computer management system. Although there are many such systems, they all typically offer hardware and software products that provide billing and accounts receivable, appointment scheduling, financial accounting, electronic billing, and practice management reporting. They enable you to use a modem to bill Medicare and Blue Cross/ Blue Shield, allowing you to bypass the clearing house and permitting your invoice to be handled in a more time-efficient manner. Such systems do not come cheap.

Petty Cash

All income needs to be deposited directly into your bank account so you will have documentation of what income you have received. However, you will need money in your office that can be readily available to you, for stamps, sodas, and miscellaneous expenses. This is petty cash. Take petty cash out of the bank account by writing a check payable to petty cash. Document the check as being an expenditure on your ledger. Write the disbursements on your accounting worksheet.

Bank Accounts

The IRS has specific requirements each therapist must follow in order to establish her or his income. All bank deposit slips, when totaled up, represent the total income. It is best to have a bank account that represents only one income source, such as your psychotherapy practice. If you blend your business with your personal account, you run the risk of paying taxes on your personal money. When submitting deposits, take a moment and write on your deposit slip a note as to what the source of the deposit was. If the deposit is coming from another source of income, clearly note this on the deposit slip. If a client's bounced check is redeposited be careful not to record it as two deposits.

Develop the habit of balancing your checking and savings accounts monthly. To overdraw could result in embarrassment and a loss of professional credibility.

Obtain a bank credit card to use for situations when you may wish not to use a check. These include purchasing supplies or paying for entertainment and travel. Not only will the credit card enable you to track your business expenditures easily, but it also will help you develop a credit history with the bank.

The IRS requires that you maintain old bank records for 3 years. I would recommend keeping them for the life of your practice, as not only income tax audits but legal claims from former partners may require proof of purchase.

SEVEN

Legal Aspects of a Private Practice

In contemporary society it is impossible to establish a private psychotherapy practice without serious recognition of the legal implications. These are seen in issues such as "informed consent to examination and treatment, voluntary and involuntary treatment, professional negligence (malpractice), liability for acts to third parties, confidentiality, evidentiary privilege, record keeping, billing practices, employment contracts, staff privileges, peer review, advertising, relationships with nonphysician health care providers, and insurance for health care" (Talbott, Hales, & Yudofsky, 1988, p. 1059). States may vary in how they consider the above issues. Therefore, an attorney who understands psychotherapy can counsel you on legal issues affecting your practice in your particular state. In this chapter, some of the typical legal issues impacting psychotherapy are explored.

Malpractice

No business is lawsuit proof. In general, in most states mental health professionals face a lower risk of lawsuit than do physicians. Perlin lists numerous reasons for the low incidence of lawsuits against psychiatrists, many of which may apply to psychotherapists:

> general reluctance of tort law to provide money damages for emotional injuries; difficulty of proving in a court of law an applicable standard of care and a causal relationship between the breach of the standard of care and the alleged injury;

psychiatric medicine remains somewhat of an enigma to most trial lawyers; stigma which patients fear might result from making public their psychiatric history; patient's reluctance to sue as a result of emotional ties to his/her psychiatrist and/or the patient's belief that successful psychotherapy requires full cooperation with the psychiatrist; many patients' inability to either formulate clear expectations or assess the "success" of their treatment; the ability of trained psychiatrists to therapeutically deal with patient hostility and thus avert a suit; and the frequency with which many patients see their psychiatrists (Meyer et al., 1988, p. 15; Perlin, 1988, p. 1).

Liability Insurance

Each therapist should carry her or his own professional liability insurance, regardless of whether she or he is independently employed or employed by an agency or organization. Judgments against the therapist can be high. The insurance carrier will pay the settlement amount, as well as the legal fees, if the coverage is adequate. There are some exceptions. Currently a number of carriers will not pay if sexual misconduct is proven. An organization also may not provide coverage if they believe the employee stepped outside the guidelines of the job description, and declare the employee to be personally liable. If the lawsuit comes up after your employment has terminated, your former employer is less likely to be invested in offering you legal coverage.

In addition, an employer may cover an employee and then go to court and ask for restitution from the employee for the expenses incurred for the legal costs. Liability insurance is still reasonably inexpensive. I feel every practicing clinician should seriously consider obtaining his or her own insurance policy, independent of institutional insurance inclusion. If you plan to do contract work or provide inpatient work, you will probably be required to carry your own liability insurance.

Most professional organizations sponsor, and some private insurance companies offer, liability insurance. The liability carrier usually provides coverage for legal representation and payment of damages (should the case go to court). Remain knowledgeable about the nature of your liability insurance and know what the limitations are. For example, as noted earlier, many insurance carriers will not cover in cases of proven sexual misconduct.

Liability insurance changes from time to time. Many insurance companies are moving away from offering the occurrence policy in favor of the claims-made policy. The difference between the two is simple: Under the occurrence coverage you are covered for all circumstances during the covered policy year, whereas under the claims-made policy you are covered for the claims so long as the policy is in effect (*Psychotherapy Finances,* 1991c, p. 2). This means that under a claims-made policy you will have to be insured this year to be covered for an event that occurred 5 years ago, even if you were insured at that time. If you should retire or give up the policy, you can purchase a "tail," which provides you coverage for any claims made during the policy's covered period.

What to Do If You Are Sued

If you receive notification that you are being sued, notify the insurance carrier immediately. Failure to do so can result in the abridgment of professional liability insurance coverage (Wright, 1981, p. 1536). Not to realize that a lawsuit is a serious problem will delay immediate legal advice and possibly endanger your legal position.

Generally the insurance carrier will provide you with good legal representation, as they are interested in minimizing their payment of damages in lawsuits. However, if the complaint is before a professional ethics committee or a state regulatory agency, coverage may not be provided. Dishonesty, fraud, malicious acts, or omissions may not be covered. Keep in mind that the attorney has been hired by the carrier to represent you. Although her or his intentions may be honorable, future work comes from the insurance company and not from you. If you are uncomfortable with the legal representation being offered, it may be wise to consult with an attorney at your own expense. Do not fall victim to the belief that it is a clinical issue and that you can "talk it out" with the individual who is suing you. You should not be speaking with anyone about the case other than your attorney (Woody, 1988, p. 194). Remember the adage: "Be your own lawyer and have a fool for a client."

Psychotherapists do not like lawsuits because they feel vulnerable and out of control. Denying the problem (flight), viewing it solely as a manifestation of a client's psychological problem and believing it will never be pursued to court, is a misconception. Responding with combative countersuits against the plaintiff (fight) and believing that a show of dominance and control will intimidate the client into withdrawing his or her claim instead may force the client into a more rigid, defensive position and result in an escalation of aggression from the client (Meyer et al., 1988, pp. 17-18). Manipulation of clinical records will only cause greater problems for you as well as your client, resulting in anything from embarrassment to legal charges being pressed against you.

Therapists can begin to practice defensively. This means avoiding clients whom you fear may become litigious, or failing to pursue overdue payments from clients for fear of angering them and having them sue. The most effective way to manage lawsuits is to learn how to run an ethically and legally healthy practice. Keep clear and accurate records. Keep clear and accurate boundaries with your clients.

Five Components
of a Malpractice Lawsuit

There are five components of a malpractice lawsuit that a plaintiff must satisfy. First, the therapist must have neglected to do something that he or she is responsible for doing (Meyer et al., 1988, p. 2; Perlin, 1988, p. 2). The second component is substantiating that the plaintiff was due reasonable care from the psychotherapist. This is established by determining that a professional relationship existed. The third component of a malpractice lawsuit holds that the care from the psychotherapist was breached, either overtly or covertly. The guidelines are that the knowledge or skill used was below the standard of care generally accepted by other professionals. Fourth, even if the minimal standard of care was not provided, in order to successfully sue the client must prove that injury resulted. Last, the client must convey that the psychotherapist's negligence resulting from this departure from a conventional standard of practice was the cause of the harm incurred, and that the client's problem or injury otherwise would not have occurred (Reamer, 1987; Woody, 1988, pp. 11-12). It is here that the burden of proof lies with the client.

Most lawsuits are settled out of court. Yet, problems still result for the psychotherapist. Lawsuits are emotionally draining because the cases may go on for years before a settlement is reached. They consume your time preparing for depositions and courtroom testimony. Lawsuits are financially costly because of legal costs, potential loss of income, and possible settlements against you. Although an out-of-court settlement does not mean the psychotherapist is guilty, it still will become a blot on his or her record (Woody, 1988, pp. 2-6). It may affect his or her position in the community and impact negatively on obtaining referrals, especially if there is publicity about the case. Too many out-of-court settlements may also affect licensure or credentialing with hospitals and other facilities. Even if he or she has done nothing wrong, it is very expensive to defend him- or herself, so his or her insurance carrier may insist on an out-of-court settlement to make the suit go away.

Liability in Supervision

Not only clinicians but supervisors also may be vulnerable to liability issues. They could be at risk for failure of their supervisees to obtain client consent, to protect third parties, to develop proper treatment plans, to refer to specialists when needed, or to provide sufficient supervision or cross-coverage in the supervisee's absence, as well as for not improving inadequate record keeping and for concealing sexual involvement with a client (Ballinger, cited in Reamer, 1989, pp. 445-446; Besharov, 1985, pp. 166-167; Cohen & Mariano, 1982; Hogan, 1979).

To minimize the likelihood of a legal suit being placed against you as a supervisor, be certain to maintain a consistent schedule of supervision, and provide information necessary on education about confidentiality, crisis intervention with suicidal clients, intimacy and other boundary issues with clients, and appropriate methods to terminate clients (Reamer, 1989). Make sure your supervisees understand all the above. Urge your supervisees to let you know immediately about problems with their clients. Supervisors are the easiest targets for litigious clients.

Liability and Contracts

Watch out for the potential risks inherent in the hold-harmless clauses that may be included in contracts with hospitals, managed care companies, or employee assistance programs. Hold-harmless clauses mean you will take on the responsibility and liability.

Your insurance company provides coverage to you. This does not extend to any obligation that was undertaken when you signed the hold-harmless clause. That is, if both you and the contracted agency are sued, your liability insurance may not cover you for protection against damages assessed by the agency.

Because avoiding such contracts would mean a reduction in caseload and income, private practitioners are going to want to be involved, but not at such personal risk. You may wish to ask the agency not to include the hold-harmless clause, but they may not agree to do so. In the future liability insurance companies may develop a rider, at a reasonable charge, to our existing liability insurance that will provide the necessary protection.

Causes for Malpractice

Some typical causes for malpractice actions are described below.

1. *Treatment without informed consent.* Treating without the client understanding the choices, right to refuse, and risks is illegal and unethical. This only applies to competent adults. The following information

must be shared in order to satisfy the criteria for informed consent: an explanation of the procedures and their purpose, the therapist's role and qualifications, risks that may occur, the benefits that can be expected, alternatives to treatment that also may help, a statement that the client can inquire about the procedures at any time, and a statement that the client can withdraw her or his consent and discontinue treatment at any time (Margolin, 1982). Barker (1984) notes that "only when a client is institutionalized, a minor, or judged incompetent to make decisions is there an exception. Even then, consent must be obtained from the person legally responsible" (p. 53).

2. *Sexual misconduct.* Many lawsuits involve sexual impropriety. This is particularly critical, as insurance policies often exclude coverage for this type of professional liability claim. All professional organizations condemn sexual involvement with a client. The impact of a sexual relationship with a client can have measurable, adverse psychological implications for the client. In a study done by Feldman-Summers and Jones (1984), clients who had sexual contact with their therapists reported anger, mistrust of men and therapists, and psychosomatic symptoms. Time and energy were diverted away from the therapeutic context of the relationship to the sexual relationship. Not only were preexisting problems not being addressed or resolved, but new problems also arose.

3. *Failure to warn.* Not notifying a third party of a client's violent proclivity will result in the therapist being viewed as negligent. The now infamous case *Tarasoff v. Regents of the University of California* (1976) put this responsibility onto therapists. The threat of violence must be made against a specific individual.

4. *Breach of confidentiality.* Problems can be prevented by developing written consent forms that stipulate the name of the individual about whom information is to be disclosed; to whom the information will be disclosed; the purpose, extent, and time limit of the disclosure; and the client's ability to revoke the consent. Clients also need to be informed about the limitations to confidentiality. Breaches of confidentiality are always unethical. In states with laws regulating confidentiality, it is illegal to breach confidentiality.

5. *Misuse of therapy.* This may include accepting money or favors from clients. One must be cautious not to abuse one's power with a client, but to use the trusting relationship to the client's benefit.

6. *Failure to advise client of risk of therapy.* As no treatment is foolproof, no guarantees can be made. After all, the client must be the one motivated for success to occur. Clients do need to know what the risks

of therapy are. For example, in marital counseling, if one partner grows and the other does not, is the marriage in greater jeopardy?

7. *False imprisonment.* This involves holding a client against her or his will, typically in a psychiatric hospital.

8. *Limits on ability.* This situation arises if you treat a client when the client should be referred to another professional, such as treating someone with high blood pressure with relaxation techniques rather than first referring the client to a physician. Another example would be a therapist treating a child without any training in working with children.

9. *Misdiagnosis and inappropriate treatment.* The client must prove that not only was the diagnosis incorrect but also that it was arrived at negligently (Meyer et al., 1988, pp. 30-32). This may occur when the cause of the problem turns out to be organic rather than psychogenic in nature. A referral to a physician at the beginning of treatment can prevent such occurrences. Liability for improper treatment also may occur when treatment is inappropriate, such as "suggesting that clients act out hostilities toward others, giving business advice to clients, or demanding that clients change jobs, move, get divorced, or change their circumstances as a condition for continuing the therapy. Obvious mismanagement of transference phenomena may also lead to liability" (Meyer et al., 1988, p. 28).

10. *Failure to prevent suicide.* This consists of having knowledge of client's suicide risk but failing to take appropriate measures to protect client from hurting himself or herself. Negligence also may result if an inadequate examination is utilized by the therapist. Using a standardized format for interviewing clients will provide for protection against preventable liability (Meyer et al., 1988, p. 38).

11. *Confining or not confining a client to an institution.* If a client is kept in the hospital based on wrongful information from the therapist, it may be a cause for malpractice. Or, malpractice may occur if a client is erroneously discharged from the institution based on information, or lack of information, from the therapist.

12. *Inappropriate termination and abandonment.* Termination must not be too sudden or during a crisis; otherwise it may be viewed as abandonment. The client can terminate abruptly, but the therapist cannot. The therapist must attempt to work through the client's termination concerns. Arrangements for the client to receive treatment from another therapist must be made, if indicated. Obtain a consent from your client to allow you to provide copies of your client's records to the new therapist.

13. *Assault and battery.* Assault and battery entail threats or using physical confrontation with a client. The client need not have sustained bodily injury, as it is unlawful to touch another person's body without her or his consent (Meyer et al., 1988, p. 41).

14. *Defamation.* Communicating something injurious either verbally or written about the client is characterized as defamation.

15. *Failure to collect payment in appropriate manner.* This includes behaviors that harrass the client or communicating confidential information while attempting to collect the fees. Also included is intentionally misdiagnosing a client to provide eligibility for third-party payments. The therapist can then be sued by either the insurance company or the client, lose his or her license, and face criminal prosecution. Liability insurance will not protect the therapist, as the actions were premeditated.

Prevention

The ideal plan is to avoid, or to minimize, the likelihood of being sued for malpractice. Below are some suggestions for how to achieve this.

1. *Maintain a good, honest, open, trusting relationship with the client* (Greenburg & Greenburg, 1988, p. 61). This involves communicating with the client, even when the client withdraws in anger. Process the client's negative feelings with her or him, be critical of your own behavior, and evaluate what impact your anger could have on the client's behavior. Clients can accept human failings and mistakes. As a clinician it is important to acknowledge when an error has occurred. Sometimes clients sue as a last resort when they feel they have not been heard.

   A patient in a major teaching medical hospital had his leg amputated due to physician error. The physicians minimized the patient's wife's needs to talk about her feelings and avoided her. I maintained close communication with both the wife and the physicians. I recommended that the medical team meet with the woman, who was extremely angry and becoming suspicious of the avoidant physicians, but the physicians refused. Two months later the woman sued the entire medical team and hospital personnel—except me—for medical malpractice.

2. *Do not enter private practice unless you have sufficient clinical experience and sufficient credentials and licenses.*

3. *Have a good rationale for what you are doing.* It must have clinical justification. Avoid unconventional treatment that does not conform to minimally acceptable clinical standards.

4. *Maintain good records.* Keep them up to date and nonjudgmental. Failure to keep records is in itself grounds for a malpractice charge (Kachorek, 1990, p. 100).

5. *Respect your client's ethical and religious beliefs.* If they conflict with yours, refer the client to another therapist.

6. *Avoid abandonment by providing your client with several names of therapists should your client wish to change therapists.* Consider yourself as the therapist until the client establishes contact with another therapist. Send your client a termination letter indicating the recommendations for treatment and names of therapists who are possible referrals.

7. *Do not identify yourself as a specialist unless you have specialized training, certification, or expertise.* A higher degree of treatment will be expected of specialists. Instead, refer to other therapists, physicians, or attorneys. Market yourself carefully. Do not accept all types of patients. Only accept those whose problems are compatible with your training.

8. *Treat minors only with parental consent.*

9. *Warn potential victims of violent patients of the potential dangers raised by the client.* As noted earlier, *Tarasoff v. Regents of the University of California* (1976) was a case in which a student attending the University of California shared with his therapist at the school treatment center his intent to kill a former date. He was apprehended by the university police but released because he was considered to not be a risk. The student killed the woman later on. The court decreed that the woman had the right to be notified by the therapist of the potential danger and that the right to privacy ends when the public is at potential risk and when a threat is made against a specific person.

10. *Terminate noncompliant patients.* Communicate this termination verbally and in writing. This will protect you from professional responsibility for patients who reject your recommendations and, therefore, may be at serious risk to themselves or others.

11. *Avoid hugging or kissing patients.* They may expect a hug at the end of the session. Explain that therapy is a nontraditional relationship, and that it would not be beneficial to them if you related to them as do others in their lives.

12. *Avoid gift giving and accepting gifts.* Never accept an expensive gift. Sometimes it may be appropriate to accept a token gift, and then only very infrequently. Always discuss the motives behind the gift giving.

13. *Keep current with professional literature.* Attend conferences, read books and journals, and consult with colleagues so you are updated in your field (Greenburg & Greenburg, 1988, p. 61).

14. *Maintain your professional liability insurance coverage.* Although it will not prevent you from getting sued, it certainly will reduce the cost.

15. *Be aware of ethical issues.* Ignorance here is not bliss. When in doubt, turn to your professional organization for guidance (Greenburg & Greenburg, 1988, p. 61).

16. *Receive training for the "what-if" situation relating to client violence.* Remove potential weapons from your office.

Privileged Communication

Privileged communication is a legal term for a privilege conferred by the law that protects clients by preventing information shared in predetermined relationships from being disclosed without the client's permission. In the case of therapy the privilege belongs to the client. The client may waive this privilege. If the client chooses to waive this privilege, it must be done in whole, not in part. Also, once it is waived, it cannot be reinstated.

Not all states extend privileged communication to all psychotherapists. Generally, doctor-patient privilege is recognized, and psychologist-patient privilege is not uncommon. It is important to know how the state in which you practice treats privileged communication with regard to your profession: whether you are included and what exceptions exist.

Exceptions to protection from discovery will exist when society or an at-risk child needs protection. If involuntary commitment proceedings for inpatient psychiatric treatment are initiated for the purpose of protection from self-injury, or if a mental health examination is ordered by a judge, the client's communications may be disclosed (Woody, 1988, p. 132). If the therapist has knowledge of a client's intent to cause harm to another individual, the therapist is then responsible for notifying authorities under the "duty to warn" ruling. Some states require the disclosure of information concerning certain crimes.

Confidentiality

Confidentiality means you cannot discuss anything about a client with anyone without the client's permission. Breaches of confidentiality are unethical. In some states breaches are illegal. A client can sue if her or his confidential information is disclosed to someone else without her or his permission.

Considerations in maintaining confidentiality include the following:

1. Confidentiality, and its limits, should be discussed at the beginning of therapy. This includes clarifying that parents may not have access to all information about their adolescent in therapy, and that information will need to be shared with the insurance company.
2. Obtain a signed consent for release of information from your client before disclosing any information. This includes instances of releasing information to the client's insurance company, as well.
3. Keep records and any other identifying information on a client locked in a file cabinet.
4. Notify your client of any situation that requires you to breach confidentiality, such as reporting to Child Protective Services or providing information required by a subpoena or court order.

Selecting an Attorney

Ideally, you already have a working relationship with an attorney with whom you reviewed the contracts on your lease when starting up your business. This attorney can either help you or can assist in referring you to an attorney who specializes in legal cases involving psychotherapists.

When interviewing attorneys you should determine whether they have represented other psychotherapists in the past and what percentage of their cases are settled out of court. You do not want an attorney who is eager to go to trial. Consider your own comfort level when talking to the attorney: Is this someone you feel you can trust, who will return your telephone calls, and who will communicate with you?

Subpoena

A subpoena is a summons by the court to appear at a specific place and time. Although usually it is to appear in court, it also may be to attend a deposition. Some subpoenas only require that the psychotherapist appear, whereas other subpoenas require that specific documents, such as notes, recordings, and videotapes, be brought to court or the deposition as well. Failure to answer as a witness or to bring the documents will be viewed as contempt of court, and may result in a fine or imprisonment (Meyer et al., 1988, p. 228).

At times psychotherapists are subpoenaed by clients or by adversarial parties to give testimony about a client. If you believe your testimony would pose harm to the client, inform your client so he or she can challenge the release of this information. Also, consult your attorney about the possibility of having your subpoena squashed. If this is not possible, inquire about privileged information. If all of the above efforts to prevent the release of information fail, ask the judge to review the records in chambers so harmful information may be screened out. If your client's attorney requests a meeting with you, meet only with your attorney present.

Depositions

Depositions are recorded testimonies taken prior to court. These enable attorneys to learn more about the case prior to the trial. Although depositions take place outside the courtroom, the person is under oath and needs to answer the questions completely. Deposition records will be submitted, and perhaps read, in the courtroom.

As with any courtroom trial, the opposing attorney will attempt to discredit the psychotherapist who is being deposed. This can include attacking personally or professionally, and generally trying to upset the therapist.

Prepare for a deposition much as you would a trial. Review your notes and any other relevant material you have on the patient. Be able to back up any theories you have with professional literature. Finally, it is important to have predeposition meetings with your client's attorney so you, as a witness, can help educate the attorney on what questions to ask.

Only answer questions within your professional expertise. Answer the questions but do not volunteer additional information. It is normal to be nervous. Answer slowly and at your own pace. Do not rush and risk saying the wrong thing. It is acceptable to say that you do not know the answer to a question.

Court

There are two reasons to have to attend court: Either you will be testifying as an expert witness or you are the defendant in a malpractice suit. The area of therapy that deals with individuals who are involved with the law is known as forensic psychology.

One of the most difficult concepts for the psychotherapist to comprehend is the uniqueness of the courtroom. The legal arena is an adversarial environment. It is different from the mental health environment, in which relationships are developed, other people's integrities are protected, and professionals try to be impartial. Each attorney's responsibility is to represent her or his client, even at the expense of the other client or expert witnesses. Prior to appearing in court to testify as an expert witness it is advisable to desensitize yourself to the courtroom atmosphere by observing a trial in process. Select a trial with similarities to the case in which you will be testifying.

In the event that you are testifying as an expert witness, you can expect to be asked about your knowledge, skill, experience, training, and education (Meyer et al., 1988, p. 222). As an expert witness you can expect to be given specific notification as to when to appear, as your time is valuable and it would be wasteful to sit in court for hours waiting to be called. Ask the attorney to call you at your office when she or he is certain about when you will be called to the stand.

Do not talk with anyone else while waiting to testify. Even an innocent conversation with a stranger in the parking garage can have significant impact on a case should the stranger turn out to be a member of the jury.

All pertinent records of the case should be reviewed by the psychotherapist prior to arrival at court. Bring an updated copy of your curriculum vitae. Do not bring any original copies of your records, as they may be entered as evidence. Bring only copies of records.

Dress with the jury in mind. Jewelry and clothing should be conservative. Much of the jury's opinion of you will be based on appearances. Conservative dress will reduce the barriers between you and the jury.

The expert witness influences the jury's determination as to responsibility and guilt. Therefore, you should be alert to transference and countertransference issues that might tarnish your research and testimony. One helpful technique I use is to decide whether my testimony would be the same if the preparation was for the prosecution rather than the defense. Having the opportunity to testify for the plaintiff and the defendant will not only heighten your awareness of this sensitive issue but also increase your credibility as an expert witness.

Your testimony may not be fully acceptable to the attorney, who does not want specific aspects of your report or records to be shared with the jury. It is important to explain clearly to the attorney that to testify, you need to be free of bias or omissions that would affect the integrity of your testimony.

In the courtroom direct your communication to the jury. Your role is to help the jury, and the judge, better understand intricate issues relating to a specific case. Do not be intimidated by the legal process. Remember that you are not the one on trial. Do not view the process as adversarial. It will only make you feel powerless or defensive. Rather, speak honestly, and without bias or professional jargon.

Fees for Depositions or Courtroom Appearances

You can expect to be financially compensated for the time spent testifying as an expert witness. Discuss your fees with the referring attorneys for whom you will testify, and confirm your conversation with a letter. Charge for your time either by the hour or by half-day increments, including travel. If you have been asked to arrive at the courtroom by a certain hour but do not testify until later, it is acceptable to charge for the waiting time. This is justifiable as you are having to reschedule your office hours and cannot be available to receive clients, thereby reducing your normal income.

Do not accept contingency payment. It is unethical. The opposing counsel will ask what you are being paid and will interpret this as you being paid for your opinion, not your time. This will make you look like a hired gun, which will discredit your testimony. You should be paid as compensation for professional services rendered.

There is a tendency to identify with the party who is paying your fees. It is also important to recognize that there may be strong pressures from the hiring attorney to have the psychotherapist report from an advocacy rather than an impartial, informative position. In contracting with the attorney indicate that the report will be as complete, objective, and unbiased as possible, with the possible inclusion of positive and negative findings.

Depending on your comfort level with the attorney, you may request payment for a deposition either before or immediately afterward. Unfortunately, it is not uncommon for attorneys to stall or fail to pay therapists once the service has been rendered. After your services are rendered, they tend to be minimized in value by others. Perhaps it is best to follow the attorney's adage: "Get payment while the tears are hot."

Lawsuits are expensive, tiring, and emotionally draining. But is that reason to abandon our private practices and change careers? Of course not. It is, however, reason to select choices wisely and make good legal decisions about the type of practice you are going to develop. Knowing the legal implications of your practice decisions will help prevent panic and the development of a defensive practice.

We live in a litigious society, but it appears that for the most part therapists are taking care of their practices. This is evidenced in the relatively low malpractice insurance premiums. Perhaps this is because of the nature of our business. We tend to question our treatment plans, and are aware of the limits of our practice. We use therapeutic contracting and encourage feedback from clients in the treatment, so consensus and open communication are likely to be maintained. This enhances positive relationships between the therapist and the client. People tend not to sue those whom they like. They also accept human errors. If we can continue to maintain these types of relationships with our clients for therapeutic purposes, we will not have to become paranoid about lawsuits, and will be able to minimize our risk in litigation.

EIGHT

Safety Issues

Safety issues will arise from time to time. Concerns for the safety of your client, others in your office, your family, and yourself are best dealt with by being proactive rather than reactive. Therapists confront danger to themselves and others on a daily basis. Some are beaten, raped, stalked, intimidated, abused, or sued. It is impossible to avoid all at-risk clients. Prepare ahead of time what you will do in emergency situations involving suicidal, battered, and/or dangerous clients. Careful and timely intervention can mean the difference between a negative or a positive income. Clients need to be screened for possible risk both personally and clinically.

Suicidal Client

Suicidal clients are fragile and lack the ego strength to be able to make the proper decisions for themselves. Depending on your clinical assessment of the severity of the threat, you will want to use some or all of the efforts described below in attempting to stabilize your client. Even when the behavior is manipulative or attention seeking, remember that there is no guaranteed way to assure that an individual will not carry out a threat to kill himself or herself. Several steps should be taken with potentially suicidal clients.

1. *Assess suicide risk.* A client is at high risk if she or he has highly lethal methods; has psychiatric problems (especially a borderline personality); is in poor health; is feeling depressed, impulsive, immature, highly dependent, or hostile; is isolated socially and living alone; has a suicide plan; has financial difficulties; uses drugs or alcohol; is anti-

social; or has made previous attempts. At least 10% of those who attempt suicide will successfully commit suicide at a later time (Dorpat & Boswell, 1963). Obtaining a thorough mental status examination will help determine the suicidal risk potential in your clients.

2. *Contract.* If you have determined that your client is not at immediate risk of harming himself or herself, have your client sign a therapeutic contract. The contract states that the client will not do anything to hurt himself or herself, and that if he or she has the impulse to do so that he or she will call you first. If your client has a supportive family member, have the family member sign the contract as well.

3. *Contact support system.* Obtain permission from your client to notify someone with whom she or he has a close relationship of the suicidal ideation or threat. Preferably the person you notify will be a family member or someone who has a strong investment in and feeling of responsibility toward your client. I like to make this telephone call in front of my client so no fantasies of possible secrets and plots are maintained. If your client will not grant you permission you still need to make this call. This breach of confidentiality is permissible because your client is at risk. Although clients may express considerable anger when they learn of your action, they generally are able to work through this anger through therapy.

4. *Remove apparent weapons.* Inquire as to how the person would kill himself or herself, if the client has a plan. If the client plans to shoot himself or herself, ask that he or she remove all guns and give them to a friend or neighbor for safekeeping. If he or she would select pills, have the client take all prescriptions to someone else or have him or her dispose of the pills. Get the client's written consent to notify his or her physician. You may suggest that only limited prescriptions be written for a while. Tell significant others of potential weapons.

5. *Monitor status of client.* If the plan is not to hospitalize your client, schedule more frequent office visits or telephone calls. Scheduled telephone calls can help your client by offering structure and decrease the likelihood of you receiving too many telephone calls during the day. A failure to call the therapist or show up for an appointment should be followed by a telephone call from the therapist to the client. If the client cannot be reached, call the significant other.

6. *Voluntary hospitalization.* In cases in which you believe the client is at too great a risk to remain at home, even with the support of significant others, hospitalization needs to be pursued. If the client will go voluntarily and has adequate insurance, you can arrange with a psychiatric hospital for your client to be admitted. If you know of a psychiatrist,

you can notify the physician of the new admission, and give enough history to make it clear as to why you recommended inpatient treatment. If not, the psychiatric hospital will assign your client a psychiatrist from a list of attending physicians who practice at that facility.

7. *Involuntary hospitalization.* Should your client refuse to admit himself or herself voluntarily to the hospital despite your strong recommendation to do so, turn to the family to pursue commitment by the court. If the family refuses to intervene, you will need to do so yourself. Although the procedure will vary depending on where you practice, typically it will involve you filing commitment papers that justify legal intervention. A judge will review them and, if in agreement, then will arrange for the police to transport the client to the hospital.

Involuntary hospitalization should be a last resort. It is traumatic for the client and may cause irreparable damage to the therapeutic relationship. Also, clients often are angry when hospitalized involuntarily. Such anger can cause them to defocus from their issues and thereby result in lengthier hospitalizations.

The first client I ever hospitalized was almost an involuntary hospitalization. My action was based on my assessment that she was highly suicidal, and most probably a "completer." She had a target date and a way to kill herself. She was putting her affairs in order. With her reluctant permission I contacted her family, but their response was, "She's just jerking your strings." I monitored this client very closely, often talking to her several times a day on weekends, which is when she would decompensate. For 2 weeks I recommended inpatient treatment for her but she refused. I told her that if she was out of control, I would have to be in control. I did not elaborate but was considering having her committed, if necessary. On the day before her target date of killing herself, I filed commitment papers. The constable called me at 3:00 P.M. and told me he was ready to pick up my client and that I would have to go along to identify her. I asked for a 1-hour postponement, and called my client again. Perhaps because she knew that something was going to happen, she agreed to go to the hospital if I would meet her there. I agreed and called the constable to cancel the commitment process. We met at the hospital and during the intake process she performed magic tricks for me. I believe she was communicating that it was magical that she had come in.

Family members came to town once my client was hospitalized, and stayed at her home. They were shocked to see how everything had been put in order. What upset them the most was the calendar with the targeted suicide date circled in red with a note, "Where am I?"

Battered Client

At times the victim has a family member who is violent. Often it is a husband who abuses a wife, but it also may be a grown child abusing an elderly parent. This client often avoids accepting help. There are several steps to take with this client.

1. *Identify the victim.* Abuse victims are quite adept at covering up their injuries and making excuses. Use direct questioning if you suspect makeup, missed appointments, or unseasonal clothing is being used to cover up indicators of domestic violence.
2. *Evaluate safety in returning home.* Although it is your client's choice as to where she or he goes to live, you ought to apprise her or him of alternative options, including shelters or a family member's or friend's home.
3. *Determine whether children are at risk.* Are children involved in the domestic violence? If so, you will need to contact Child Protective Services.
4. *Consider client's legal rights.* Advise your client of her or his legal rights in pressing criminal charges against the abuser or obtaining a protective order to prevent additional attacks. Refer your client to an attorney to learn about the legal implications should she or he consider an option other than returning home.

Violent Client

There are two types of violent clients: those who could present harm to you and those who could present harm to someone else. It is your responsibility to know what to do in the "what-if" situation should a client become threatening to you or others.

■ Danger to Therapist

Often the violent client gives "notice" of intent prior to striking the therapist. Listen to your client. Help your client remain in control. Do not minimize what a client is capable of doing. The smart therapist will plan ahead for the possibility of encountering a dangerous client and take necessary precautions.

1. *Office decor.* Keep sharp and heavy objects out of the office. They can readily become weapons. Position your chair to be closest to the door. This will be critical in the event of needing a quick exit and ensuring that you are not blocked from leaving the room. Identify ahead of time what items can be quickly used to provide a shield for you, such as a cushion or a lightweight desk chair.

2. *Self-defense.* Learn basic self-defense techniques. Local hospitals may offer classes as a community service, as they offer them for hospital staff. If your client becomes threatening, assume a defensive posture in anticipation of an attack. Do not directly face your client. Remove your necktie or earrings. Protect against a kick or punch by wrapping one arm around your neck and the other around your stomach. If knocked to the floor, keep your feet pointed at your client and block further attacks with your feet. If being choked, push your chin down to allow for maximum air and blood circulation. If being bitten, push your body part farther into your client's mouth and squeeze your assailant's nostrils (Tardiff, 1989, pp. 19-20).

3. *Avoid isolation.* Do not schedule potentially abusive clients when no one else is in the office. In particular, this includes evenings and weekends. Once I had to see a potentially violent man early in the morning before my support staff arrived. Rather than take personal risks, I arranged to meet the man at a psychiatric hospital nearby and held my session there.

4. *Intervene immediately when danger arises.* Do not stay with the escalating emotions, but set limits. Either remind the client that he or she needs to get in control or the session will end, or leave your office and have another staff member accompany you into your office. Often an out-of-control client will get back in control in this situation. Do not let your own denial of the client's potential volatility prevent you from protecting yourself from a dangerous client. Use a calm, nonjudgmental voice when speaking with a dangerous client. Never lose control of yourself. Remain sitting to avoid intimidating your client. Listen empathically and avoid giving interpretations or asking disturbing questions. Help your client examine the consequences of becoming violent.

5. *Commitment or preventative custody.* As with the suicidal client, you may need to consider arrangements that will provide protection for your client and/or others. This is particularly important if your client has a plan for hurting someone and has a history of being impulsive and hurting others, and has the means to hurt someone. Involve family members if possible. Notify the police if the risk of danger continues.

6. *Document events and actions.* Record your observations, assessments, and recommendations.

■ Danger to Others

In situations in which a client presents a danger to someone else, you have both an ethical as well as a legal obligation to protect the potential victim. The following are steps you might take.

1. *Decide the potential risk.* Determine whether your client has a history of impulsivity or hurting others. Does she or he have a specific plan to hurt this individual? How does she or he view the consequences of pursuing such a plan? Is she or he abusing drugs or alcohol? Is she or he psychotic?
2. *If risk is demonstrated.* Notify significant others as well as the potential victim. Consider either voluntary or involuntary hospitalization.
3. *If no immediate risk is demonstrated.* Consider referral for a medication consultation. Monitor the client closely with increased outpatient therapy.
4. *Document events and actions.* Record your observations, assessments, and recommendations.

Child-Abusing Client

It may become apparent during the course of treatment that your client is a suspected child abuser. Most states require that a therapist report any suspected child abuse or neglect to Child Protective Services. Mandatory disclosure of suspected abuse to a government agency often results in an uncomfortable dilemma for therapists, as they fear fracturing the therapeutic relationship. The following steps can reduce this discomfort.

1. *Discuss legal requirements.* Let the client know that you have no choice but to report the suspected abuse or neglect to Child Protective Services. Not to report the case could result in fines and criminal charges being placed against you.
2. *Explain the process.* In as nonjudgmental a way as possible, inform your client of what he or she can expect once you contact Child Protective Services. Your client will appreciate your openness.
3. *Document events and actions.* Record your observations, assessments, recommendations, and communication with Child Protective Services.

Litigious Client

Individuals who have a history of suing professionals, who do not own responsibility for themselves, who tend to blame others for their problems, or who do not want to get better are at risk for suing their therapist when their problems do not disappear.

Careful screening at the beginning of therapy is critical. Clearly identify the limitations of your role as a therapist. Reach for unverbalized expectations of your client so unrealistic expectations may be corrected. Include in your routine intake interview a question about your client's history with lawsuits.

Go with your gut feeling about your clients. One client who sues you can wreck your whole career. Remember, insurance carriers typically will settle (with a payment) rather than run up costly legal fees. Your innocence will not be enough. Select your clients carefully so you protect yourself and those around you.

NINE

Marketing

Marketing is the heart of your practice. If it ceases to occur on a regular basis, your practice will suffer a slow death. Despite its importance, marketing often fails to receive proper attention and respect from many psychotherapists. Perhaps this negative perspective developed as a result of observing physicians and attorneys struggle within their own professions about the ethics of marketing one's practice.

It used to be that a therapist could have a spontaneous practice. With little or minimal work, it just happened. Times have changed. Competition is high among practitioners. Word of mouth alone no longer suffices. It has become a business necessity to market ourselves. Wise professionals are learning not only to accept marketing but also to embrace it as an opportunity both to educate the public and build their practice.

For the hesitant minority who still view marketing as unbecoming behavior, consider the following situation. You are at a social gathering and someone you do not know approaches you and states that she is going through a difficult divorce and understands that you work with people in these situations. She asks about your therapy. Would you describe your practice to her? If so, you have just marketed yourself. Let's face it: If we cannot sell ourselves, we will end up working for someone who can.

Understand what marketing is. It is not gimmicks, the "hard sell," or hustling potential clients. Rather, it is the process of ascertaining clients' needs and determining how your services can be matched with those existing needs.

Be proud of marketing. It is found in every business. Debbie Field, of Mrs. Field's Cookies, was marketing when she first put her cookies (which weren't selling well) on a tray and stood outside her store offering free samples to anyone who was interested. Coca-Cola is marketing when they help support the Special Olympics. Some cartoons, including the Teenage Mutant Ninja Turtles, which entertain our children, are developed for the sole purpose of marketing items for sale.

Ensuring that new clients will come into your office must be done on an ongoing basis. Do not expect instant gratification from marketing. The marketing contacts you make today will bring in business tomorrow. If you do not make any marketing contacts today, you are unlikely to have the business tomorrow. You have to be a thinker *and* a doer rather than simply a thinker when marketing your business.

Consistency is the name of the game. Recognize that every encounter with someone is a marketing opportunity. I recall the time my father was visiting me from out of town. As a chemist, he wanted to visit some engineers at a laboratory near my home and asked me to join him. He assured me the visit would only be an hour at most. The visit stretched from early morning into lunch. I was bored until I learned that one engineer's wife was an attorney specializing in family law. I seized the opportunity to discuss my work with the engineer. He ended up giving my business card to his wife. She subsequently became a strong referral source for me. We even conducted seminars together, entitled "Emotional and Legal Issues Associated with Divorce," which served as an excellent source for referrals. Six months later, the other engineer referred his daughter to me for outpatient counseling. Four years later I am still receiving referrals from this attorney. How very productive that one day turned out to be for me! You must take advantage of opportunities when they present themselves and create them when they do not.

Professional Goals and Objectives

To market effectively you need to establish goals and objectives, develop marketing strategies, determine how you will allocate your resources, and monitor the results. Developing goals and objectives will help ensure attaining the marketing results you want and will decrease lost time. This planning stage of marketing requires that you discipline yourself to give thought to your future. If you do not set realistic goals and objectives, you run the risk of higher costs and a lower caseload. Goals define what you expect to achieve. Without such planning you are likely to run higher advertising costs, lose sight of specific plans, and spend money haphazardly. You run the risk of getting caught up in the day-to-day operations, thereby losing the ability to make plans. If you fail to set goals, your caseload will be negatively affected, as you will not be pulling in the necessary clientele.

Objectives are the road map to attaining your goals. Objectives will help guide you through the difficult times, as they consist of measurable ways your goals will be achieved. Put your objectives in writing.

Learn to be action- and goal-oriented. Designate a period of time during which you can sit at your desk and write without any distractions. List your goals in order of importance, and follow this order. Divide the goals into short- and long-term goals, and list them according to priority. Review the short-term goals weekly on a specified day. Review the long-term goals quarterly to ensure that you remain focused on carrying through your plans. Otherwise, they are doomed to be forgotten as are our New Year's resolutions. This review also enables you to evaluate what problems are precluding growth.

Goals need to be flexible and broad but realistic, challenging, and objectively measurable. Be honest and realistic with yourself about what you hope to achieve and what obstacles may present themselves. Setting goals too high can create frustration. Setting goals too low can result in disappointing results. Visualize each goal so you can envision what the accomplishment will look and feel like. Have a backup plan you can pursue should an obstacle create a barrier, and plan how you can avert or minimize the obstacle.

Objectives should be specific and measurable and will thereby indicate exactly what you should be doing to achieve your goals. They should identify the hows, whens, and whats that you need to do to achieve the results. They should identify prospective clients: who and where, how you will reach them, how much it is advisable to advertise, and what type of advertising you will use. They should identify the competition: Who are they? What are their strengths and weaknesses, and how do they do their marketing? Set your basic strategy for developing referrals, a budget for advertising, and a deadline when positive results should be experienced from advertising. It is the objectives that keep you from procrastinating and provide the motivation to work toward the goal. I plot out my objectives on a calendar, enabling me to have constant visual reminders of what I need to be doing during the week.

Do not feel the need to adhere to goals rigidly. Expect disappointments. Feel free to make the necessary modifications in your goals when such disappointments occur. For example, if your goal is to introduce yourself to eight internists and five gynecologists each week, and you then realize that these contacts are not as productive as contracting with managed care companies would be, then make the necessary changes in your goals. Perhaps you will then want to set a goal of writing to six managed care companies each day for information and contracts.

Remember: Markets are never static. They are fluid. As soon as you establish objectives and goals the market will change. Marketing is a continuous function. Successful therapists are those who keep abreast of marketing strategies, build successful programs, and continuously change them to ensure that fresh ideas keep them ahead of the competition.

Referral Development

There is a lot of competition out there. This means you will need to be creative and identify potential resources to market that have not been saturated by other professionals. This means working long hours, being persistent about developing necessary contacts, and always being on the lookout for new marketing opportunities. Remember that you will get out of your referral development just what you put into it. The next sections provide suggestions for developing referrals.

■ Professional and Social Groups

Affiliate with professional and social groups that may become good sources of contacts for referrals. Engage in community activities. Attend meetings. Join organizations. Involve yourself with religious and voluntary agencies. Connect with self-help groups and inquire about being available for question-and-answer sessions or for presentations. Keep in touch with colleagues and other professionals. Stay current with the activities of local training institutions. Volunteer to participate in relevant activities at clinics or hospitals.

Do not expect immediate gratification. It may take months for others to learn to trust you and to understand your profession fully. Get actively involved so others have the opportunity to observe you but try to select activities that will reflect your capabilities. If you have the opportunity to make a presentation to your professional or social group on a mental-health-related topic, take it.

■ Find a Niche

Look for unmet needs in the community. Do the schools need someone to talk about coping with suicides? Does the community have any support groups to help with a recent crisis, such as an earthquake, an explosion in a chemical or manufacturing plant, or a flood? Does the community hospital emergency room want an inservice on how to deal effectively with aggressive patients? Start assessments, talks, or groups to meet the needs you discover. Be creative in identifying unmet needs. Do not simply duplicate what your competitor is doing.

■ Be Creative

Stay one step ahead of your competition. Be creative and be the first to identify a need for a service. Do realize, however, that the competition will react quickly and copy what you are doing. They may even improve on it.

I started a free adolescent therapy group. It was very well received by the community and the schools in particular. I was overwhelmed with referrals. Many of the parents decided to continue with family therapy as well, which was at my normal fee. I told other therapists of my success, which unfortunately led to me having a corner on the market for only 6 months. After this, the psychiatric hospital I was using for my admissions at that time decided they would follow suit. They started free adolescent therapy groups in several locations in the community, setting themselves up in direct competition with me.

■ Understand the Marketplace

Do not assume you know what is wanted or needed. Be adaptable and continually reassess your understanding of what the marketplace is and who your potential referral sources are. This will include physicians, the judicial system, schools, insurance companies, hospitals, self-help groups, churches and synagogues, word of mouth, and so on. Do not become inflexible or overconfident; both can result in failure. Educate the marketplace so they will come to you rather than go to others. Let others know your experience, publications, particular interest, or certification that is applicable to a given market. Get beyond your modesty and fear that you will be bragging. Not to educate others is to expect that they can read your mind and automatically know to refer different populations to you.

■ Refer to Other Practitioners

Refer to nonpsychiatrist practitioners for medication consultations. Jackson notes that although "a surprisingly large number of office visits to non-psychiatrist physicians result in prescriptions for antipsychotic or antidepressant drugs," and while "non-psychiatrist physicians see almost as many outpatient mental health and substance abuse patients as psychiatrists," the physicians refer only 3.3% of these patients to mental health professionals (Jackson, 1991). If you refer patients to these physicians, there is a likelihood the physician will do some lab work and may develop a permanent patient. The physicians will then refer back to you.

■ Work With the Media

Develop good relationships with the media. Ask the media to use you as a reference for mental-health-related topics. With newspapers, begin by calling the publisher and asking with whom you should speak. With radio, call the program director. With television, call the assignment editor. Once you have the contact individual's name, write a follow-up letter expressing your interest, and include a curriculum vitae, business card, and practice brochure, if you have one. This information will probably be placed in a reference file.

Accommodate the media and give interviews on short notice. Inquire about writing a column in the newspaper. Write a letter to the editor. Contact the large daily newspaper in your city; if you receive a negative response, contact local weekly newspapers.

■ Acknowledge Referrals

Communicate with each referral source as soon as a referral is made. Always determine how new clients were referred to you. This will let you know what form of advertising is working. Acknowledging these new referrals is an important tool in maintaining referral sources. Acknowledgments enable you to thank someone who has done you a favor. In all cases, obtain a release of information consent from the client before you engage in any verbal or written communication with a referral source (see Figure 4.6, discussed in Chapter 4). This is a form that clients sign giving the therapist permission to release information about their status, treatment, diagnosis, and prognosis to specified individuals. Without such permission the therapist cannot even acknowledge or deny that a client is coming in for therapy. Most clients will readily consent to signing this release form. I tell them it is a courtesy for me to let the referral source know that the client followed through with the recommendation for therapy. Also, if appropriate, I mention that the consent form allows the referral source and me to work as a team in treating the client. I allow the client to read the information I am sending. I document in my records that the client either read it or was offered the opportunity to do so.

There are several ways to acknowledge a referral. The method selected will probably be based on who referred the client to you. Some professionals, such as physicians or some mental health professionals, may consider receiving a telephone call to be burdensome. In this case I send an assessment sheet (Figure 9.1) detailing the presenting problem, diagnosis, treatment plan, and next scheduled appointment. Always stamp the top of the assessment sheet "Confidential." When I feel that the referral source would

COUNSELING ASSOCIATES *Of* HOUSTON
_____

17101 MAIN STREET, STE. 100
HOUSTON, TEXAS 77068
TELEPHONE: (713) 548-1898

Date:_____

Re: _____

Dear Dr._____ ,

Thank you for referring your patient to me for psychotherapy.   I appreciate your confidence in me. The following is a summary of essential findings:

Diagnosis:

_____

_____

Treatment Recommendations:

_____

_____

_____

_____

Next Appointment:

_____

Signed:_____
            Eileen S. Lenson, ACSW, CSW/ACP, BCD
            Psychotherapist

Figure 9.1. Assessment Sheet

appreciate a less formal, more personal form of feedback, I send a brief letter. In this situation I take the opportunity at the closing to market myself briefly (Figure 9.2).

For schools I send a copy of the release of information form the client has signed, which gives permission for the school officials to communicate with me regarding the student. By sending the school counselor a copy of this release, valuable time is saved waiting for the parent to go into the school

COUNSELING ASSOCIATES *Of* HOUSTON

17101 MAIN STREET, STE. 100
HOUSTON, TEXAS 77068
TELEPHONE: (713) 548-1898

February 26, 1993

Dr. J. Doe
222 South Little Drive, Ste. 400
Houston, TX 77090

Dear Dr. Doe:

Thank you for referring Jane Smith to me for psychotherapy services. She was treated for depression at the psychiatric hospital and made excellent progress. She was discharged home on February 21.

While in the hospital, Ms. Smith worked on family of origin, self-esteem, assertiveness and boundary issues. She is following up with outpatient psychotherapy with me and is seen individually and in my women's group.

Her prognosis is very good if she continues with the therapy, which I am confident she will. If you have any questions, please feel free to contact me at 548-1898.

I am taking the liberty of enclosing a few fliers describing groups I am leading currently. Once again, thank you for the referral.

Sincerely,

Eileen S. Lenson, ACSW, CSW/ACP, BCD
Psychotherapist

EL/ky

Enclosures

Figure 9.2. Thank-You Letter to Referral Source

to sign another release. I can then call the school counselor to determine whether she or he has information pertaining to the adolescent that would be helpful in my treatment. It is a comfortable and beneficial way of expediting the sharing of information, and it enables me to become better acquainted with new school counselors.

For other referral sources I may not want to obtain information but just acknowledge that I received the referral. For instance, if a satisfied client

Eileen S. Lenson, ACSW, CSW/ACP, BCD
17101 Main Street, Suite 100
Houston, Texas 77068
(713) 548-1898

Date____/____/____

Dear _____,

Thank you for referring _____ to me for psychotherapy

services. Your expression of confidence is greatly appreciated.

Sincerely,

Eileen S. Lenson

Figure 9.3. Thank-You Acknowledgment Card

NOTE: Be sure to send this card in an envelope, as this would be a breach of confidentiality as a postcard.

refers a new client to me, or if a colleague who already knows much about
the client and would not benefit from the redundancy sends me a client, it
will not be appropriate or necessary to provide the referring source with
clinical information about the new client. In these cases I send an acknowledgment card thanking them for their confidence in my professional services
(Figure 9.3). A 4 × 6 card (similar to the type used for open houses) can be
used to convey a simple message of acknowledgment for the referral. By
having these cards preprinted with a line for the client's name and a line for
your signature, the card is easily managed by you and easily read by the
recipient. Send it after the first session in a sealed envelope.

■ Contact Potential Referral Sources

Send a customized form letter to prospective referral sources introducing
yourself and briefly describing your services (Figure 9.4). Include a note at
the end of the letter that you will be contacting them in a week. Mark this
date on your calendar, Day-Timer, or computer program so you are sure to
follow through with your commitment. When you make contact, determine
whether they qualify as an eligible referral source. If so, inquire about the
possibility of setting up a time to meet. To avoid wasting your time, select
those who are the gatekeepers, the ones who actually make the referrals.
Determine this by simply asking, "Who makes the decision to refer to thera-

COUNSELING ASSOCIATES *Of* **HOUSTON**
_____

                                                              17101 MAIN STREET, STE. 100
                                                              HOUSTON, TEXAS 77068
                                                              TELEPHONE: (713) 548-1898

August 27, 1992

Mr. John Doe
Big Town High School
3112 Woods Lane
Spring, TX 77379

Dear Mr. Doe:

I am a psychotherapist in the Northwest Houston area, and I would like to introduce you to my Free Adolescent Therapy Group. The group has been in progress since last Spring and has been most successful in dealing with adolescents and their issues.

The group is open-ended, and it meets every Thursday night from 5:30 to 6:30 P.M. I find that adolescents who have not been in therapy and who have been resistant to addressing their issues elsewhere, respond positively to my group.

I would welcome new referrals from you, and I have enclosed a couple of fliers for your review. Once a referral from you to my group is made, I have the teen's parent(s) sign a consent for release of information so that we may communicate about his or her issues.

I also have a free drug screening program and have included fliers on this as well. I will call you in a week to discuss this with you further. In the meanwhile, please feel free to call me if you have any questions or need more information. Thank you.

Sincerely,

Eileen S. Lenson, ACSW, CSW/ACP, BCD
Psychotherapist

EL/ky
Enclosures

Figure 9.4. Self-Introduction Letter to Prospective Referral Sources

pists?" Reach out to those referral sources who have the potential to target large groups of individuals, such as clergy, physicians, and school counselors. Identify referral sources who will refer clients capable of paying for your services. Do not be discouraged if people do not want to meet with you. This search for new referral sources is a "shotgun" approach but can pay off in the long run.

■ **Establish a Simple Referral Procedure**

Encourage referral sources to inform you when a referral has been made. I noticed that only a small percentage of referrals made to me would actually follow through with calling for an appointment. To increase the likelihood of a potential referral making an appointment, I suggested to several of my referral sources that they verbally let me know when a referral had been made. If I did not hear from the potential client within an agreed-on period of time, I would call the referral source back and let them know the status. The referring source often would then call the potential client and help work out any resistance issues he or she might have with regard to calling for an appointment.

As a result of this proactive approach to receiving referrals my caseload increased considerably. Referral sources felt better knowing that the clients were being seen, and they appreciated knowing I would track the clients until they entered treatment.

■ **Conferences**

Present at conferences. You will get name recognition as being an expert in a specific area. Surprisingly, it takes very little to be "recognized" as an expert. Other professionals will refer to you if you have an expertise they do not have. Be visible.

■ **Public Talks**

Give free "talks." Talks are great. People will see you as the expert, you will appear ethical, and you will be viewed as providing a community service. At the height of my marketing period I was giving one or two talks per week, and found it to be one of my strongest marketing tools.

There are a few ways to help ensure that your talk becomes a way of developing referrals and not simply a public service. Always have handouts available with your name, agency, address, and telephone number on each page. This ensures people of having access to your telephone number even if they lose the first page. I also often staple a business card to the front page of the handout packet.

Prepare for your talk by practicing with a minute timer so you know exactly how long your presentation will be. Preparation will also allow for you to develop familiarity with your talk so you will not have to read it. Once you are familiar with your talk, reduce it to outline form. Then become even more familiar with your talk and reduce the outline to 3×5 notecards. After your presentation consider turning your talk into an article to be submitted to either a professional or a lay publication.

Only talk for one half to three quarters as long as the time allotted. It will be more effective if you use various methods to connect with people on the feeling rather than the cognitive level. All too often we want people to see how smart we are, so we load them down with facts and information. The audiences go away thinking we are smart, but do not consider coming to us for therapy. It is more effective, and a better marketing tool, to get people to talk to each other and to share their feelings. For example, if you are giving a talk on communicating with your adolescent, you could say, "There may have been times in your own family when you felt that one family member was not listening to the other. Let's take the next 2 minutes for you to share with your spouse your own observations. Then we can discuss it." Instead of people walking away saying, "Isn't he smart?" they'll walk away thinking, "He understands me." You are more likely to get referrals from those who feel you understand them.

At times you may be speaking at a church, school, or place of business and someone else will be introducing you. This is often awkward for this person, as she or he may know little about you. The result can be an introduction that leaves out important information or gives incorrect facts. I have found people to be grateful if they are given a brief introduction they can either commit to memory or read. Call the person prior to the scheduled date of the presentation and offer to do this for her or him. If she or he is receptive, send a brief letter with the introduction (Figure 9.5).

When scheduling your talk be careful not to select times that may encounter community conflicts. I learned this the hard way. I organized a 3-hour seminar, rented a hotel conference room, sent out a major mailing, advertised on the radio, and had handouts for 100 attendees available. Unbeknownst to me, I had chosen Super Bowl Sunday! I confess to being one of the three Americans who are oblivious to sports events. Needless to say, the turnout was negligible. I have since learned to note sporting events, major church events, holidays, and other community activities that may conflict with any planned lectures.

Talks can be held anywhere. One of my most successful presentations was held at a YMCA on folding chairs in an unattractive room. Talks can also be held at schools, libraries, or your office if you have the space. Unless you can expect a large attendance from the congregation, avoid using churches for your presentations. Some people will feel shamed if they experience emotional conflict in a house of worship. Wherever you select, make certain that it is easy to locate.

I always request that interested individuals preregister for my talks by telephone RSVPs. This allows me to develop a mailing list. It also enables

COUNSELING ASSOCIATES *Of* HOUSTON

17101 MAIN STREET, STE. 100
HOUSTON, TEXAS 77068
TELEPHONE: (713) 548-1898

August 27, 1992

Ms. Jane Franklin, R.N., B.S.N.
Houston Northwest Medical Center
710 F.M. 1960 West
Houston, TX 77090

Dear Jane,

Following is a brief introduction I prepared as per your request:

"Eileen Lenson is a psychotherapist in private practice in Northwest Houston. She works with individuals, couples, families, and various therapy groups. She gives talks and writes articles on mental health-related topics. Eileen is also an Allied Health Professional at Charter Hospital in Kingwood."

Also, I am enclosing some brochures of a workshop on assertiveness that I am presenting on November 4, that I thought might be of interest to you.

I look forward to seeing you again soon.

Sincerely,

Eileen S. Lenson, ACSW, CSW/ACP, BCD
Psychotherapist

EL/ky

Enclosure

Figure 9.5. Introduction for Presentation

people to become a little more comfortable with calling a therapist's office, smoothing the way should they decide to follow through with therapy after the presentation. Also, it gives me a rough estimate of how many people I can expect and allows me to ensure that I have a sufficient number of handouts.

Allow for a question-and-answer period after a talk. It permits people to have the opportunity to participate, get their questions answered, and get a better sense of your views. At the end of my presentation I ask that attendees fill out an evaluation of my talk (Figure 9.6). Although I am looking for

COUNSELING ASSOCIATES *Of* **HOUSTON**

17101 MAIN STREET, STE. 100
HOUSTON, TEXAS 77068
TELEPHONE: (713) 548-1898

EVALUATION

Thank you for joining me today. To help me prepare future presentations, please complete this form. Thank you.

NAME:_____

ORGANIZATION: _____

MAILING ADDRESS: _____

_____

PHONE: Home:_____ Office:_____

STRENGTHS TODAY: _____

_____

_____

SUGGESTIONS FOR IMPROVEMENT:_____

_____

_____

COMMENTS: _____

_____

I would like you to contact me regarding:
(Please check)

_____ Free consultation and assessment
_____ Free adolescent therapy group
_____ Adult therapy group
_____ Put me on your mailing list

Figure 9.6. Evaluation of Presentation

feedback on my strengths and weaknesses, I also wish to provide each individual an opportunity to request more information from me. They can check the appropriate space adjacent to the service that interests them. It may be a free evaluation or information on a specific group I am leading. I follow up within 2 days by calling each person. Because I ask questions, offer help, and show concern, people believe in me. I am able to develop a relationship that may help in forming a therapeutic trust.

Do not charge admission for your talks. Instead, anticipate that you will get referrals afterward.

■ Reduce Your Rates When Appropriate

Reduce your charges to accommodate an important referral source's client. Reducing your rates to make therapy more affordable to specific populations you want to attract is "business smart." Referral sources you are cultivating will be pleased and more inclined to refer others.

■ Offer Free Services

Offer free services that will bring in clients you otherwise might have missed. My free adolescent therapy group brings in adolescents who most likely otherwise would have not started therapy. Once an adolescent is in the group I may identify needs for individual and family therapy. I share my recommendations with the parents, and fee-based therapy often is initiated.

Another free service I offer is drug and alcohol screening in conjunction with an interview and assessment. I arranged a contract with a drug laboratory to accept referrals I make for urine analyses of specific drugs and alcohol. The laboratory then charges me, not the client, for the service. The results of the screens are communicated to me by the drug laboratory, and I share the results with the client in a second free, brief interview. Many referrals are identified in this manner, resulting in this program being a cost-effective method of bringing in appropriate referrals.

Last, I use 20-minute free evaluations to help potential clients decide whether they have a problem and whether they wish to see me. If they identify an issue to address in therapy and wish to have me as their therapist, we continue the session and I charge them for the hour. If they do not wish to enter therapy with me, the evaluation ends after 20 minutes at no charge to them. Be very creative in thinking up different ways to bring in prospective clients.

■ Accept All Referrals

Never, never turn down a referral simply because you are too busy. Offer to function as a consultant. Or, stretch your day and see the client. A full schedule today does not guarantee a full schedule next week or next month. I have found that by overextending myself a little today, I guarantee not losing the referral source. There are natural slowdown periods during the year, such as the end of school, the month of December, and holidays. Therefore, I know that if I overextend myself at one point in the year there will be time to relax and catch up later on.

■ Create Packages

Offer packaged sessions. If you are a Certified Alcohol and Drug Abuse Counselor (CADAC) or have comparable chemical dependency training, you may wish to develop an intensive outpatient program offering comprehensive therapy, education, and experiential intervention and market it to employers. If you enjoy couple counseling you may wish to offer a program extended over several weeks on preparing for marriage and market it to clergy. When a recession occurs you might consider offering outplacement counseling for those who have lost their jobs and market it to corporations.

■ Network

Creatively interface with other professionals. Ask other professionals—physicians, dentists, lawyers, accountants, retailers—what types of problems they are having in their offices and identify how you can help. For example, if a pediatrician is being burdened by noncompliance from mothers who do not have their children take medication for hyperactivity, offer to give "brown-bag" lunch talks in the waiting room. If a plastic surgeon has disappointed clients following cosmetic surgery, offer to give a free assessment (let the surgeon pay you, however) to each patient to determine realistic expectations and risk for postsurgery disappointment.

Offer to do inservices for those referral sources who recognize problems experienced by their office staff. For example, if an attorney's support staff are having difficulty managing client anger, offer to address this topic with them. If a physician's office staff lack skills in working with terminally ill patients, provide an inservice. Not only will you get client referrals but you will get staff referrals as well.

■ Get on Referral Lists

Get on the referral lists from managed care companies, preferred provider organizations (PPOs), employee assistance programs (EAPs), health maintenance organizations (HMOs), and psychiatric hospitals. It often is not easy locating these contacts. The information changes so rapidly that lists are quickly obsolete. I found the best system is going through the Yellow Pages or contacting local chambers of commerce for listings of local businesses and calling them directly. Local medical and psychiatric hospitals will have lists of those companies they have contracts with and generally are agreeable to sharing the information with you. Sometimes the newsletters from professional organizations will have advertisements from companies selling lists of managed care organizations and employee assistance programs in your state. Inquire about the frequency with which lists are updated. As this field changes rapidly, I would be wary of any list not updated within the past 12 months.

Become knowledgeable about EAPs in your area by joining the International Association of Employee Assistance Program Professionals, and associate with the chapter in your community. Membership should enable you to attend monthly chapter meetings (great for networking) and have access to the list of EAP members.

Although this is discussed in greater detail in Chapter 6, below is a brief description of how a psychotherapist interfaces with managed care, PPOs, EAPs, HMOs, and psychiatric hospitals.

Managed Care Companies

Managed care companies will develop panels of providers they feel can offer effective services at contracted rates to their members. Psychotherapists finding panels to be closed should continue to make inquiries about being reviewed for the panel every 6 months. Attempt to identify services, such as working with specific populations, offering specific treatment techniques, or speaking other languages fluently, that other therapists are not offering. This can result in the awarding of a contract.

I believe managed care companies have received a "bad rap" in the mental health field. Therapists who develop a good relationship with the managed care companies are often rewarded with a consistant number of referrals. A good working relationship results in greater trust from the managed care company, allowing for fewer telephone consultations and, at times, more sessions approved.

If you move from one geographical area to another, these relationships can often continue, as many companies are national. This can ease the transition and expedite the establishment of a new practice in a new location.

Preferred Provider Organizations (PPOs)

Many times a potential client will request a referral from his or her employer or insurance company, who in turn will give the client a list of several therapists who are on their approved provider lists. Some insurance companies give their customers an incentive for using a provider who has agreed to specific accordances. This incentive often consists of a reduced charge for therapy services. At times there is a limit on the number of allowed outpatient visits. Many PPOs are looking for providers who can offer short-term therapy.

Local employers who are using PPO coverage may provide you with an opportunity to sign up as a provider, assuming you have successfully treated some of their employees. Once you are on the panel of providers, get a list of the physicians on the panel and let them know that you would like to work out a cross-referral arrangement.

Employee Assistance Programs (EAPs)

Businesses and industry often establish employee assistance programs (EAPs) that offer assessments and referrals to employees and their dependents. Usually they do not provide the counseling but refer employees to community therapists. Developing a relationship with your local EAPs and getting on their referral list can be an asset for building and maintaining your business. Usually they will accept your current fee schedule.

Health Maintenance Organizations (HMOs)

Health maintenance organizations provide comprehensive health care at a nominal per-visit charge to the patient. HMOs require that the patient visit only those health-care providers who are employed by or under contract with the HMO. If a psychotherapist becomes a provider, the HMO will establish the fee basis, which typically will be less than the open market.

Psychiatric Hospitals

Psychiatric hospitals are usually interested only in the inpatient, and day treatment, not the outpatient practice. Often, people in the community will call hospitals and ask for referrals for outpatient therapy. The hospitals develop a referral list of therapists whom they feel comfortable with and whom they know will refer back to the hospital should the referral need inpatient treatment at a later date. Establish a relationship with the hospital marketing director as well as the interventionists (staff who take the calls and refer out to the therapists) so you can be placed on a referral list.

Contact the hospitals and inquire about regularly held professional meetings that may be of interest to you. These may include grand rounds and allied health professional monthly meetings. Excellent opportunities for networking, these meetings must be attended frequently to be beneficial.

■ Be an Expert

Present yourself as an expert in specific areas. Referral sources do not want generalists. They want someone who will be able to understand their client's clinical issues. Also, let your clients know that you have expertise in areas other than that for which they are being treated, so they may refer you to others for counseling.

■ Be Persistent

Do not give up on a prospective resource you are wanting to establish a relationship with. Probably you are not the only psychotherapist trying to establish a referral relationship with the resource. The competition will never stop trying to reach this individual—why should you?

■ Work Smarter, Not Harder

You may not need to work harder, but rather may find it worthwhile to try something different. If giving public presentations is not bringing in clients, do not increase the number of speeches. Rather, look at other ways, subjects, or locations to make contact with the community.

■ Network Again

Networking not only reduces the loneliness that can result from being in private practice, but also enables you to develop a file of contact people you can reach out to. When you meet colleagues at meetings and conferences, send them a short note telling them you enjoyed meeting them, include a brochure, and suggest keeping in touch.

If you are affiliated with a psychiatric hospital, be visible. Meet with your clients during the time of day when you are most likely to encounter other therapists and psychiatrists. Try to join a colleague for a meal in the hospital. You can make great strides in developing a relationship over a relaxing meal. Schedule networking time when you go to the hospital to meet with your clients. Get to know the staff; they can be instrumental in promoting you. Get on hospital committees as a way of getting to know and develop relationships with staff, allied health professionals, and physicians. Besides resulting in referrals, professional contacts enable the sharing of important therapeutic or billing information.

■ Make Contacts Through Current Clients

As therapy nears an end with clients, let them know of your interest in working with other population groups. Give them two business cards. Suggest that one is for them to keep should they wish to return in the future. The second is for them to give to a friend who may benefit from therapy at some point.

- Offer Checkups

Provide "10,000-mile checkups" on former clients. At the end of treatment with a client, enter her or his name in your calendar for 3 months from that date. When that date arrives call your client and inquire how she or he is doing. Clients generally will be very appreciative of your interest in them. Do not solicit new business at this time. Therapists typically are resistant to calling clients. They hide behind issues of closure, boundaries, and ethics, but really they are afraid of rejection from the client.

- Use Unfilled Time to Market

Market during your unfilled clinical hours. Do not make the mistake of eagerly filling in your unfilled clinical hours with low-paying clients. You will be better off in the long run using that hour to market actively to potential referral sources who are capable of making good referrals.

Cold Calls

Cold calls entail going out into the community, meeting prospective referral sources, and asking for the opportunity to discuss their needs and the services you have to offer. It is this part of marketing with which many psychotherapists are most uncomfortable. However, objectifying the steps and understanding the purpose of the contact will help remove some of the uncertainty and fear.

There are two ways to make a cold call. The first is to simply show up at the prospective referral source's office and request an opportunity to meet. The second is to call ahead of time and schedule with either the individual or the secretary a time to meet. The key in selecting which way to make a cold call is usually the marketing contact's occupation. For instance, physicians generally schedule an hour around lunchtime during which they meet with drug company representatives and other "salespeople" wanting to share information with them. The office receptionist will be able to schedule an appointment for you during this time. School counselors, on the other hand, tend to be less in control of their days and may suggest that you come at a less specific time, such as early morning or after the lunch hour. School counselors typically arrive at work 30 minutes before the students. I have found this to be a good time to meet with them. You may wish to bring a dozen doughnuts for these "sunrise" meetings. Other counselors from surrounding offices may express an interest in your doughnuts and stay long enough to benefit from what you have to say about your practice.

Limit your own talking and encourage the referral source to talk so you can learn who they are and how their agency or work setting fits into your practice. Identify what their needs are and how your practice can accommodate them. Ask who their most difficult case is, and suggest they send that case to you. You will be meeting the needs and wants of the prospective referral source, and will develop referral loyalty from them.

Concentrate on what is being said. Consciously be aware of developing a good relationship, complete with warmth and rapport. This may mean you need to spend a few social minutes talking about a topic unrelated to your work. You have to start where they are and gently move them to where you want them to be. It really is the same practice you would use in therapy with a client.

Observe verbal communication as well as body language for signs of rapport. Maintain good eye contact. Attempt nonverbal mirroring. People tend to like people who are like themselves, and people refer to those whom they like. Develop a firm handshake that conveys confidence. Position yourself squarely on your chair but lean forward slightly to convey interest in the other person.

Instead of "teaching" others about you, be "teachable," or their minds are likely to wander off. People speak at between 100 and 150 words per minute. People listen at between 400 and 500 words per minute. If people are bored, they will tune you out. To avoid this, ask what problems their agency has and how you may be able to help them. Ask good probing questions so you can understand what their needs are. Ask questions to clarify, not to confront. Consider developing a list of questions before you start.

Identify what you hope to achieve during the meeting prior to leaving your office. If you are clear about your agenda, then it will be conveyed to your referral source. If you are unprepared, you run the risk of compensating with too much talk. Tell the potential referral source what therapy services you have to offer and how the services achieve their goals. Always solicit feedback on how they feel about it, so you will know whether you have communicated enough information about your services. If they have reservations, listen to them nondefensively and be ready to acknowledge any shortcomings. Bring appropriate fliers, brochures, giveaways, and newsletters. Always bring business cards. (I keep a box of fliers and business cards in the trunk of my car so I am never caught at a meeting in short supply.)

Ask for a business card from the person with whom you are meeting. I write brief notes to myself on the back side of the business card so I can remember special information I have received. I store these cards in my card file. If you have the opportunity to meet or talk with this person in a few months, you can reflect back on the notes. This will greatly enhance their feelings for you.

Take few notes during your meeting. This is time-consuming and distracting. Spend a few minutes on returning to your car to jot down important notes after each marketing contact.

Never leave a cold call without asking for business. This is how you close a meeting. Too frequently psychotherapists are hesitant to ask for business. They develop relationships, ask probing questions, and do a good needs assessment but fail to ask for business. This one omission changes the meeting from being a business marketing event to being a social event. (Some psychotherapists are bewildered about why they do not get referrals—they did not ask for them!)

Everyone has to develop his or her own style of asking for business, and it helps to practice a few alternative approaches prior to the meeting. Suggestions on asking for business include, "Do you feel you will have a need (or be able) to refer clients to me for therapy? I know it requires confidence in a therapist to be able to refer to her. I would appreciate it if you could try a referral to me. We could then discuss how the client was benefited. I do believe you would then develop the trust for future referrals," or, "Would you feel comfortable referring clients to me?" or, "How many clients a week are you usually referring to therapists? What percentage do you believe would benefit from coming into my practice?"

At the end of the meeting it is also wise to network and ask for names of other business contacts who may find your services helpful. School counselors may know of other school counselors, and general practitioners may know of other general practitioners, to refer you to. If contacts are provided for you, ask whether you can use the referring person's name when calling on these contacts. I have found that this lends me automatic credibility and opens doors to wonderful marketing contacts I otherwise might not have had.

Always, always, *always* drop the new contact a brief note to thank him or her for the time spent with you. This is your opportunity to share any additional information about your services that you may not have had the opportunity to talk about. Because I write frequently for mental health magazines, I sometimes include a copy of an article I have written, should it be applicable to a topic we discussed. Send your note, including a business card, within one week of your contact with the prospective referral source. It will communicate caring, efficiency, and good organization, all reflecting well on your clinical skills. Record your own notes of the meeting on a "Marketing Referral and Development Contacts" sheet (Figure 9.7) (derived from the referral development form used at the former Laurelwood Hospital, PIA, Houston, TX).

If an office staff individual was particularly helpful to you, write a short note to this person as well. Surprisingly, it is often the office manager, especially in physicians' offices, who selects the therapist for a referral.

MARKETING REFERRAL AND DEVELOPMENT CONTACTS

CONTACT: LAST NAME   FIRST NAME   DATE OF CONTACT

_____YES/NO_____
AGENCY OR ORGANIZATION   THANK YOU SENT?   DATE SENT

TITLE

STREET ADDRESS   SUITE/APT. #   CITY, STATE   ZIP

PHONE NO.: _____

_____YES or NO_____YES or NO_____YES or NO_____
     MAILING LIST   ASK FOR BUSINESS   NEEDS ASSESSMENT?

PURPOSE OF CONTACT: _____

CHANGE OF ADDRESS   CITY   STATE   ZIP   PHONE

WHO ELSE TO CONTACT?

PERSONAL NOTES:

_____

_____

_____

FOLLOW-UP:

DATE:_____   TYPE OF ACTIVITY:_____

_____

_____

_____

_____

Figure 9.7. Marketing and Referral and Development Contacts

Although the most effective cold calls will be person-to-person, you may at times find that you need to depend on the telephone to make these contacts. Make the calls yourself rather than having your secretary do so. If the person you are calling has to wait while your secretary gets you for the call, the person called is likely to become resentful. Your marketing call will fail before it has even begun.

Because you are at a disadvantage not having eye-to-eye contact, you need to pay close attention to your tone of voice. Surprisingly, if you smile when you are talking, your voice will be positively influenced and will be more likely to convey friendliness, openness, and warmth.

Avoid temptations to involve yourself in other activities when you are on the telephone. Do not deceive yourself into believing that the other person cannot hear you. (I once conducted a pre-interview on the telephone with a therapist who wanted to join our practice. She continued to eat throughout the entire telephone discussion. I felt this reflected poorly on her and did not consider her as a serious applicant.) People can hear pages turning, staples stapling, nails being filed, dishes being washed, and other such distractions. Rather than convey the message that the person you are talking to is not important, make the decision to hold off on all other activities.

Although most prospective referral sources will like a cold-call meeting with a therapist who is warm, polite, respectful, helpful, and friendly, some potential referral sources will consider cold calls annoying. They do not wish to be interrupted. They may view you as not being busy and, therefore, not successful, because you are out in the community making contacts. Some may reluctantly give you a couple of minutes. In this situation take the couple of minutes offered and only continue meeting if requested to do so. Otherwise, honor your agreement and leave. The best way to approach those individuals who do not wish to meet with you is to acknowledge quickly that this is an inopportune time to talk and then leave. Suggest setting up an appointment at a mutually acceptable time.

After meeting or talking with someone, add their name to your mailing list. Follow-up mailings will enable them to continue learning about your achievements while not forgetting you.

Selling Your Services

Many psychotherapists do not like to think of themselves as selling anything. However, we are all salespeople. Anyone who has convinced someone else—a parent, sibling, spouse, or child—to do something *is* a salesperson. In fact, we frequently "sell" reluctant clients our services. This does not mean selling is being manipulative. Rather, it is helping others understand where to go to receive good therapy.

Keep in mind that you should not be promising more than you can provide. Also remember that when you are "selling" you also are providing needs assessments, consultations, and perhaps identifying diagnoses (Bly, 1991, pp. 11-12). You are a highly trained specialist with multiple objectives when making contact with a prospective referral source.

Thirteen factors will help you successfully sell your services.

1. *Visualize your presentation.* Envision yourself having a successful presentation. Too often people sabotage themselves by going into a presentation only remembering the past failed presentations. We tend to move toward that which we see. So, visualizing success helps us achieve it.

2. *Sell, don't tell.* The person in control is the one who asks questions. The prospective referral source will be more likely to listen to you if he or she is expected to answer you. This presents a more dynamic approach for you. If the other person directs the discussion, you can appear ineffective. Do not, however, confuse this with believing you should perform "third-degree" interrogation of the referral source.

3. *Be friendly and enthusiastic.* View others as potential friends. People typically have a resistance to sales and will quickly tune out. It is important to establish trust and develop a rapport within a few moments. A good opening will help you here. You have about 30 seconds to achieve this goal.

4. *Ask "yes" questions.* Subtly getting the person into the frame of mind where she or he is agreeing with you will help later on when you are "closing the sale," which is when you are about to ask for business. It will then be harder to say no to you. Good yes questions or statements include: "It can really be frustrating working with ADHD adolescents in the classroom, can't it?" "It must feel good to know that you are able to get kids in need the proper help!" "You and I must really love this work to commit ourselves to working with such difficult populations." "Will you feel comfortable referring an ADHD student to me for treatment?"

5. *Begin with open-ended questions and end with close-ended questions.* This enables you to move from general to specific facts. It captures the other person's attention and enhances his or her investment in listening.

6. *Be planned, not canned.* Know in advance what your agenda is, but allow for spontaneity. Individualize your presentation to match the person's needs.

7. *Be truthful.* If you have obtained the appointment with a promise that you will just take 5 minutes of their time, honor your commitment. Stay longer only if you are invited to do so.

8. *Be helpful.* The person may share concern about a client. Be generous and share whatever suggestions you can. This helps the person feel friendly and trusting toward you.

9. *Identify the type of person with whom you are speaking.* People tend to be either visual, auditory, or kinesthetic in the way they learn and receive information. Communicate information based on their manner of learning and making decisions. It will enhance rapport because they will believe that you view things the same way.

   Approximately 35% of the population are visually oriented. You can identify them by their tendency to stare into space. These people make decisions based on what they see. Speak to them in descriptive terms so they can visualize a picture of what you are describing. These people place importance on eye contact. Use brochures, handouts, and giveaway items for visually oriented people.

   Auditory people react to your voice, especially its tone, pace, and rhythm. They will make decisions based on how you talk about your programs. They constitute approximately 25% of the population.

   Kinesthetic individuals, who constitute approximately 40% of the population, deal with their intuitions. If they trust you and feel that you are honest and caring, they will develop strong affections for you and will refer on that basis (Johnson, 1988, pp. 8-9).

10. *Discuss costs only at the end of the meeting.* The emphasis of your presentation should be on the value of your services. Do not explain, defend, or apologize for the price. It is based on the quality of your work.

11. *Acknowledge what the referral source will gain.* Most people will either consciously or subconsciously wonder what they get out of making a referral to you. If they do not ask, take it upon yourself to let them know. If you are meeting with an attorney, he or she will welcome the knowledge that a client can call someone else for emotional support. If you are meeting with a physician, she or he will be glad to know that there will be another professional to help monitor compliance with the medical recommendations. In all cases acknowledge that you will, at times, need to make cross-referrals to other professionals.

12. *Always close.* Approximately 50% of all sales calls end without any attempt to close. Typically psychotherapists do not ask for business. Ask whether what you have discussed makes sense. Will they give it a try? When could you expect a referral? Ask for the business.

13. *Do not worry about objections.* Objections convey interest. Do not be defensive. Listen thoroughly to the objections. Acknowledge accurate

problems that they address and identify how you will make the necessary changes. Sometimes people will share objections because they are resistant to being told anything. More often, it is a way of requesting additional information.

Maintaining Referrals

Psychotherapists are often bewildered as to why referral sources and clients leave and go to the competition. Typically it is because of the quality of service they have received, such as feedback, telephone calls, respect, and appreciation, rather than the quality of therapy. The following suggestions can be helpful in these areas.

1. *Transform an inquiry call into an appointment.* When asked about your fee, do not make the mistake of simply quoting it. Instead, stress your expertise, interest in working with this type of client, reasonable hours, and so on (*Practice Builder,* 1989a).

2. *Send a letter to new clients.* Welcome new clients to your office with a letter stating that you are pleased they have chosen you to be their therapist. If they have not yet come in for their first appointment, send information about your practice: a brochure, résumé, or article you have written (if appropriate). Remind them of your hours of availability, whom to call in the event of an emergency, and that if they have any questions they should call you. This will be appreciated and discourage "therapist shopping."

3. *Maintain contact with clients.* After your vacations, if former clients fail to follow up with further appointments, call them. They will feel valued. They may have terminated because of the anger and abandonment they feel about your having left. I have my secretary call all my regular clients the week before I return from vacation and offer to schedule an appointment for them for the week I am back in the office. This reduces a loss of continuity for the client in therapy, and reduces the likelihood of premature terminations.

4. *There is no such thing as referral loyalty.* Referral sources are fickle. They may refer to a therapist simply because they ran into him at a function or at the neighborhood grocery store and his face and name are easy to recall. They also may refer to the therapist whom they believe can offer the best services. Constantly remind referral sources of yourself by keeping them on a mailing list and sending information about new programs, groups, or seminars you are conducting. An

occasional telephone call is also an effective reminder of your services. If referrals drop off from a referral source, call and ask why. Use this opportunity to describe the other types of clients whom you see, and whom the referral source may be sending elsewhere.

5. *Take referral sources out to lunch periodically.* This gives you the opportunity to spend time with them and learn more about what services they need. People tend to feel nurtured by food and will transfer that positive association to the time spent with you. Do not drink alcohol, even if your guest does, because it may inhibit your ability to think clearly. Besides, you will be returning to the office and it would be inappropriate to have alcohol on your breath. Afterward, follow up with a brief written note thanking them for their time and addressing any key points.

6. *Send a card, or a gift if appropriate, to referral sources during the holidays.* This helps keep the memory of you alive and lets the referral source know that he or she is important to you. I feel most comfortable keeping the cost of the gift low, lest the referral source feel I am trying to "purchase" referrals.

7. *Call "no shows."* It demonstrates caring on your part. It will also make you money. After all, if that "no show" fails to return, what have you lost in income? If you have a number of "no shows" over the week, what have you lost in income that week (*Practice Builder,* 1985b)?

8. *Follow up with clients once after they have terminated therapy.* Clients who invested in therapy will interpret your interest as caring. A phone call will remind them that you are still there should they need additional therapy. It also will remind them of a resource should their friends or family need counseling. Remember clients and former clients on their birthday with a warm but professional card. Keep them on your mailing list so they are informed of any talks you have given, articles or books you have published, or areas of treatment you have expanded into.

9. *Evaluate your practice.* Look at the number of referrals you lost due to dropouts and then consider what your responsibility is. Be honest with yourself. Did you keep clients waiting? Did you return phone calls? Did you call them when appointments were missed?

10. *Flip through your card file from time to time.* This will remind you of referral sources you have not had contact with in a while. I keep everyone's business card in my card file. If I have 15 or 20 minutes of unstructured time, I will call a couple of the referral sources simply to remind them that I am still around and to reestablish communica-

tion. In this way a broad base of referrals is not only developed but also maintained.

Set a goal to make a specific number of calls each week. I call those with whom I have not had recent contact and provide them with friendly updates. Sometimes instead of calling I send reprints of an article I have written that may be of interest to them or copies of newspaper articles that remind me of them. Of course, I also use my card file to provide a list of the people to whom I wish to send season's greetings cards.

11. *Remember telephone etiquette.* Be certain that the secretary or whomever is handling the telephones is consistently polite and friendly. If hostilities are allowed to develop, the client may terminate and you will never know why. Have a friend call your office and answering service from time to time to check on pleasantness, helpfulness, and follow-through. (I used this method to discover that my answering service was rude and was putting people on hold for long periods of time. I will never know what it cost me in business.) Be certain that reliable and clear messages are taken for each call received, including the caller's telephone number.

Soliciting Client Feedback

Develop a system that will provide you with feedback on client satisfaction. This is often difficult for or even distasteful to clinicians. Yet it can be done tastefully, ethically, and with clinical good judgment. Remember, it is not what you are doing that counts: It is client satisfaction that counts. After all, if your clients are not satisfied, you will not be able to practice effectively. The system that probably works best is to develop a confidential questionnaire and send it with a self-addressed, stamped envelope. Ask questions regarding their satisfaction with the therapy, billing, and length of session; reason for selecting you to be their therapist; what they wish the therapist would do more or less of; and why they terminated therapy.

Advertising

Word of mouth may never be enough to bring in the number of new clients necessary to maintain a strong practice. You will need to have advertising that is strong and effective. Advertising should attract new clients or referral sources as well as remind people that you are still available, as even good referral sources can forget you unless reminded. Advertising will continuously inform or remind people of you, stimulate inquiries, spread the benefits of your practice, increase your name recognition, build your image in the community, and persuade people to consider using your services.

Before advertising you need to ask yourself these questions: Who are the people I want to target? Where are these people located? Why should the people consider responding to my advertising? What sort of message do I want to deliver? Can I offer a reason to believe in the benefit of my services? What tone and manner of advertising do I want?

Never engage in advertising that will compromise you professionally. Keep in focus the need to maintain credibility. Do not leave total responsibility for writing or designing ads to professional salespeople. They will not know your business like you do, and liberties they may take in promises, ethics, colors, typeface, or style may detract from your credibility. Make all details your responsibility. No detail is unimportant. Remember: Nothing in advertising is neutral or casual. Casualness brings about calamities. Be certain to "sign off" personally on all ads prior to their being placed.

Never spend more for advertising than you can afford to lose. To avoid financial problems, pay in cash for advertising. It will help you be organized. A rule of thumb for determining what to spend is as follows: 3%-5% of your monthly income if you want to maintain your current practice level, 5%-7% if you want to enlarge your practice, and 7%-10% if you want to enter new marketing areas (Conlee, 1990, p. 161; *Private Practice Update,* 1991, p. 1). Avoid a crash advertising program. They seldom pay off. Rather, develop a long-term approach.

Advertising is an investment. For every dollar spent, you should get a return through increased revenue. However, your "return" might take months to actualize. It is unlikely that if you advertise on Monday you will experience a significant increase on Tuesday. Do not advertise unless you are making a 2 to 1 or 3 to 1 return on your investment (personal communication with Bob Wright, Director, Professional Practice Development, Gulf Pines Hospital, Houston, TX, 1990). If an advertisement is not bringing in the desired return, change the ad by offering a different or free service, or drop the ad. Be prepared to repeat your advertising: Repetition aids retention.

All advertising should be kept clear and simple. In good advertising, less is more. Avoid clutter and allow white space to accent your words. Good quotes are effective eye-catchers. Be original, creative, and avoid "me too" advertising. Maintain a single-mindedness with regard to communicating your message and what you intend for the potential client to do after he or she takes in the message (personal communication with Bob Wright, Director, Professional Practice Development, Gulf Pines Hospital, Houston, TX, 1990).

You will want to become familiar with various advertising methods that may be used to promote your services. Before settling on what type of advertising you would like to do, select several newspapers, magazines, and fliers and analyze the ads placed by your competition. Note how other psychotherapists advertise themselves. Look critically at the ads and make your own notes regarding how you want to simulate or avoid what they have printed. Look at current trends. Whatever you do, be original. Identify a niche. Advertise in publications that your prospective clients, not your colleagues, are likely to be reading. Do not let anything out of your office that reflects poorly on you (whether it is a flier, handout, letter, or business card). After all, nothing you do with regard to advertising is neutral. It will either increase or decrease your credibility.

■ Direct Mail

Everyone is familiar with direct mail. Direct mail is the paraphernalia clogging your mailbox that you often throw away without opening. Nuisance mail to some can be your vehicle for developing new business. For you, direct mail is an opportunity to reach a large audience of potential clients.

Direct mail can be as simple as a letter, a self-mailer (mail that folds up rather than being inserted in an envelope), or a card or as extravagant as a detailed color brochure. Direct mail is economical. The post office can give you a bulk rate permit, although quantity bulk mailings can be slow. Allow extra time for delivery. Three weeks is not uncommon. If the prospect of folding, inserting, labeling, and applying postage is overwhelming, contract with a mailing house to do the job for you. There are professional direct mail companies that specialize in this field.

One advantage of direct mail is that you are not competing with other ads; the reader is looking at your mail exclusively. The piece also is likely to be saved, or even posted, if it applies to a general public.

Mailing lists can be rented. The Yellow Pages have a listing of mailing-list companies from which you can select a couple to make inquiry calls. You will want to mail to targeted populations, so identify what desired demographic groups you wish to target, based on age, marital status, economic status, and occupation. Not identifying specific demographics results in a shotgun approach, which will be wasteful. Ask whether the mailing lists are regularly updated.

Even if you decide to rent mailing lists, develop your own mailing list using the zip codes of clients and referral sources you already have. The client list includes active clients as well as addresses you obtained from completed evaluations at previous presentations. These targeted zip codes are indicative of the areas from which you are most likely to obtain referrals. The response will generally come from within a 15-mile radius.

Do not use mailing labels. People are more likely to throw away labeled envelopes than those with typed names as the former are less personal.

A self-mailer will get opened even if the addressee has moved, whereas an envelope may get forwarded or discarded. A few thousand words can be delivered to targeted populations by self-mailers. Be aware, however, that the postage will increase with the number of pages you add and that prospective clients do not want to read a lot of copy. They do not have the time or desire to know a lot about you at this time. Do not spend voluminous amounts of space on words trying to educate them. It is unnecessary and may result in you losing a prospective client. Although economical, the self-mailer's primary drawback is that it looks like an advertisement. A study shared by *Practice Builder* pointed out that the performance rate of the number 10 envelope is typically 35%-40% better than the self-mailer (*Practice Builder,* 1984c, p. 4).

If you prefer to use an envelope rather than a self-mailer, include a cover letter, a business card, and a brochure. It is also helpful if you have a postage-paid reply card attached to the mailer or enclosed in the envelope so the reader can check interest in different areas. Have a place for the reader to put his or her name, address, telephone number, and best times for you to call.

At times direct mail can be ineffective. To enhance its performance, have an attention-grabbing title but avoid the temptation to make it cutesy or gimmicky. The topic is serious, and you run the risk of offending readers if they feel their problems are being taken lightly. Use a good quality glossy paper.

Try to include simple, short, catchy phrases. Start out with an opening statement that grabs the reader's attention, such as "Has Your Teenager Fired You as a Parent?" Identify problems the reader can relate to, and then offer services to solve the problem. Use the word "you" a lot.

Make the paragraphs short. Use subtitles to help break up the copy (*Practice Builder,* 1984a, p. 4). Play with different styles of type to keep reader interest. Describe why you are qualified to help the reader with this problem. Give the reader directions on how to call you for an appointment or write for further information. Avoid testimonials, as they appear to violate confidentiality.

You will know the success of your direct mail within 2 to 3 weeks, as 80% of the responses will have been made. You can expect a 4% return from direct mail. If you receive 10%, you have had a high return.

Send direct mailers regularly, either monthly or seasonally. Vary color, size, and print style so as to "prevent habituation and to keep the response up" (*Practice Builder,* 1984b, p. 8).

■ Newspapers

There are newspapers, and then there are newspapers. There are business journals, local papers, and papers that are designed to reach specific industries, trades, and professions. I have found that my best advertising dollar is spent if I concentrate on advertising in newspapers that have a circulation within 15 miles of my office. The free weekly, local community papers often meet this need perfectly. They typically provide you with a high circulation at low cost. Do not waste your money on advertising citywide.

Newspaper advertisements are good in that you can include as lengthy a message as you wish to or can afford. Visual images can be used to compliment your message. New ideas, workshops, or programs you are offering can be effectively marketed through newspaper advertising. Place as large an ad as you can comfortably afford, as the size of the ad will be important in attracting attention.

People buy benefits, not products. Include in the advertising benefits such as evening and Saturday hours—readers learn they do not have to miss work. Another benefit to describe is that insurance is accepted, reducing the client's financial concerns. Provide solid information, tips, and advice. Use a strong, positive headline. It is all the better if the headline offers a service.

Design your own ads. After all, who knows your practice better than you? Avoid the use of psychological jargon. Be certain the ad can be read and understood by most readers. (Procter & Gamble had to drop "concentrated" from their ads because many readers thought it meant the product had been "blessed by the Pope" [*Practice Builder,* 1984b, p. 6].) If you are uncertain whether your ad text is too advanced, ask others to read it. Then ask whether they understood what the ad said and whether they know what the message is asking them to do. Decide what populations you are targeting and write the ad with those individuals in mind. Do not clutter your ad with multiple messages. It will appear stronger if one clear theme is conveyed. Keep the format simple.

Start with several small ads and track the effectiveness of each. Then withdraw the ones that are not effective. Consider increasing the size of the successful ads. Use a heavy black border around your ads to make them stand out on the page. The smaller the ad, the thicker the border you should use to make it noticeable. Use white space in the ad to emphasize your written copy and to make it more appealing to the reader.

David Ogilvy suggests inserting an extra space between paragraphs to increase readership by 12%. He also recommends using an oversized first letter in the body copy to increase the readership another 13% (David Ogilvy, cited in *Practice Builder,* 1988). To personalize your ad, consider using your

TABLE 9.1 Readership Breakdown

Market	Sunday Location	Daily Location
Affluent males	Business	Business
Middle-income males	Sports	Sports
Affluent females	Business	Women's
Middle-income females	Main news	Women's
Affluent men and women	Business	Main news
Middle-income men and women	Main news or TV section	Main news or TV section

SOURCE: *Practice Builder,* 1985d, p. 9.

photograph or drawings. Use not only your agency's name but your own as well to enhance name recognition.

Have your ad professionally typeset. Hand deliver the ad to the newspaper camera-ready. To save the expense of a professionally typeset ad, have the publication provide you with camera-ready copy for your approval prior to insertion. Do not mail it in. Use this opportunity to develop good relationships with the publication staff. At this time, ask for specific placement of your ad. Ask for it to appear on the right-hand side of the page above the fold line. This is where most readers direct their eyes first. Be very appreciative if they do this for you. By doing all of the above, you are assuming responsibility for the design, production, and delivery of your ad, thus reducing the likelihood of embarrassing or costly mistakes.

If you plan to place your advertisement in a daily newspaper, select the placement based on the population you hope to target. For instance, a study performed by *Practice Builder* (1985d) determined the breakdown of readership to be as shown in Table 9.1.

As with all advertising, one-shot advertising will not bring you any benefits. The community needs to be continually reminded of you. Lay out a program or campaign and submit ads to the newspaper on a regular basis. This helps develop name recognition over an extended period of time. I typically advertise biweekly. Be aware of specific seasons or holidays that may stimulate more business and warrant extra ads.

■ Magazines

The readership is broad, but advertising in magazines is costly. Because you would be advertising to an area that is broader than you can service, the money will be wasted. Unless it is a very local magazine ready to offer you discounted rates (which they may do if they receive last-minute cancellations), choose another medium for advertising.

■ Brochures

Brochures should be carefully written, impressive-looking packets of information about you that can be used widely for advertising your services. One benefit of brochures is that they can be updated at minimal cost. Brochures also can be tailored to the specific needs of the client population you are targeting.

They should be left in your waiting room for new clients, and hopefully may be passed on to a friend. You can drop brochures off at physicians' offices, distribute them at workshops or talks, and leave them in hospital lobbies. They can even be sent with a cover letter in direct mailings to potential or current referral sources (*Practice Builder,* 1984f, p. 2).

The content should include your credentials and training, awards won, and appearances made on radio and television. This information reassures potential clients that you will understand their problems. Identify the populations you work with and the office procedures regarding making an appointment. Be sure to include identifying information such as the agency's name, address, telephone number, and simple directions. Write out words rather than abbreviating. Do not include psychological jargon or personal information. The brochure should be clean, polished, and professional in appearance.

The brochure also should be developed for easy reading. Subheadings aid in this goal. Use lots of paragraphs as well as short words and sentences. Grab the reader's attention by making the headline a benefit rather than your practice name. If the printed word does not help convince the reader to buy your services, do not include it (*Practice Builder,* 1988, p. 3). After all, if your intent is to inform the reader, you are printing up a public service document at personal expense!

Always use a good quality, heavyweight paper for brochures. There are two basic styles of brochures you should consider. The first is the single sheet of paper folded into thirds, with different categories of information placed on each section. The second is more expensive. It opens like a folder, with your name, agency, and address on the cover. The inside contains pockets for informational sheets, a biographical page with your photograph (Figure 9.8), and fliers advertising your groups and special events. Although initially more costly, the second style of brochure allows you to update information or target a different audience simply by printing new inserts. Select bright colors and avoid color patterns that are passé, even if you happen to like them.

Mistakes do happen. If the printer goofs, she or he will have to reprint the brochures. But if you goofed, you will have to live with the mistakes. Therefore, request that the printer give you a proof of the brochure so you can review it for errors. It is less costly to correct errors at this point.

Eileen S. Lenson _____

Ms. Lenson is a Psychotherapist on staff at Charter Hospital of Kingwood.

- Ms. Lenson is a Certified Social Worker - Advanced Clinical Practitioner with special certification in trauma resolution therapy and clinical hypnosis. She is also a Board Certified Diplomate in Clinical Social Work, a Licensed Certified Social Worker in the State of Maryland, and an Academy Certified Social Worker. Ms. Lenson received her Masters degree from the University of Maryland, Baltimore.
- In addition to her work at Charter, Ms. Lenson maintains a private practice with special emphasis on the treatment of depression, grief, marital problems, chemical dependency, family problems, co-dependency, and sexual abuse. Clients include adolescents, adults, families, and couples on an in-patient basis. Ms. Lenson also conducts adolescent and women's group therapy sessions.
- Before becoming associated with Charter, Ms. Lenson held the position of Social Work Supervisor for the George Washington University Medical Center in Washington, DC, and taught courses on ethics at the George Washington University Medical School.
- Professional membership includes the National Association of Social Workers. Ms. Lenson is also a published author and a public speaker in her field and is a frequent guest on local radio shows.

 CHARTER HOSPITAL OF KINGWOOD

17115 Red Oak Drive, Suite 230
Houston, TX 77090
(713) 444-6577

Figure 9.8. Biographical Sheet With Photograph

You may have concluded that a brochure sounds too expensive for your budget. Do not overlook the ability to produce a brochure on your home computer. Or, maybe you simply do not want to invest the time required to send out a polished product (and you should not be sending out anything that reflects poorly on you). Then consider what a subscriber to *Practice Builder* came up with: a postcard with interesting pieces of information (*Practice Builder*, 1991, p. 6). Send these "postcard tips" out on a regular basis and wait to hear the positive reception from the recipients. This is a fresh and inexpensive way to keep the community aware of your services.

■ Handouts

Booklets, lists of support groups, or fact sheets on specific interest groups, such as adult children of alcoholics or codependents, should be accessible in your waiting room for interested clients. Although you did not write them, you can still benefit by stamping them with your name, address, and telephone number. They are likely to be picked up by clients to be given away. What a wonderful marketing tool!

■ Yellow Pages

Typically therapists find the telephone book a poor source of new referrals, although this does vary geographically. In a more transient community in which people have not developed relationships with traditional referral sources, many people will be more reliant on seeking out services on their own and will turn to the telephone book. This is not to imply that advertising in the Yellow Pages holds no value, for even those who are referred to your practice through trusted physicians, school counselors, clergy, and others often will check you out in the Yellow Pages to confirm your credibility.

List your services by name as well as by specialty, such as psychotherapist, marriage and family counselor, and counseling. Study the listings in the Yellow Pages and try to identify a service you provide that will separate you from the others. If others repeatedly advertise drug and alcohol screening, do so in your ad but add in large letters EVENING HOURS AVAILABLE. In this way you will be capturing interest by telling readers what you have and securing business by introducing your benefits. Help the reader select you by including bulleted statements such as "We care," "We are here to listen to you," or "Emergency care provided."

The competition, although not advertising evening hours, probably offers them. A prospective client who wants evening hours will be more likely to call your office first. Put in anything that helps capture a client's attention and gives her or him a reason to notice you over the other advertisements.

Due to the increase in managed care and HMOs, prospective clients have less choice in selecting a therapist, if they want maximum reimbursement from their insurance carrier. Therefore, the number of individuals using the Yellow Pages to select a therapist will decline, as the selection of a therapist is being decided for them by their insurance companies.

If other mental health professionals are not using the Yellow Pages, use a 1-inch advertisement. This provides you with the best return on your investment. It looks classy yet unintimidating. When it comes to the size of your Yellow Pages advertisement, bigger is not necessarily better—unless you have a lot of competition. If this is the case, buy an advertisement slightly larger than that of your competition (*Practice Builder,* 1984d, p. 4).

Keep in mind that the ad will run for a year and cannot be changed once it has been placed. For this reason select your ad carefully and only after cautiously studying the competition. Look at other advertisements critically. Determine what ads jump off the page at you and which ones are difficult to read or do not motivate you to respond. Use two to three different typefaces and thick letters for easy reading (*Practice Builder,* 1984d, p. 6).

Do not automatically renew each year without first evaluating the ad's effectiveness and assessing whether you want to update the message. If you are not yet in private practice but plan to be soon, consider placing your advertisement in the Yellow Pages prior to the establishment of your practice. Otherwise you may lose out on the benefits of the Yellow Paged listing for your first year in business.

Only use the main Yellow Pages book. Forget advertising in the smaller regional books. When was the last time you pulled one out to look up a telephone number?

If a client informs you that she or he used the Yellow Pages to locate you, ask the client what it was about the advertisement that attracted her or him. Keep notes on this feedback and incorporate it into your refinement of your advertisement for the next year.

■ Radio

Radio commercials are productive because they allow you to select your specific audience due to special demographic appeal of station programming. Select the radio station and time of day based on the population you want to listen to your advertising. The radio station salespeople have the demographics on who is listening to what show at what specific time. The length of message is more limited than in the newspaper but it is repeated frequently. It is personal and allows you to speak directly to the audience. It is powerful because you can use the word "you" and give facts.

To be successful, you (or the radio announcer) must speak 150 words per minute. This is fast but necessary to keep people invested. Communicate only one idea to avoid diversions or confusion. Once you have people's attention, you will want them to react. Provide facts. Give them excitement at the end of the announcement. Direct them to call *today* to sign up for the group or call *today* for a free consultation.

To develop your message fully, you will need to spend 60 seconds on each advertisement, with your telephone number being repeated two or three times in the message. For you to obtain a response, the listener will need to hear the message between five and seven times. Therefore, do not pursue this form of advertising unless you are willing to make the financial commitment (*Practice Builder,* 1984e, p. 7; *Practice Builder,* 1985c, p. 6).

The drawbacks to radio advertising are its lack of visual images and the cost. Negotiate cost with the radio station sales representative. The first price list they bring out will probably be the most expensive. Most stations will negotiate from their published rate card or put together "packages" for you. Be sure they understand your budget limitations. Ask them to donate some free advertising to match the paid advertising you will provide. Do not compromise the airing time of your advertisement for cost. The best times are the commuting hours to and from work. Look for cheaper rates if you want to advertise during "slow" times, typically summer and January (*Practice Builder,* 1984c, p. 5).

■ Television

Television is a powerful medium. It combines sight, sound, and motion. As with radio advertising, you can either write the copy for television advertisements or use an agency. You have to have a good opening because most viewers have a remote control and only give you 3 to 5 seconds to grab their attention. The tone of the advertising must reflect the demeanor of your practice. Finally, you must have a strong, catchy ending.

Consider advertising on a local cable station, if available in your area. It often is less expensive and can be discriminatory in targeting specific audiences or populations. Ask for data on the number of viewers. You may be wasting your money if the viewership is too low. Advertise during nonprime-time hours, which include nighttime. It will be less expensive and you are more likely to target insomniacs and others with mental health problems.

To do a television ad well, you may need to use an advertising agency or the television production department to provide you with the necessary help. The cost of producing the commercial can be high. Television stations, because of the research they have done, can help you identify the time periods and stations that will best reach the populations you want. The greatest drawback to television is the cost. Typically the costs will be higher than any other form of advertising.

■ Seminars

Providing seminars can not only increase your name recognition in the community but also pay well. You can either sponsor your own seminar or write to companies that sponsor and market seminars and offer to be a seminar leader.

Select a subject area that you are skilled in and believe would be of interest to the community. Plan out a schedule that would last one half day to a full day, and allow for an in-depth discussion on the topic. To keep attendees from getting restless, try to select a mix of formal instruction with experiential exercises. This will satisfy both the left- and the right-brain people.

Arrange for someone, perhaps your secretary, to register people when they arrive, give name tags, and distribute necessary handouts. If you are having the event in a hotel conference room, your secretary also should be in charge of temperature control should the room become too stuffy or cold, and he or she should help coordinate the arrival or cleanup of drinks and food.

If you are hoping to attract professionals to your seminar, look into obtaining continuing education units (CEUs). To do so, contact the respective professional organizations. They will send you an application packet to complete and charge you a processing fee. Plan ahead if you wish to offer CEUs, as it is a lengthy process.

Advertise your seminar in the newspaper. Place the ad on the two Sundays prior to the seminar to benefit from the sizable readership, and on a weekday just prior to the seminar to obtain the impulsive attendance. If your seminar is free, also announce it in the "Calendar of Community Events" (*Practice Builder,* 1988, p. 11).

■ Billboards

When I first moved to Houston, Texas, I was appalled by the number of billboards cluttering the highways. Four years later I had come not only to accept but also appreciate this aspect of Houston's culture and arranged for a billboard of my own. This 40-foot by 28-foot billboard advertised free drug and alcohol screening. I used three bright colors and very few printed words. My telephone number was the largest printed item on the billboard. The location for the billboard was one block from my office so I would be attracting the traffic that regularly travels by my office. This better ensured that I would reach prospective clients.

As billboard readers have only 10 seconds or less of exposure to your message, it must be simple and catchy. Convey one message only with emotional appeal. The wording must be prominent and highly visible. To increase the effectiveness of a billboard, have the advertisement moved to different sites on a prearranged basis with the billboard company. A physician successfully advertised his vasectomy services using this rotating sign process. One client told the physician that he finally came in for the surgery because it seemed that the signs were following him around town reminding him to have the procedure performed!

After 1 year I had not received one telephone inquiry that I could directly trace to my billboard. Research states that billboards enhance name recognition. They do not necessarily bring in immediate business. They do, however, support other forms of marketing you produce. Billboards can be expensive. If you have a large marketing budget, billboards can prove to be a good investment. If you have an affiliation with a psychiatric hospital, you may wish to ask for their assistance in payment for such advertising.

A cousin to billboards is position advertising: outdoor and transit advertising (on buses, taxis, shopping carts) and signs. These forms of advertising often are less expensive.

■ Advertising Agencies

An advertising agency can help you by making recommendations on the approaches you should take in marketing. They can help you write your copy and make contacts with the media, identify target markets, and determine how to spread word of your services.

They may charge you on a flat-fee basis, a commission basis, or a combination of the two. They also may require a minimum billing before accepting you as a client. Speak with several advertising agencies before selecting one. Establish a written contract prior to having them do work for you. Speak with others in the field for recommendations. Be certain the agency you wish to work with understands the mental health field. Ask for exclusivity within a specific geographical area so the agency is not representing you as well as your competition.

■ Marketing Consultants

A new industry growing in the mental health community is people who sell their marketing services to therapists. These consultants offer to make community contacts, drop off your business card and brochure, and bring in referrals for you. The problem with this is that potential referral sources and clients are buying the representative, not what is being offered—the therapist. There is no substitute for you, the clinician, getting out into the community and making personal contacts.

■ Psychiatric Hospitals

Psychiatric hospitals depend on referrals from health-care providers. Therefore, they often are willing to share marketing expertise and assist with expenses of allied health-care professionals whom they believe may refer future patients. Such help may range from a marketing department representative reviewing your goals and objectives and sharing her or his expertise to sponsoring a seminar with the accompanying advertisements in the newspaper and/or on radio. Hospitals also may agree to pay for advertisements in the newspapers about your general services or pay portions of your overhead. They are also a source of referrals of inpatients who need to be followed for individual and family therapy.

As you undoubtedly have been cautioned, there is no such thing as a "free lunch." I have known both reputable and disreputable psychiatric hospitals. Reputable hospitals will provide marketing assistance with the expectation that when you have a patient appropriate for inpatient treatment you will consider placement at their institution. Disreputable hospitals, on the other hand, will be very generous with their outlay of financial support and may attempt to woo you with dinners and theater tickets, but then apply pressure for you to meet admission quotas. They will offer you a reciprocity of referrals for each referral you make to their inpatient treatment. These hospitals often are attempting to fill beds, not necessarily to provide good treatment. Financial and treatment decisions are being made without the client's awareness and consent. This unethical process has negatively influenced many good psychotherapists and resulted in greed casting a shadow on the therapist's good judgment and our profession in general.

■ Medical Hospitals

With the advent of the Diagnostic Related Grouping (DRG) system, medical hospitals found their billing system changing, census dropping, and length of stay shortening. This is because under the DRGs, insurance is based on the diagnosis rather than the length of stay.

To survive, hospitals have begun courting mental-health-care professionals to help provide specialty services in the hopes of attracting patients to their facilities. The opportunity for providing specialized services, such as developing and overseeing new programs or providing in-house consultation to a hospital, is increasing. This may include being available to staff on a consultation basis when they are having problems dealing with a difficult situation, such as a burn victim or a death; providing stress management courses for coronary artery bypass graft patients; or working with eating disorder or pain management patients.

■ Free Advertising

Believe it or not, with a little chutzpah, ingenuity, and motivation, you can get free advertising. It is yet another way to get your name and services in the media. Free advertising can be obtained through the newspapers, radio, or television.

Newspapers

You can write press releases on groups, workshops, presentations, or other relevant projects with which you are involved. Write a release as you would write for the newspaper, to maximize readership. Keep the press release to approximately 100 words, double-spaced. Answer the following questions in your press release for maximum interest: who? what? where? when? why? and how? Top it with a three- to four-word catchy title. Include an offer to send a free pamphlet if the reader calls or writes you. This ensures the inclusion of your telephone number and address. Put the most important information in the first line. You will lose 20% of the people by the second line. Either put a specific release date at the top or put "For Immediate Release."

If you know a journalist or editor, call him or her and try to develop an interest in your project. If you do not know anyone, call the newspaper or magazine and obtain the name of the person to whom your release should be sent. Never address it "To Whom It May Concern" or "Editor." A name will better ensure it getting printed or aired. Follow up on your mailing and call the specific individual to whom you sent the release. Ask whether she or he has any questions. You may also wish to ask a newspaper editor whether she or he would like to write an article about a specific part of your practice.

If you are hosting a free event, such as a talk or seminar, you can send an announcement of it to the newspapers and the radio and television stations. Accompany it with a professionally prepared picture of yourself. They may publish it as a public service announcement free of charge.

If writing is one of your strengths, consider sending editors either an outline of an article or a completed article you would like to have published in their newspaper or magazine. Include a cover letter detailing your other writing experiences and why you are qualified to write on this topic. If you get no response, write the editor that you are withdrawing your article and then submit it to another publication.

Publications do not always pay for submitted articles. Ask what their policy is. Minimally, you should be able to expect a blurb at the end of the article with your name, title, agency, and telephone number. Sometimes a publication will not pay for the article but will place an ad free of charge. Once the article is accepted for publication, suggest additional topics to the editor for future articles you are willing to write. If a newspaper interviews you or publishes an article you write, get professional copies of it and use it when marketing.

Radio

The way to advertise for free on the radio is to write talk show hosts about a topic on which you would like to speak. Ask to be interviewed on radio. Come prepared with a list of suggested questions you can give the host, should he or she not be familiar with your work and have difficulty identifying interesting and pertinent questions to ask you. Prior to the actual taping, tell the host of special groups, seminars, or professional projects you have that may be of interest to the station's listeners. Because you are an interesting guest who is voluntarily speaking, the host probably will be pleased to accommodate you and give you free plugs.

When you come, bring a blank cassette tape. The host will tape a copy of the interview for you. When you leave, give the host and the receptionist a business card. Days after the tape has aired, people may call the station and request your telephone number. If your host has your telephone number handy, he or she will be more likely to give it out.

A good time to contact the radio stations is 4 to 6 weeks prior to your providing a service to the community, such as a workshop, or after you have been involved in a current community problem (such as a task force on cults or Red Cross involvement with flood disaster victims), or during holidays.

As with the newspapers and magazines, write the producers of the radio stations to inform them of human interest activities you are involved in that may interest the community. If it is a free event they will be especially likely to give air time to present your project. Once you have been invited to be on the radio, drop a note to your clients and referral sources, suggesting that the show may be a topic of interest to them.

Television

If you happen to be in the right place doing the right thing, or if you know of someone with connections in television, you may be lucky enough to get interviewed. For those who are not as lucky, take the time to write the production managers of the news or talk shows that you believe will appeal to the populations you wish to target and suggest a topic you would like to present on television. Because hosts often do not know your topic as well as you do, take a list of suggested questions that the host may use. Always be courteous, both during the interview and afterward with the host and the receptionist. As with radio, leave your business card and follow up with a fitting thank-you note.

The audience will want to receive something from you. If you are talking on a topic of general interest, you can spontaneously offer to send material on this topic if the viewers send you a self-addressed, stamped envelope. This way you are getting your address out to the public while developing your own mailing list. As with a radio appearance, drop a note to your clients and referral sources notifying them of your appearance and suggest that the topic may be one of interest to them.

■ Newsletters

Newsletters enable you to market your ideas. They keep your name current in the community, both with clients and with referral sources. Select a regular timetable for mailing them out—either seasonally or monthly, but no less frequently than quarterly. Otherwise, you will lose your name recognition. Send them just prior to and during your busy seasons. (Do not waste your time and money sending newsletters during your slow seasons.) For example, send newsletters all through November and December for the topics of holiday blues, compulsive spending, or chemical dependency.

Avoid sounding too professional. It will only come out stuffy, and no one will read it. Use short words and short sentences. Remember: This is a newsletter to the public, not a presentation at a national conference. Do not just inform. If you do, you are wasting your time and postage. Instead, offer a motivation to call you, such as a free group or seminar.

Have newsletters professionally typeset. Consider using your letterhead as the first page but identify that it is a newsletter. Have a great headline to ensure readership. Eighty percent of all readers fail to get beyond the headline (*Practice Builder*, 1985a, p. 9). Newsletters reflect the quality of your office, so do not shortcut the expense and have them photocopied. Newsletters can be small, up to four pages. Do not charge readers for your newsletter.

Use your newsletters to accompany any mail that leaves your office. Send them to professionals with cover letters, offering to help with any difficult cases. Then follow up the mailing with a telephone call (*Practice Builder*, 1985a, p. 9).

■ Open House

An open house marks the beginning of a new practice, opening a second office, an introduction of new equipment, or the joining of a new colleague. It offers an opportunity to have other professionals become acquainted with you and your office. It also affords you the opportunity to invite potential referral sources whom you have not yet met. Only professionals, not clients, are invited.

A 3-by-5 or 4-by-6 invitation should be mailed out announcing the open house hours. Offering it on a weekday may encourage more attendees than would a weekend. Have the open house from late afternoon to the early evening, allowing for guests with varying work schedules to arrive when it is convenient for them. Serve food that is easy to pick up with the hands. Serve nonalcoholic beverages.

To increase the likelihood of attendance, call the people you have invited and tell them you are hoping they will be able to attend. Open houses typically are poorly attended, probably because of the lack of a personal touch. No one wants to respond to an impersonal invitation. If you have invited several attorneys, tell each attorney this on the phone. Do likewise with other professionals. They will attend because they see their own networking opportunities.

Although the open house is a marketing concept, do not be too obvious with your guests. Make them feel comfortable and develop a personal relationship as a foundation. People tend to refer to those whom they like, so make them feel comfortable. Get them to talk about themselves so you begin to identify needs they may have in the way of referrals.

■ Promotional Items

Giveaway items promote goodwill while also advertising your personal or agency name and business telephone number. The types of gimmicks you buy will depend on your budget and the age of the client you are hoping to attract. What is important is to select items that will receive regular usage. Post-it Note Pads, tote bags, umbrellas, calculators, desk clocks, and coffee mugs are good for adults, as everyone from physicians to housewives has a need for them. Keychains, pencils, pens, sun visors, and T-shirts are attractive to teenagers. I found the spongy "anxiety" brick, which is red and looks like a brick, to be in great demand by the adolescents in my practice. They can crunch the brick up and toss it as a way of coping with their anger. The beauty of these items is that the user is reminded of your practice with each usage, as your name and telephone number are printed on each item. If a competitor begins using the same product giveaway as you have, drop the item and select another. Develop a pattern of being original.

Whichever marketing tool you select should be based on meeting different client markets. Do be cautious about selecting only one method because it is familiar and comfortable to you. A risk lies in the public associating you with only a narrow position or ability—for example, "can give speeches but can't write." To reach the various target markets best, you need a diversified and coordinated advertising effort that promotes your services.

Personal Image

An implicit but rarely acknowledged element of marketing is personal image. A positive personal image conveys respect, seriousness, and confidence and generates trust. Return telephone calls in a timely fashion. Be courteous and on time.

Once, while sitting in the waiting room to meet with a psychiatrist, I overheard a woman loudly complaining to another about being kept waiting 40 minutes for her appointment. She repeatedly complained about the doctor's tardiness with keeping appointments. She also mentioned the name of another physician who, when tardy for his appointment, did not charge her. This woman's complaining was highly uncomplimentary negative publicity. Would it not serve one's professional image to have a policy of not charging if late for the session?

Be neat. Dress a little better than do your clients. It will convey accomplishment and respect. Forward reports to others on time when requested. Do not make false promises to your clients. Communicate with other professionals about mutual clients as needed. Be cautious of conveying "hype" rather than sound marketing. Convey credibility. It is like "old money." It means you will not be flashy but will be trusted. Not communicating a positive presentation establishes a barrier to being understood and, therefore, to receiving referrals.

Summary

Being service oriented, I initially did not realize that marketing would be so demanding. Marketing, done correctly, is a way of life. It requires a commitment of time, money, and consistency. It means doing what you must do when you need to do it, like it or not.

Marketing begins as soon as you have office space. As you will not begin with many filled client hours, you will need to spend your time marketing. I began my practice by marketing 40 or more hours per week. It was ego-deflating, tiring work. The deferred gratification and rewards for my hard work did come, but only much later. Being a "go-getter" is critical for a healthy practice. Think of marketing as an investment in your future.

To market successfully is to remind yourself that you must have a business relationship as well as a therapeutic relationship with each client and prospective referral source. It is difficult to find the balance between focusing on other people's needs over your own, not crusading, and concentrating on therapy. Heed my warning that therapeutic skills alone will never be sufficient for building a successful private practice. Marketing skills will get the clients in your office.

Reading books on marketing and learning from other types of businesses will help in your continued quest to identify who needs your services and how to prevent your competition from taking over your share of the client market. Do not be intimidated by the competition. No matter how competent they may appear, remember that they cannot do everything well. Try to identify a portion of the market that they are not currently servicing adequately and seek it out for yourself. Everyone has their own strengths and weaknesses. Good marketing entails knowing the competition's weaknesses.

Never stop looking at changes you can make. Can you shorten the waiting time clients have to endure to get an appointment with you? Can you return telephone calls more expeditiously? Can some charges be reduced? Can your image be enhanced? What improvements can you make in the services you are presently offering?

Basically, what I am addressing is responsibility. To market yourself most efficiently, you must accept 100% responsibility for your actions. This means discarding blame and excuses. It means developing a system to identify why clients never reach your office and why others leave you prematurely. This honest, ongoing self-appraisal, which involves communication and listening, is necessary for your practice to be able to problem solve effectively and reach its fullest potential.

Remember: Good marketing can help your private practice compensate for problems in poor cash flow, undercapitalization, recession, and unestablished name recognition. You do not need to have high name recognition to have a successful practice. You simply have to have the self-discipline, commitment, and motivation to follow the steps I have recommended. Sporadic quick fixes will never achieve success. Finally, make everything you do in marketing count. You can never afford to be casual, as casualness brings casualties.

TEN

Ethical Aspects of a Private Practice

It is good business to be ethical, which means doing things the right way. It reflects the manner in which you view and treat clients, employees, and the community. If you are ethical you are more likely to be trusted. If you are unethical, you risk lawsuits. Without ethics, greed and immorality are likely to result and will dramatically affect your business. Once ethical issues are "side stepped," decisions easily and quickly become amoral. Decisions to lie, to buy or steal clients, or to do whatever is necessary to build and develop one's practice often will be made in response to pressure to meet overhead or keep up with the competition. People who make such decisions feel trapped and do not recognize the consequences of their behavior. Their reputations will be damaged and may never be restored once ethical conduct is ignored.

Ignoring ethical issues can have a more devastating effect on your practice than can poor marketing tactics or poor collection procedures. The ethical issues never go away, so it is always best to incorporate your ethical values with your professional objectives.

You cannot justify unethical behavior with the defense that other practitioners are doing the same and that you must do it to keep up with the competition. Last, you cannot hide behind unethical behavior through an addictive dependency, afraid to make changes because of the dependencies you have developed. You cannot rely on the law to provide guidelines for professional conduct, as much unethical behavior is legal. Rather, the code of ethics furnished by your profession can help.

Practitioners are being held more accountable for their actions today than in the past. Therefore, it is worthwhile to review the ethical conflicts a psychotherapist is likely to encounter, such as value differences, confidentiality, privileged communication, informed consent, contracts, premature termination and abandonment, termination, continuing nonbenefiting clients, emergencies, boundaries, sexual misconduct, professionalism, admitting to psychiatric hospitals, group therapy, and access to records.

Value Differences

At times clients will come to sessions with issues that conflict with your own value system. You will need to work through your own feelings, away from the session. If you cannot, you may need to refer the client to someone else. When referring the client to another therapist, do so in a manner in which the client does not feel rejected but rather that communicates a concern that the client receive the best therapist for that issue.

It is ethical to refer out cases with which you are not personally or professionally comfortable. However, it is best to recognize what types of clients are likely to stimulate countertransference and to avoid accepting them into your practice to begin with. It will then be less disruptive than referring out at a later time, to you as well as to the client.

Confidentiality

At times therapists confuse confidentiality with privileged communication. Confidentiality is the "laws or rules of professional ethics that regulate the disclosure of information obtained in psychotherapy" (Knapp & Vande-Creek, 1987, p. 1), whereas privileged communication is a "legal term dealing with the admission of evidence into court" (Knapp & VandeCreek, 1987, p. vii).

Confidentiality refers to the use of information (Everstine et al., 1990, p. 828). Confidentiality is the client's right not to have communication shared about him or her. It is the client's right to disclose important personal information to a therapist without fear of having that information shared with others. With few exceptions, the client has the right in therapy not to give up his or her right to confidentiality. All of the mental health professional groups view this ethical issue in a similar manner in their code of ethics.

Although in theory most therapists would agree to the necessity of confidentiality, in practice it often is not treated in the required cautious, consistent manner. This can be due to confusion by the therapist as to what information is confidential and the proper manner for it to be shared with others. Therapists vary as to the extent of confidentiality they adhere to: from not sharing at all, to disclosures in specific situations, to perhaps unintentional slips at a cocktail party. The following are situations in which confidentiality was breached by three different therapists.

1. A nurse in a psychiatric hospital approached a therapist and mentioned that the therapist's new admission was a neighbor of hers. The patient was admitted to a separate unit from the one the nurse worked on. She expressed concern that the patient had recently begun looking run down and depressed, and asked the therapist how the patient was doing. The therapist replied, "Much better, now that she is in a treatment program." This patient's confidentiality was violated.

2. A therapist had her clinical notes for a client sitting in her car, easily visible to the public. She parked her car at a restaurant and went inside. This client's confidentiality was violated.

3. While relaxing at home with his family, a therapist received a call from his office about a client in emotional distress who wanted to speak with the therapist as soon as possible. He returned his client's call in the presence of his family members. This client's confidentiality was violated.

You can see that it is probably best to treat the disclosure of all information with extreme caution. As therapists often assume a variety of roles, they may find themselves tempted to share information about a client without permission. This may be in a family setting, as one consultant to another in an agency, in a supervisory session, to insurance carriers' utilization review committees, or via computerized records. The computerized brains of insurance companies do not ensure that the information will be contained in one office.

The therapist may be liable to the client if confidential information is disclosed without permission. In *Leggett v. First Interstate Bank of Oregon* (Schwartz, 1987), a jury awarded a plaintiff $27,000 for lost earnings and $150,000 in punitive damages against a psychologist for breach of confidentiality. Failure to respect a client's right to confidentiality with unauthorized disclosure of information can result in therapist liability to the client in money damages (Schwartz, 1989, p. 225). Be knowledgeable about what constitutes confidentiality in the state in which you practice.

So what is considered to be confidential? The answer is: all information about your client. You cannot even acknowledge that the client comes to your office without the client's consent. Three criteria are involved when considering a client's ability to provide consent: being competent, being fully informed, and voluntarily giving consent (Everstine et al., 1990, pp. 831-832).

Exceptions do exist. Therefore, full, unconditional confidentiality should never be promised a client. You may be required by law to furnish privileged information if ordered by a judge. Your records may be subpoenaed. It is expected that you will breach confidentiality if you suspect child abuse or neglect. Other criminal investigations, such as investigations into billing practices, also may result in the disclosure of confidential information (Schwartz, 1989, p. 225). If your client presents a physical risk to himself or herself or others, you may need to share information with family members, police, and judges, especially if an involuntary civil commitment is sought. If you are required to release records due to compulsory legal actions, inform your client. The privilege is also waived if your client sues you (Wilson, 1978, pp. 111-133). If you are getting supervision or discussing a client within your office staff setting, you do not need to worry about breaching confidentiality.

If you are leading a therapy group you will want to involve the group members in the confidentiality issue in the first session. Some states have criminal penalties for breaching confidentiality by group members. Make certain that your members are informed by providing them with a written statement about not disclosing confidential information. To protect yourself have them sign a statement that they understand the group rule and agree to abide by it (Kearney, 1984, pp. 19-20).

Privileged Communication

Privileged communication helps protect the client from having her or his communications shared in a courtroom by the therapist without the client's permission. As the privilege belongs to the client, the client is capable of voluntarily waiving this privilege. Although this can be done verbally, it is recommended that you obtain a written relinquishment of this release indicating to whom and for how long the privilege is valid so as to ensure no misunderstandings at a later time (Schwartz, 1989, p. 223). This privilege is not applicable in the following situations: if the client waives the privilege; if a client files charges against a therapist, such as malpractice, or criminal investigations, such as insurance inquiry into billing practices; if the client divulges a plan to hurt himself or herself or someone else or to commit a crime; if child abuse or neglect is suspected; if the client is a minor and requires legal action; if a client needs emergency lifesaving involvement; if the therapist needs to collect charges on unpaid invoices; if the client's state makes him or her a risk at work to others; if the client is hospitalized involuntarily; if claims are filed for life and accident benefits; or if information is shared in the presence of a third person (Wilson, 1978, pp. 111-133).

Each state is responsible for determining whether they recognize the therapist-client privileged communication. Each therapist is responsible for understanding her or his own state's licensing and regulatory statutes that address privileged communication. In situations where a case is going to court, the therapist can always petition the court in a request for confidentiality. If it is refused, the therapist must provide the requested information or be found in contempt of court.

Informed Consent

You will need to obtain informed consent from your clients regarding their anticipations in treatment with regard to "goals, expectations, procedures, and potential side-effects" (Keith-Spiegel & Koacher, 1985, p. 122), as well as in disclosing confidential information. Too often clients come to a therapist's office looking for treatment but failing to recognize that review of issues and feelings that have not been previously addressed can result in outcomes far from what they had expected.

> Mrs. K came to therapy for help with her adolescent daughter. After a few sessions it became clear to the therapist that Mrs. K was depressed, enmeshed with her daughter, and would benefit from some individual sessions. Family counseling helped Mrs. K focus on her own issues, reduce her codependency, and resolve family of origin conflicts. Mr. K made no changes. Mrs. K grew emotionally, but outgrew her husband. Mr. K resented the changes she made. They divorced the following year. Mr. K blamed therapy.

It can help to explain to clients at the beginning of therapy that personal growth may have both positive and negative side effects, as changes in people's emotional well-being may affect other aspects of their lives.

Informed consent enables you to disclose specific information about a client to another party. Obtaining informed consent is more than obtaining a signature on a release form. *Informed* consent involves properly informing the client how and to whom this information will be shared. Rozovsky (1986) identifies six criteria necessary for consent to be considered valid:

1. Absence of coercion and undue influence. The client needs to have had the choice and not been pressured.
2. Clients must be capable of providing consent. The client must have the ability to comprehend the facts.
3. Clients must consent to specific procedures. The consent forms cannot be so vague that the client could possibly be confused as to what he or she is consenting to.
4. Depending on state law, permission must be either written or verbal, implied or expressed.
5. The client must have the right to withdraw consent. Once the statement is signed, the client should be able to change his or her mind.
6. The client must have adequate information about the decision. The nature and purpose of the release of information must be clear (pp. 8-41).

Always get written consent to release information. Have the release written in simple language. A written document will help provide an accurate accounting that permission was granted to be communicated to other specific parties. Memories fade over time and a signed release will remind clients who may have forgotten giving their permission. Rather than having a client sign a blanket consent for disclosure of information, you may wish to consider a specific designated time period during which the consent is valid. This may be based on an arbitrary time period such as 3 months, duration of treatment, or for a specific purpose. Include the name of the person the information is to be released to and why. The client must sign the consent form freely and not be forced or pressured to do so, and must be permitted to refuse to sign. Never obtain an informed consent without discussing the options should the client wish not to sign, and the potential risks in signing (or not signing) the form.

Contracts

To focus the purpose of the therapeutic relationship, a simple, written contract will help clarify the "goals, expectations, and boundaries of therapy" (Hare-Mustin, Marecek, Kaplan, & Liss-Levinson, 1979, p. 7). The contract will address ethical issues by informing clients of the process of therapy, anticipate possible areas of misunderstandings, detail the cost and payment schedule, and address limitations of confidentiality, as well as emphasize that freedom of choice exists for the client. The contract can be handled as part of the intake process. A sample of forms to be used is included in Chapter 4.

Premature Termination
and Abandonment

What is the correct way to end therapy? How do you arrange for sudden endings? How do you handle a client you do not wish to treat? What do you do if you plan to be out of town or if you are moving?

You have the right to select your clients. You have the right to terminate treatment once the client is no longer benefiting. You do need to be careful not to terminate in such a manner that your client feels she or he has been abandoned. You can protect yourself from being sued for abandonment by conscientiously preparing for cross-coverage in the event you are inaccessible, or by transferring clients to other therapists.

It is your responsibility to be accessible to your clients 24 hours a day in the event of an emergency, unless you have contracted with them otherwise. Because no one can be expected to sit by their telephone at all times, use an answering service and pager or frequently call in to an answering machine. Letting your clients know you are available by phone 24 hours a day in the event of an emergency is important. It will reduce feelings of inaccessibility between sessions and may avoid any feelings of abandonment. When you are inaccessible to patients, such as when you are on vacation, it is necessary to make arrangements for cross-coverage. Be certain to choose someone who is reliable and shares your values in providing continuity of care.

If you are going to be transferring clients out to another therapist because you will be taking an extended leave or vacation or because you are closing your practice, be careful to do so in an orderly fashion. Identify a therapist with proper training to continue providing treatment in an uninterrupted manner. Have the therapist join you for a couple of sessions so your client will have reassurance that the new therapist understands his or her issues. It will also help the client to see cohesive teamwork between the two therapists.

Be cautious about terminating prematurely. Reasons may include a client's lack of funds, noncompliance by the client, or when therapy needs to continue but you are ending it due to negative transference. You are not expected to like every client who comes to you. But should this happen, seek out supervision so you can try to work through the problem by better understanding your feelings. If a client is having financial problems severe enough to prevent her or him from coming in on a regular basis, consider reducing the hourly rate to a sliding fee scale, cutting the session time in half, or meeting less frequently. If none of these are viable options, discuss with the client her or his readiness to be referred out.

There will be situations in which you will refer clients out. If you are too busy, do not have the available hours to meet when the client requires, the client cannot afford you, the client is failing to progress, or you do not want to work with that type of client, inform the client of your limitations and refer out. You are not expected to accept each client who is referred to you. However, if you choose not to accept a client, you should provide the client with a list of other appropriate therapists. Explain your limitations (e.g., no experience with chemical dependency or sexual abuse) so the client is not rejected and abandoned.

Termination

Most therapeutic relationships will end when both you and your client agree that maximum clinical benefit has been achieved. It is comforting to reassure the client that he or she may return if the need arises at a later time. You cannot abandon the client merely because he or she does not have the funds to pay you. You may terminate when the client is noncompliant.

I was treating a woman as an inpatient at a psychiatric hospital. She had been suicidal. After 4 weeks of intensive treatment, she was discharged to her parents' home. The discharge recommendation was that she not live with the man she had developed a relationship with while in the hospital. The concern was that she was not stable enough to cope with a new relationship at that time and needed her family to provide stability.

She had agreed to this arrangement and signed a contract that she would adhere to it. Two hours after discharge she moved in with the new boyfriend. Two days later she was in the intensive care unit for a failed suicide attempt.

Because she violated the contract and undermined our treatment, I found it necessary to terminate treatment with her. I was not angry, but felt it to be important to help her understand that there are limits and consequences she needed to live by. I visited her in the hospital to explain why I was terminating. She understood. This meeting was therapeutic and minimized any possibility that she might feel abandoned.

You also may terminate when it becomes evident that a referral to a specialist is indicated. It is appropriate to terminate when the goals in treatment have been achieved. It is acceptable to terminate when no progress is being made.

Clearly document in your clinical records the reasons for termination and the recommendations you made. This will protect you in the future should a client fail to follow up on your recommendations.

It is always important to terminate clearly and formally with a client, and to provide the reasons for doing so. Formal termination marks the ending of your responsibility for this individual. Do this by sending your client a letter.

Continuing Nonbenefiting Clients

If no specific goals are being sought in treatment, and the client is being maintained in therapy to meet the therapist's emotional or financial needs, then unethical choices are being made. Some clients are going to develop dependency needs. Some of these dependency needs must be met outside of therapy—not in the therapeutic relationship. Using the client's "fears, insecurities or dependency" (Keith-Spiegel & Koacher, 1985, p. 129) to continue therapy poses ethical issues. Sometimes it is the therapist who develops dependency needs. Be aware that it is unethical to keep a client in your practice beyond when necessary due to monetary dependency.

Boundaries

It is important to establish clear boundaries in your psychotherapy practice. Sometimes there are no easy answers as to what decisions you should make. Situations will arise when you encounter a client in a social setting; when friends, neighbors, or colleagues seek treatment with you; when a client wants to become friends; or when you want to make self-disclosures to the client. What do you do?

If you encounter a client in a social setting, I would recommend that you do not acknowledge the client unless you are acknowledged first. This permits your client a sense of privacy and confidentiality.

Regardless of how detached you may believe you can be, I recommend against treating those with whom you share a personal relationship. You cannot maintain your objectivity and remain friends. To have a dual relationship as a therapist and a friend "jeopardizes the therapy by introducing possible motivational contaminants for both participants" (Ethics Committee, 1987, p. 734). The individual cannot have the freedom to open up and take risks, knowing that he or she will have to relate to you outside of the session.

Avoid a client's suggestion to "get together," even after therapy has terminated. It is best for the client to see you in the therapeutic role, not as your private self. Once you develop a personal relationship, some of the "magic" of the therapy sessions may come undone. It is better to inquire of your client as to what she or he is looking for in a personal relationship, and to avoid any social contact with clients outside the office setting. It may be that termination is difficult, or that she or he has difficulty with boundaries, or that she or he is lonely or having sexual feelings for you. Through exploration you can gently identify what lies underneath your client's desire for a personal friendship. At that time you can establish clear limits as to the professional boundaries.

I know of a psychoanalyst whose secretary told him, in front of a client, that his wife had called. The analyst fired his secretary that day for making a disclosure about his personal life. Few therapists would respond quite so strongly, but it does raise the question of when a self-disclosure is justified. Each therapist needs to evaluate the motivation behind such disclosures. Are they being shared for a therapeutic purpose? If not, they probably do not belong in treatment.

Sexual Misconduct

All professional ethics codes emphasize the importance of the therapist not exploiting the trusting relationship with a client to meet the therapist's own needs, be they financial, emotional, or sexual. To exploit a client's trust carelessly through intimacy or sexual activity is ethically insensitive, acting-out behavior. As such encounters are emotionally charged, the client can become confused between reality and fantasy, causing significant adjustment problems thereafter.

Sexual misconduct is more likely to occur between male therapists and female clients than vice versa. It is best not to engage in any physical contact with your clients, such as kissing or hugging, and always to keep your behavior above reproach. Work out your countertransference issues in your own therapy, not in sessions with a client.

Psychiatric Hospitals

You must be careful not to exploit the client for personal financial gain by hospitalizing too readily or hospitalizing for a longer stay than necessary. This can happen when hospitals reward frequently admitting allied health professionals with additional inpatient and outpatient referrals. Or, the hospital may offer help with a therapist's billing, overhead, or with other perks. If a therapist is receiving referrals or financial assistance from a hospital, this information should be disclosed to any client being referred to the hospital for treatment.

Although there is clear benefit to being hospitalized to certain clients, you must be wary of ethical choices you are making when in a competitive psychiatric hospital environment. Certain rights and freedoms are taken away from the client once he or she is in the hospital. Therefore, the benefits versus the risks of hospitalization must be considered prior to admission.

Group Therapy

The ethical responsibility of group leaders differs from that of therapists conducting individual therapy sessions, in that group leaders have to concern themselves with the group as a functional system. They have to determine ahead of time how the various psychological needs of each group member are going to have an impact on the other members. Special care in selecting group members must take place to ensure that the group process will not have harmful effects on any member.

Availability of Records

As therapy is demystified, and as clients assume more responsibility for knowing what is in their clinical records, more requests are made for access to clients' records. The records should be shared in a professionally sound manner so as to prevent the client from misunderstanding and being injured needlessly from incorrect interpretations. The therapist needs to be able to answer questions and explain psychological terms. For this reason records should only be shared when reviewed with the therapist. If we are to encourage our clients to dispel the dysfunctional secrets in their lives, we need to comply and not fall into the trap of "protecting" the client and not disclosing our observations.

This also means we have to assume responsibility and be cautious about what we include in our notes. Any irrelevant, biased, or incorrect information may be challenged, and the client will have the opportunity to request that the data be amended.

The therapist should always explore the client's agenda for seeing the clinical records. If a trust issue is at stake, it will be necessary for the client to address it directly with the therapist. Family members generally are denied access to the clinical records of another adult. Being the "insured" does not entitle one spouse to review the records of the other.

Supervision

Keeping focused on your responsibility to promote the welfare of your client will ensure a quality, ethical practice. This will ensure that the client is being referred to other therapists when requiring intervention outside your expertise, and is not being kept as an active client longer than necessary due to therapist greed. It will keep you aware of potentially damaging projections of your own biases onto the clients, and will help you avoid self-disclosing for the wrong reasons. A good ethical practice will also preclude you from changing the client's diagnosis to assure payment from the insurance company, as doing so would develop a fraudulent relationship with the client and the insurance company. In other words, honesty, both with yourself and with your clients, will ensure that you provide a practice of high caliber and integrity.

We as therapists are fallible human beings with very real vulnerabilities, biases, limitations, and needs. Ongoing supervision can help prevent crossing the line between ethical and unethical behavior. You may seek individual, group, or peer supervision. All too often supervision is sought for the purpose of satisfying licensing requirements, but ceases once the therapist is experienced and more confident. Instead, supervision should be obtained throughout your practice.

ELEVEN

Retirement Planning

Generally the last consideration the independent practitioner makes when establishing a private practice is a retirement plan and estate planning. Yet, it is crucial to think of your future today. Clinicians often fail to recognize that the benefits from their salaried position provided a large financial savings for them—a savings that has now been lost as a private practitioner, and that the clinician must obtain on her or his own. When planning for retirement, you must take into consideration how much it will cost to live 3 or 4 decades from now. If you started your private practice at a young age and worked 40 years, and if inflation averaged 5% per year, it would cost $351,000 to equal what $50,000 would purchase when you started.

Tax-deferred retirement plans enable you to invest income and not have to pay income tax on the investment or interest earned until the funds are withdrawn after age 59.5. (In other words, they are not tax free. You have been able to postpone payment for a period of time.) Tax-deferred plans differ from taxable investments or savings accounts, which are taxed annually on the dividends and interest (Kissel, 1983, p. 291).

Set up a reserve fund for retirement. This will prevent you from pulling out money for daily living expenses. You can do this by making investments that will offer you shelter from taxes. Learn the legal and tax decisions affecting any retirement plan you invest in. Do not simply trust financial advisors. Monitor your own retirement assets. All too frequently an individual will want to sell you an investment that will provide him or her with income but be in dissonance with your needs.

There are a wide variety of plans developed for the purpose of providing you with income following your retirement. Listed below are the most frequently used retirement plans to consider. Each category is addressed in a brief manner, with the hope that you will then become more familiar with options available for funding your retirement. Prior to making decisions on the selection of a plan, consult with your CPA or financial advisor. This individual will be able to explain each category in greater detail and make recommendations based on your unique needs.

Individual Retirement Accounts (IRAs)

IRAs are the simplest retirement plans to set up. IRAs are tax-deferred accounts that work well with any other retirement plan. They produce earnings that will not be taxed until you begin having the funds dispensed. There is a $2,000 maximum contribution that the individual can contribute each year. You may set up multiple IRAs. But do be careful of annual fees the institutions may charge to manage your accounts.

The IRA is tax favored in that the full amount of the contribution may be tax deductible, and the earnings are tax deferred until you receive the money as a retirement benefit. There will be a penalty for early withdrawal. The longer you have until retirement, the more you will benefit from a nondeductible IRA. When considering an IRA examine your personal situation closely. Review your age and liquidity concerns, the length of time you have to retirement, the rates of return you can get on competing investments, and your federal and state tax rates (Price Waterhouse, 1992, p. 71).

Simplified Employee Pension (SEP)

The SEP is a relatively new retirement program. It is a plan, which provides the funding of a retirement benefit for the eligible employees of the employer, to include the ability to fund a benefit for the employer himself. SEPs are simple to establish—it is a matter of simply filling out a form—and administer. The SEP participants can make tax-deductible contributions to either an individual retirement account (IRA) or individual retirement annuity.

You are allowed to vary the amount of your investment from year to year. This is a flexible quality that some other plans do not offer. The ceiling for contributions equals 15% of your earnings, up to $30,000.

The SEP is one of the only retirement plans exempted from annual administrative fees. It is considerably less complicated than other qualified plans. The contributions are not subject to FICA or FUTA taxes, or IRS or Department of Labor forms.

Keogh Plan

Keoghs allow the self-employed to save for retirement in a similar manner to those who are employed by someone else. A Keogh's primary function is to provide an employer-sponsored qualified retirement plan. Your tax liability is reduced by being able to deduct any Keogh contribution from your income tax return while not paying on any earning from this contribution until you withdraw the money at retirement.

There are two plan types: defined-contribution plans and defined-benefit plans. Defined-contribution plans allow you to make annual contributions that are large enough to guarantee a predetermined amount per year following retirement. Defined-contribution plans come in two types: profit-sharing plans and money-purchase plans (Price Waterhouse, 1992, p. 75).

■ Profit-Sharing Plan

This retirement plan offers a flexible approach to making contributions. You are not obligated to make an annual contribution should your business expenses require that you put your money to other uses. The contributions are tax deductible and can be based on profits.

Although profits are no longer required in order to make a contribution, the contributions must be "substantial and recurring." The employer contributions are tax deductible. Employees are not taxed on the annual contributions or earnings.

For profit-sharing plans, contributions are allowed to be 25% of net earned income or $30,000, whichever is less. A maximum of 15% of the payroll may be contributed and deducted by the corporation.

Qualified part- and full-time employees must be included in this plan. The contributions for the employees must be made at least at the same percentage as made for owner-employees.

Dependent upon the participant's income and filing status, he or she may invest in a profit-sharing plan as well as take a deduction for IRA contribution. Anyone can have an IRA, but only some can take the deduction. The amount of distribution available at retirement will be determined by the amount of money contributed over the number of years as well as the value of the account when taking distributions.

■ Money-Purchase Pension Plan

With the money-purchase pension plan, a larger contribution is allowed, but the employer commits to paying a set percentage of the employee's salary each year. This means the employer is obligated to make the same percentage contributions regardless of his or her income—or pay a penalty. The flexibility of other programs does not exist here. The contributions are tax deductible. The earnings are allowed to accumulate tax deferred.

The maximum amount of contribution an individual is allowed to make is 25% of the total salary, but not more than $30,000. Depending on the their income and filing status, participants are allowed to take the deduction for an IRA.

Defined Benefit Plan

With defined benefits contributions are a function of the amount of benefit that is promised or defined at the beginning of participation. The employer contributes an actuarially determined amount each year to the plan. (An actuary is an individual employed by the insurance company to calculate the risks and premiums on a statistical basis.) There is little flexibility with the amount of contribution the employer makes, and consistent contributions may need to be made regardless of one's income. Penalties are imposed for failure to make estimated quarterly contributions or overcontributions to the plan. Retirement benefits are guaranteed; therefore, the precise contributions must be made, regardless of profitability made, in order ultimately to reach the predetermined "defined benefit."

As of 1992 the cap in annual payouts for this plan comes to the lesser of $111,221 or 100% of your average annual earnings for the three consecutive years in which your earnings are the highest (Price Waterhouse, 1992, pp. 77-78). The contributions are tax deductible and not taxed at the time to the employee. The earnings accumulate tax deferred. Participants also may have an IRA; however, only some may take the annual reduction.

This plan is attractive to older employees because it enables them to make larger contributions, enabling them to obtain substantive retirement benefits even though they are close to retirement. Predetermined payments are issued each year after retirement.

Costs of administering this plan are higher than other retirement benefit plans because of actuarial costs. It is also complex and difficult to comprehend.

Target Benefit Pension Plan

This plan has components of both the defined-benefit and the money-purchase plan. The contributions are decided based on the guidelines of the defined benefit plan, and the actual benefit is based on the account balance, like the money-purchase plan (which is a defined-contribution type plan).

An actuary determines what amount the employer may contribute each year. These contributions are tax deductible and not taxed at the time to the employee. The earnings accrue on a tax-deferred basis. There is no flexibility with the amount of contributions one makes, as the obligation continues, year after year.

This plan is attractive to older employees, although they may not benefit as greatly as they would with a defined benefit plan. It does offer employees with permanent life insurance benefits that will not either expire or cost a lot to convert at time of retirement. The investment risks depend on the amount of contributions, the number of years one has until retirement, and the return on the investment.

401-K Plan

Congress provided for the 401-K plan to offer tax incentives that allow deferral of personal income taxes on the contributions to and earnings of qualified employer-sponsored retirement savings plans, and deductions from taxable corporate income of employer contributions to such plans. The employee may either accept cash (through salary or bonus) or have it deferred into a retirement plan. These contributions are not taxed at the time, other than Social Security and unemployment taxes, and any contributions the employer makes are tax deductible. The earnings accrued in the plan are tax deferred.

The 401-K can have several features. The employees can contribute on a pretax basis without any employer contribution. Or, the employer only can make contributions to the 401-K for the employee, which does not involve any reduction or deferral of the employee's salary. Or, the plan can have both employee contributions and employer contributions.

Often the employer will contribute or "match" what the employee is contributing up to a certain amount. The employer is not obligated to contribute as part of a 401-K. However, if one employee is matched, every employee must be matched.

There is an expense to putting the plan into effect and keeping it in compliance. 401-Ks are quite popular.

Social Security (FICA)

Social Security is a retirement plan that provides benefits when contributors reach either 62 or 65 years of age, whichever they choose. Most people will find that they want to have other sources of retirement benefits in addition to Social Security.

Most employed people are required to pay into the Social Security system. The self-employed practitioner who is incorporated will contribute to Social Security at the same rate as the solo proprietorship practitioner.

Corporate Pension Plans

One of the primary benefits of incorporating is to obtain tax-favored retirement plans. These may include pensions, profit-sharing plans, or stock bonuses. Unlike other retirement plans, the investor is not limited by the amount of money he or she contributes, offering considerable flexibility in selecting the amount of contribution he or she wishes to make.

Tax-Deferred Annuities (TDAs)

Clinicians who consult for public schools or charitable, religious, or nonprofit organizations are able to benefit from TDAs. The Internal Revenue Service determines the maximum amount that may be contributed each year. The amounts contributed from your employer are deducted from income that may be taxed federally. The contributions and interest earned are not taxed until taken out at retirement, or until you begin to receive monthly annuities. Once funds are withdrawn, you are then taxed as though they were ordinary income.

Single-Premium Deferred Annuity (SPDAs)

Insurance companies are now offering single-premium deferred annuities. After a relatively high minimum single investment, on which taxes have already been paid, the interest is tax deferred and the individual is able to withdraw up to 10% of his or her SPDA without a tax liability.

The principal investment is guaranteed. This, along with the withdrawal privileges, makes the retirement plan appealing to many investors.

Considerations in Selecting Retirement Plans

Risk. The amount of risk to your investment will vary with the type of vehicle you select. Banks tend to offer the safest investments, as they are fully insured up to $100,000.00. Brokerage firms will offer safe investments such as CDs, Treasury bills, and annuities as well as riskier investments.

Interest rates. Are the interest rates compounded daily, quarterly, or not at all?

Minimum initial investment. The minimum initial deposit varies greatly among the different plans. Can you continue to add to your plan over time?

Fees. Some plans charge at the time the plan is initiated. Others charge for premature withdrawal. Still others charge once the plan matures. If you are in a group plan that offers multiple plans, transfer fees may be attached to any changes you make.

If you will make a decision to save a percentage of everything you earn, and invest it in retirement, you will avoid the shell shock of retiring on substandard financial resources.

Even those practitioners interested in researching various investments will find it helpful to work with experts who can offer advice in preparing an investment portfolio to meet particular needs during retirement. A variety of professionals can offer such help. It may come from an attorney who specializes in estate planning or an accountant who can advise you on tax planning based on preparing your income tax returns. Both will charge you on an hourly basis. Financial consultants, who buy and sell your investments and who will research the benefits of different services, work on a commission basis determined on the investments you make. Financial planners, who help you develop an overall financial plan, are either commission based or fee based. Interview the investment professional to determine whether you are comfortable with her or his training, attitude toward taking risks, and style of communicating.

View retirement a a three-legged stool: government, employee, and employer. As a self-employed practitioner you lose two legs of the stool. To compensate for this loss, you need to put in the maximum amount in order to get back 50% of your gross income at time of retirement.

Regardless of the retirement plan you select, make it your business to know the legal and tax decisions affecting it. No advisor can be as invested as you are in the retirement accounts doing well.

Estate Planning

No one likes to think of their own mortality. Right now you probably are focused on developing and expanding, not retiring or dying. Yet, we have no control over when we die. To postpone arranging for one's estate until old age can prove disastrous. If you die without a will, the state will make decisions regarding the division of your property for you. You will have no control over the decisions made. It will also be more costly, so fewer assets will be available for distribution. It is better to take the time now to develop an estate plan.

Many people believe they are not affluent enough to qualify for estate planning. However, an estate plan is merely applying forethought to the ultimate distribution of your assets and making the distribution legal. Regular review of your estate will allow for you to make the necessary accommodations due to changes in tax laws, income, assets, and heirs.

The first step in estate planning is to create a will. Use the services of an attorney who will create a legally sound document. Include in your will who the executor will be. This is the person who will be responsible for effectuating the requests you have made in your will; paying off your debts, taxes, and burial; and putting your affairs in order. The person selected for this duty should be someone who knows you well and whom you trust. Select an executor who can cope with the time-consuming and technically demanding tasks of administering an estate. Also include in your will burial arrangements who would become guardian of your children, how property will be disposed of, and a trust you have selected to disburse funds for minor children.

All too often the costs and complexity involved with estate planning create resistance in people to develop an estate plan. There will be legal fees incurred in drawing up wills or trusts. However, the current costs will be minimal compared to the costs and delays after your death, should you not have developed an estate plan. If you wish to have control over determining how your assets will be dispersed, avoid probate, minimize your estate taxes, and make arrangements for your children, you will want to address your own estate planning.

Employees:
Hiring, Managing, Firing

Hiring

Employees reflect upon the employer. How many times have you walked away from an office angry or frustrated because the receptionist was indifferent or rude, or resolved never to shop again in a store because the staff was unhelpful?

Often your secretary or receptionist will be the initial contact for potential clients. The client will call your office and inquire about available services and schedule a first appointment. A well-mannered, professional staff person can ensure that an appointment with a new client is secured and that this client feels comfortable about coming to your office.

Hiring the right person for the right job is critical to your practice. If the staff alienates clients, premature termination of your clients is likely to increase. The unfortunate part is that your former clients may never share their reason for leaving your practice. They will assume that the staff is following your policies. This is because the clients will have difficulty separating your office staff's attitudes and behaviors from you. The anger they develop toward someone in your office will be displaced onto you. They also may feel abandoned by you. Rather than confront you, which is difficult for most clients to do, they will leave. I learned this the hard way.

I had a wonderful secretary who had a nice telephone voice and demeanor. She never personalized the anger expressed by difficult clients. She remained stable, steady, and predictable. Clients adored her and felt comfortable calling my office.

She left me for a 6-month maternity leave, during which I hired a temporary secretary. Having become spoiled by my first secretary, and being very busy, I failed to monitor the replacement secretary's telephone demeanor closely. I had assumed that she, too, would have the maturity and professionalism to handle the position as competently as my former secretary.

After a couple of months I became aware of a pattern involving angry and prematurely terminating clients. By paying closer attention, I learned that my new secretary was uncomfortable with handling certain aspects of the job. She reacted to problems with anger and defensiveness.

I stepped in and provided her with some on-the-job training. She became more knowledgeable and competent with handling difficult clients. The problem resolved itself, although I never saw my previously terminated clients again. It taught me a great lesson in complacency. It also taught me how important each employee is to the success of the psychotherapist.

The first step in hiring employees is to identify what expectations you have for each person. This is essential in order to hire the person with the right skills and temperament for the job. Develop a job description detailing the duties, skills, knowledge, and expectations for each job.

Next you need to make a preliminary screening of applicants. You can use either the classified advertisements, personnel agencies, or word-of-mouth referrals. Networking with colleagues, friends, and others may bring skilled applicants worthy of interviewing. Instruct applicants to mail their résumés so you are not inundated with telephone calls.

Once you have a list of applicants you wish to interview, arrange for interviews. Have each applicant complete an employment application prior to the interview. The employment application serves four purposes: to screen applicants for appropriateness for the specific job, to obtain all relevant information on the applicant, to help provide consistent information for all applicants, and to help prove nondiscriminatory measures taken in hiring. Standard employment application forms are available at business stationery and office supply stores.

Keep all applications and résumés of applicants whom you do not select as new hires. In the event that an applicant files a charge against you for discrimination in hiring, you will have the documents necessary to defend your position. In addition, if the new employee does not remain long at the job, or if another position opens up soon, you will have a current list of prospective employees from which to select.

When interviewing applicants have a checklist of questions to ask. This will assure you of obtaining all the information you need as well as being certain that uniformity and consistency in asking questions occurs. Inquire about experience and length of time spent at previous jobs. This will indicate stability. Sometimes a former employment may be brief, but with good justification. Avoid using tests unless they are validated for the specific job and are free of cultural bias.

Listen and be attentive to what is *not* being said during the interview. Be careful not to talk too much—you want to hear what your potential employee has to say. Do you hear negativity? If they speak poorly about a former employer, it is likely they will do the same about you. Listen to the way the applicant talks, thinks, and manages emotions. Look at the individual's poise and tactfulness.

Listen for defensiveness, one of the worst qualities I believe a staff member can have. I assess this by asking an applicant to recall something he or she did not do well in another job. We all have erred from time to time. If an applicant cannot recall a single incident, I would worry that the person either fears that imperfection is unacceptable, cannot accept criticism, or is totally unaware of how he or she performs on a job. Because this question can be threatening to the applicant, I follow up with a request that he or she recall something he or she did well at a former job and of which he or she is very proud. The second request will disclose the applicant's self-esteem.

Even though the applicant may have no experience working for a psychotherapist, you can gain a sense of how she or he would react to specific problems in the office. Ask what the applicant would do if a client with an emergency called and the therapist was in a counseling session. What would the applicant do if a client told her or him something in confidence that the therapist needs to be told? These types of questions measure an applicant's common sense, self-confidence, and ability to think for herself or himself.

Most things you need to know about an applicant are available for you during the one or two interviews. It is your job to listen and properly process this information. This is where you can use your own clinical training to avoid hiring mistakes that other employers without the psychological training and listening skills you possess may make.

Candidly share with the applicants everything pertinent about the job. Do not "sugarcoat" the duties, expectations, benefits, or work environment. Regardless of how you present the position, the new employee will quickly learn the reality. If you have misrepresented the employment situation, the employee will have feelings of betrayal and anger, and may act out at work. You will regret this.

Ask the same questions of all applicants. This will help protect you against charges of discrimination. Ask only job-related questions. Conduct interviews privately. Allow plenty of time for questions and answers. Put the applicant at ease. Stay in control and keep the interview focused on the subject of employment. Give a tour of the office and introduce the applicant to others in the office. Get their feedback later. Do not take too many notes.

Use the time to be attentive to the applicant. Use open-ended questions where applicable to encourage elaboration on responses.

Always request references, regardless of how certain you are that the applicant sitting before you is ethical and competent, and check out the references. References can reveal important information. Contact the references by telephone rather than letter. Letters take too long and may be too general to be of any value to you.

It is essential to contact former employers. A previous employer is likely to be more candid on the telephone than in a letter. Also, follow-up questions can be asked for any problem or strong areas. Many employers are afraid to say anything negative about former employees for fear of a libel lawsuit, so listen very carefully to what they are not saying. Are they damning the individual with faint praise? Are there long, uncomfortable pauses? Ask for strengths and limitations. Inquire about the applicant's work skills, reliability, ability and willingness to learn new tasks, common sense, communication skills, and ability to work independently and with others. Ask whether they would hire the person again, and why or why not.

Realize that, although salary is important to employees, it is not everything. They will want fringe benefits as well. Employees are likely to stay longer if offered benefits such as health insurance, vacation, sick and personal leave, and retirement benefits.

During the interview I strongly emphasize the need for confidentiality. Employees need to be aware that they cannot talk about one client in front of another. I also believe that no personal business of the secretary should be talked about in front of clients. Boundaries between staff and clients are critical to maintain. Prospective employees need to understand that it is unacceptable to develop personal relationships with the therapist's clients.

Other rules I emphasize include the limiting of personal calls to lunchtime and breaks, no eating during work, and playing the radio in a soft, nondistracting manner so as not to offend anyone in the waiting room. This is the time to specify what you expect in terms of employee attire. Clearly communicate what is unacceptable dress and what you expect the employee to wear.

Interview your prospective employees at least twice. Regardless of how well the first interview progressed, an additional interview will allow you to ask questions you did not think to ask initially. There may be items you want to clarify. Finally, it gives you an opportunity to obtain another glance into their sense of professionalism by the way they dress, attend to appearance, and are punctual for the appointment.

Make your hiring decision as soon as possible after all interviews are completed. Trust your gut reaction when interviewing. If you are ambivalent, do not hire the applicant. You may be picking up on a clue at the subconscious level.

Be familiar with equal employment opportunity (EEO) laws and restrictions when interviewing. Discrimination is prohibited by law. Contact the Equal Employment Opportunity Commission for information on hiring and the law. Do note that state and local laws sometimes expand EEO laws to include nondiscrimination based on other, regional circumstances.

Policy and Procedure Manual

Having a written document clearly defining your policy regarding hiring can prevent problems that may arise from misinterpretations of employer/employee relationships and that can then only be settled through legal recourse. This is an increasing problem for employers and is time consuming and costly. Include your hiring policy in your policy and procedure manual.

The policy and procedure manual should be brief, clear, and written with the intention of helping an employee understand the rules and the consequences of violating them. The policy and procedure manual should include the following:

Employment policies: Equal opportunity employer, hiring, probation period, promotion, performance evaluation

Salaries and wages: Work hours, overtime, pay dates

Benefits: Life and health insurance, unemployment insurance, vacations, leave of absence, sick leave

Policies: Work rules, dress code, tardiness, absenteeism, settling difficulties, safety

Specific policies for handling client relationships and communication: Boundaries, protection of confidentiality with regard to records, requests, verbal and written communication

When hiring an applicant immediately complete the necessary paperwork required for payroll and taxes.

Personnel Records

Personnel records should reflect the employment history of each employee. Use these records to keep the paperwork you will acquire on the employee: employment application, job description, performance, reviews, promotions, disciplinary action, withholding information, and any other significant documentation related to the individual's employment. This information can be valuable in documenting decisions you make at a later time.

If you have an employee, you have costly responsibilities regarding both state laws and the Internal Revenue Service. Each employee will need to have separate payroll records. You will need to withhold federal income and Social Security taxes, and state income and disability taxes, if applicable. You will have to work out the quarterly and annual payroll tax returns. In addition, you will need to pay the employer's portion of Social Security and unemployment taxes, obtain workers' compensation insurance, and work out the annual earnings statement for each employee. Secure workers' compensation prior to actually hiring anyone. You will want the protection it can offer should an employee sustain an injury on the job and suffer a loss of income. Business stationery stores carry prepackaged personnel record systems for your convenience. Or, you may wish to contact your local IRS office for free Circular E, *Employer's Tax Guide.*

You will need an Employer Identification Number (EIN) to complete the necessary paperwork for income tax preparation. The IRS will provide, free of charge, Form SS-4, which is the Application for Employer Identification Number. Form W-4, the Employee Withholding Allowance Certificate, must be filled out by each of your employees. They are available from the IRS.

As the regulations of each state differ, it will be necessary for you to contact your state department of employment to obtain information on additional tax withholdings, unemployment insurance, and paperwork required. If your state has a state income tax, you will be required to withhold state income tax from the employee. The same may be true for city taxes.

I have known of incidences in which therapists have attempted to redefine a secretary as a subcontractor rather than an employee as a way of avoiding the tax requirements. To misrepresent an employee as a subcontractor when in fact he or she is not can result in potential legal problems for you later on.

Secretarial Tasks

A trained and competent secretary manages the office smoothly and efficiently, saving the therapist time and work. The specific tasks performed by the secretary are varied in scope. They include but are not limited to the following:

■ Telephone

The telephone should be answered by the third ring. The secretary should use either the therapist's or the agency's name following the initial "hello" and then identify himself or herself by name. For example, a greeting would include, "Hello, Counseling Associates of Northwest Houston, Kathy speaking." A message is recorded in a telephone message book if the therapist is not in.

The secretary screens and directs callers. He or she needs to be able to make an assessment as to whether the call is routine or an emergency and respond accordingly. Callers should not be put on hold for more than 2 minutes without the secretary rechecking with them to determine whether they want to continue to hold.

■ Answering Service or Machine

First thing in the morning or after returning from lunch or an errand, the secretary will retrieve any messages that have accumulated with the answering service or machine. All messages are entered in a telephone message book. Having a copy of telephone messages can help with later retrieval of lost or misplaced messages. The date and time, caller's name, telephone number, and a brief message are noted in the message book.

Inform clients from the onset of therapy who will have access to their telephone messages if it is anyone other than you. Note that you have informed them and keep a copy of this information in your client's clinical file.

■ Scheduling and Rearranging Appointments

Systematic scheduling of appointments for clients and marketing contacts will allow for good use of the therapist's time. You will want appointments scheduled closely enough so as not to waste your time, but spaced far enough apart to allow you to take a breather, write notes, and return telephone calls.

If a client calls to cancel an appointment the day of the appointment, the secretary should advise the caller of the cancellation policy and what, if any, cost there will be to the client. Every effort to reschedule the appointment should be made at this time.

■ Receiving Clients

The secretary should welcome each client in a warm, pleasing manner. Addressing the client by name, once the client has disclosed it, will help the client feel at ease. If coffee or a soft drink is available it should be offered to the client. The secretary should then notify the therapist, if not in session, that her or his next client has arrived.

■ Generating Correspondence

The secretary will write letters, including correspondence with insurance companies, billing, ordering of supplies, marketing, termination letters to clients, communication with hospitals regarding privileges, and referral acknowledgments (Burns, 1989, p. 557). No letter should leave your office that is not perfect, as it reflects on your professionalism. A hard copy of every letter should be made for your files.

■ Filing Records

Business files are kept separately from client files. The file label should identify the contents of the file. The files are then arranged by subject and placed in alphabetical order. Client files will be accessed most easily if arranged by client's last name, first name, and middle initial. If two names are identical, add the city, town, or Social Security number to provide clearer identification (Burns, 1989, p. 558).

Clinical records for clients whom you have terminated will need to be separated from your active records. The former can be stored in a back storage room in a fireproof, waterproof, locked metal file cabinet. Do not discard old files, regardless of IRS or legal stipulations. You may wish to have the files should a client reenter therapy years later. Also, in some states you can be held liable for malpractice with a child until the child reaches 18 years of age.

■ Completing Insurance Claim Forms

Your secretary will file a claim with your client's insurance carrier for payment. Although most of your clients will have health-care insurance, the benefits will vary widely from policy to policy. Due to the complexity of filing under chemical dependency and psychiatric, most therapists prefer that their secretaries communicate with the insurance companies and complete the insurance claim forms for clients to avoid the possibility of mistakes. This aspect of the secretary's job is most important and time consuming. It should be monitored by the therapist to assure accuracy and timeliness of claims being filed.

■ Billing

If your secretary is maintaining the financial records of the office, he or she will be recording client charges and receiving payments from clients and insurance companies. Depending on how your office is set up, the billing statements may be computer generated, typewritten individually on statement forms, or photocopied from the client's ledgers (Burns, 1989, p. 560).

Accounts may be billed monthly or at the time of service. I recommend billing after each session to avoid the accumulation of a large balance. The exception is with inpatients. They are to write a check daily.

My secretary bills the insurance carrier every 2 weeks. He does this by going through the ledger cards and billing half of the accounts one week and the second half the following week. On the third week he is back to billing the first half of the ledger cards, and so on.

Again, careful monitoring by the therapist is required. It is the therapist's responsibility to assure that the work is being carried out properly.

■ Reviewing Fees

If a caller asks for a sliding fee, the secretary can simply say, "You will need to speak with the therapist about that. Would you like to leave your name and telephone number with me so I can have him call you back?" It will then be up to the therapist's discretion whether a reduction in the hourly charge is to be made and, if so, how much.

Your secretary will be responsible for quoting your hourly charge to new clients. Because people often are unaware of the cost of therapy, it can be presented in this manner: "Dr. Jones's fee is $_____ per hour. However, we do accept health insurance and a major portion of this charge may be covered. Would you like to give me your policy number and I will make inquiries as to how much you would have to pay and call you back?"

■ Collecting Fees

A variety of approaches can be used to handle collections, as clients do not always pay their bills as they are accumulating. This is addressed more thoroughly in Chapter 6. Sending letters and making telephone calls, each being progressively more urgent, is usually effective in settling the account. When calling, the secretary must use tact, understanding, confidence, and listening skills. A note of every telephone conversation must be recorded for future reference in the client's records.

■ Maintaining Client Records

Client records should be kept in two charts: one for billing and one for progress notes. For easy identification, use one color label for all records relating to billing and another color label relating to progress notes. To economize on paper, use one sheet of paper for multiple clinical entries.

All insurance forms will go into the billing file. (Keep these files locked to protect confidentiality.) Your secretary will take one original insurance form with the client's signature and type all information onto it. Several copies should be made of this form, for subsequent therapy sessions. A stamp of the provider's name will suffice here.

A copy needs to be made of all insurance forms sent to insurance companies and put in the file. They will be essential if further communication with an insurance company is required.

When the Explanation of Insurance Benefits (EOB) arrives with payment for services rendered, your secretary will compare it to the copy of the insurance form previously sent to the insurance company for accuracy in payment. The EOBs may contain payment for multiple claims. If discrepancies arise your secretary will need to call the insurance company or write a letter pointing out the problem, and speak to a supervisor if necessary.

■ Handling Mail

The mail should be opened and distributed daily. (Client communications to you should be given to you unopened.) Once the general office mail has been distributed, the secretary should process all incoming checks.

■ Making Bank Deposits

Incoming checks should be stamped "for deposit only" once they arrive. A copy of each check should be made in the event that a problem later arises. Several checks can be photocopied on each sheet of paper.

Bank deposits should be made daily. Do not leave cash or checks overnight unless in a locked safe.

■ Ordering and Maintaining Office Supplies and Equipment

To ensure that your office runs smoothly your secretary will be responsible for keeping all supplies in stock. Running out of an item can result in waste, additional expense, and poor use of the secretary's time.

■ Typing and Transcribing

All correspondence and transcribing, including dictated and handwritten correspondence and clinical notes, will be performed by the secretary. Special care should be taken to assure that no identifying documents are left in view of clients on the desk or on the computer screen, as this would jeopardize confidentiality. Be certain that all office staff understand confidentiality concerns.

Qualifications

The secretary should have dynamic interpersonal skills and personal characteristics such as "patience, courteousness, composure, good sense, tact, thoughtfulness, reliability, punctuality and flexibility" (Burns, 1989, p. 552). It is important that the secretary pay attention to accuracy and detail and that she or he value confidentiality. She or he must be honest and dependable. A tidy, professional image will be necessary to convey the proper impression for the office.

A secretary must support the ethical standards set forth by the therapist. If this standard of conduct is violated, the therapist will be at risk for negligence. The secretary helps prevent possible litigation by doing the following (Burns, 1989):

- Establishing good client rapport
- Retaining all information as confidential
- Not sharing negative feelings toward therapists to clients
- Not discussing a client's diagnosis or treatment with clients or anyone unless there is an approved reason to do so
- Keeping records current, thorough, and accurate
- Recognizing boundaries and confidentiality during office and telephone conversations with clients
- Giving the therapist any significant information learned about the client (p. 554)

It is inadvisable to hire people you know: This goes for family as well as friends. It may not be possible to have a professional relationship in the office with a good friend or relative. If you still want to hire a family member or friend, go through the steps of your standard interview, discuss the expectations each of you have, and clarify the boundaries that must exist between your personal and professional lives.

Due to budgetary considerations, you may wish to hire a part-time secretary. In this case hire someone for morning hours, so they can contact insurance companies. All too often the insurance company offices close at 4:00

P.M. Calling first thing in the morning provides greater likelihood of not being greeted with a busy signal or a tape recording.

Managing

With the first employee you hire, you become a manager. This means considering another person's needs and happiness in addition to your own. It means considering the increased overhead you will have once you go on vacation, because you will still be responsible for your employees' salary. You will have to be a role model. You cannot nap or accept personal calls during the day and then expect your staff not to do the same.

Training and supervision enable employees to be familiarized with the policies of your office, and to become an asset to your practice. My experience has been that both my secretary and I benefited from my offering training during the orientation period, and then slowly but steadily withdrawing as both he and I became confident of his abilities and understanding of the job responsibilities. This prevented the possibility of me hovering over him constantly, never allowing him to develop a sense of autonomy on the job.

Either provide the training for your support staff yourself, look for workshops that advertise enhancement of office skills or working with insurance companies, or turn to local psychiatric hospitals for information. They may sponsor such training free of charge. Consider having your secretary meet with your accountant to become familiar with the billing.

Be available on a daily basis to supervise and review with your secretary any questions or problems that may have arisen during the day. If your secretary develops a sense of trust in being able to discuss routine problems with you, and learns that it is safe to share complaints, a greater likelihood will exist that he or she will approach you with a potentially large problem that could negatively affect your practice if you did not have timely knowledge of it.

Once you have confidence in your secretary, reduce the supervision from daily to weekly meetings. You should continue the regular schedule of meetings and reviewing your employee's progress. Not to do so can result in your failure to notice billing problems or sloppy clerical practices that are developing and affecting your practice.

As you begin to delegate responsibility to your secretary so you are freed to dedicate more time and energy to your work, allow for personal differences in styles and approaches to problem solving. As long as the end result is achieved, do not interfere with the secretary's method of getting there. It may only serve to suppress her or his initiative and confidence.

You will find that by investing in such training, your practice will prosper. Over the long run it will help lower your costs with less employee turnover and more efficient work being performed, an improved work morale, and the learning of skills more quickly and efficiently.

Develop good two-way communication with your secretary. As you will be quite busy with your caseload, it is important to develop a pattern of giving and receiving nonessential communication. I developed a system with my secretary in which we each have a file in a readily accessible drawer in her desk with our names on it. Letters I write after hours to be typed, handouts I want photocopied, and ideas I want her to pursue are placed in her file. I am then able to forget about these issues and not worry about having to tell her about them at inopportune times. Likewise, my secretary can easily slip communications to me into my file. The more therapists you have in your office, the more important this type of system will be.

Talk with your secretary in a clear, direct manner. Do not use jargon, and avoid being patronizing. Conversely, do not lecture. Use appropriate facial expressions, body language, and comments to communicate to your employee that you are listening. Then look and listen for your employee's reaction.

Be fair, understanding, helpful, and compassionate. Look to be respected, not loved. Be cautious about mixing business and personal relationships. Your offer of socializing may be interpreted as a "command performance," and the employee may feel obligated to comply. Resentment may result. Be clear about what you expect from your employees. Put it in writing for all of you to review. In return, learn what your employees' goals and expectations are, and what they expect from you.

Employees are motivated when they are provided realistic challenges. Ask for their opinions. Offer diversity in their position. Motivate them to do more than robotic type activities. Encourage them in assuming more responsibility. Your support staff have a fresh perspective on the office activities and needs. Valuing their input will result in more creativity, a sense of importance and belonging, and valuable information being provided to your practice. A happy staff usually translates into a stable staff.

I encourage personal growth and advancement by expanding the roles my secretary traditionally performs. This includes him doing marketing for my practice, as well as attending conferences. It enhances his self-esteem, because he realizes that his work is valued. My office benefits when he realizes how important he is: His performance skills increase, he is always looking for better ways to do the work, and he feels valued enough to suggest new ideas.

Do not take your office staff for granted. Respect their privacy. Recognize them for what they do, and let them know they are appreciated. Remember that they are employees, not partners. Do not have expectations that they will be as invested in your success as you are. Do not expect the same sacrifices you make, such as missed lunches and long hours. You will "burn them out" at that rate.

Offering a good salary will help ensure, but not guarantee, good work performance. Many psychotherapists will not be able to offer a competitive salary. This should not be considered a deterrent to hiring competent employees, as people are motivated to work for more than just the salary. If you make sure the job is interesting and challenging, and offers the opportunity to learn new things, exercise judgment, and participate in office decisions, your secretary will have job satisfaction that cannot be measured by a paycheck alone.

Be certain that your office conditions are suitable to the needs of the secretary. If the equipment she or he is using is faulty, fix it. If she or he is unhappy about something the therapists are doing, discuss it. Keep your employees informed and involved in any changes affecting the office. This will enhance their commitment, security, and sense of belonging to the office. They will know that their job is important to your practice.

Provide recognition for performance, which will increase morale and loyalty. This may include a new title, even though the position is the same (such as from secretary to office manager), a plaque for special work performed, or lunch out on you.

All employees deserve to receive formal feedback as to how their work is viewed in their employer's eyes. Complete written annual evaluations in which weaknesses as well as strengths are objectively reviewed. Evaluations will be able to justify promotions, merit increases, demotions, and terminations. You will be able to evaluate areas for improvement to be worked on. You also will be able to focus on the employee's strengths. Tie the evaluation into a pay increase, which will increase incentive to perform well. I strongly believe there should not be any surprises in the evaluation, because over the course of the year any problems should have been shared openly and directly with your employees.

Use this as a time to review how the past year has been for the two of you, expectations you both have for the coming year, and how the employee has performed in areas you listed last time as needing improvement (Figure 12.1).

Avoid giving commissions or cash incentives to employees for bringing in new patients, as this may look like "buying" patients. The salary should be adequate without need for a bonus and quality performance should be a requirement not needing a bonus for reinforcement. Further, a low bonus can lead to big disappointment and become a disincentive. Once bonuses are introduced, you cannot take them away without creating considerable resent-

ANNUAL EMPLOYEE EVALUATION

Employee Name: _____

Position: _____

Supervisor: _____

Review Date: _____

Scale: 0 = Unacceptable
          1 = Needs improvement
          2 = Standard
          3 = Above standard
          4 = Outstanding
          N/A = Not applicable

<u>Rating</u>

1.   Prioritizes tasks and meets deadlines -------------------------------------- _____
2.   Attendance --- _____
3.   Appropriate appearance -- _____
4.   Relationship with other staff --- _____
5.   Relationship with clients -- _____
6.   Follows the policy and procedure manual ------------------------------- _____
7.   Completes billing in timely and accurate manner --------------------- _____
8.   Works independently -- _____
9.   Demonstrates initiative --- _____
10. Displays knowledge of job --- _____

Other comments:_____

_____

_____

_____

_____

_____

_____
Signature of Supervisor   Date

_____
Signature of Employee   Date

Figure 12.1. Annual Employee Evaluation Form

ment. This is because it is human nature to treat what was once a privilege as an entitlement.

As successful collection from insurance companies is both bothersome and important, consider offering an incentive program of 1% to 3% to the employee responsible for obtaining reimbursement. This will increase the likelihood of insurance forms being completed properly. It also will decrease the tendency an employee might have of not maintaining the necessary communication with insurance companies that will ensure payment.

One solo practitioner I know experienced a loss of 18% of her gross income. This was due to problems with insurance reimbursement. Clerical sloppiness in completing the insurance forms, failure to complete all the paperwork in a timely fashion, and not following up with insurance companies who either were not paying or were paying at a rate lower than initially quoted were responsible for the loss.

This therapist began an incentive-building program by offering her secretary a bonus of 3% for payments made by insurance companies. Within 90 days her loss went from 18% to 4%. With little effort she was realizing an additional 14% of her income that previously had been lost. I have not kept in touch with this practitioner, but I suspect that as her secretary has become more adept at working with insurance companies, and as the reward factor will continue to encourage innovation and motivation, she will be able to further decrease her loss rate.

At times you will need to reprimand and even discipline an employee. When this is necessary, be certain to do so in a private place to avoid shaming. To improve an employee's performance, describe specifically what you are seeking.

If the employee engages in a serious breach of performance, issue a warning letter. The letter should be signed by the employee, and a copy placed in his or her personnel file. The issuing of two related formal warning letters in a 12-month period, or three unrelated in an 18-month period, should result in immediate termination. This policy is shared with employees immediately after they are hired, so they are not surprised if you have to follow through.

Firing

Despite your best intentions and efforts, the time may come when you need to terminate an employee. Disappointments and errors do occur in hiring staff. Sometimes the most experienced interviewer will not pick up on a serious flaw in an employee, only to have it become a very major contraindicator for employment.

In cases such as these, hiring on a 3- to 6-month trial basis will enable you to observe the employee working in your office and to determine whether the completed work is suitable to you.

Once the trial period is completed, meet with your employee. Indicate what your decision is with regard to hiring this person. If you remain ambivalent about making his or her employment permanent, and want more time for the employee to be able to address specific problems, consider extending the trial period another 30 to 90 days. If at the end of the second trial period you still are uncertain whether to hire the person or not, terminate the employment. Do yourself and your employee a favor and end what is obviously a bad match. As rules on hiring are influenced by legal cases and may change over time, I would recommend you contact your local Employment Commission regarding hiring on a trial basis.

A therapist who hired a secretary under the trial basis arrangement had the unfortunate experience of hiring a borderline personality who split the staff and created confusion and anger in the office. When it became obvious that the secretary was at the center of the chaos, she was terminated. Because she had been hired on a 3-month trial basis, her employment was not permanent and unemployment compensation and lawsuits were avoided.

Hopefully you will have attempted to reconcile the problem with the employee by talking about it and clearly explaining what you expect to be done differently. If the necessary changes have not been made by the employee, then termination may be the best thing for both of you.

Sometimes therapists are reticent to terminate an employee, even though no positive changes are being made. I believe that at times therapists can experience some role confusion, which leads to maintaining instead of firing employees. We pride ourselves on developing and maintaining relationships with our clients. When they get "stuck" in treatment, we may continue working with clients, looking for a way to provide motivation for change. Being more experienced at being clinicians than employers, we fail to see the difference in our roles as therapist and as employer.

Another reason for being reticent about terminating an employee is employer's guilt. Employers feel responsible for what occurs in their office. Therefore, they share some of the blame for problems and then feel guilty when it is obvious that the employee is not working out. This makes firing very stressful for the employer.

It is difficult to terminate employees. Yet, you need to recognize when you have made a hiring mistake. It never gets easy. Not only is firing an emotional burden, but it also carries legal problems in today's litigious climate. To prepare against unwanted lawsuits from disgruntled former employees for "wrongful dismissal," develop a firing policy before you begin hiring. Give the policy to all new employees. Put a signed sheet stating that they have received this or your policy and procedures manual in their personnel file.

Should the employee be performing short of your expectations, set a specific time frame during which you want improvements to be made. Explain exactly what you expect and when you expect to see change. Try to have the unsatisfactory behavior corrected. If the problem continues, provide the employee with a written reprimand, describing the deficiency. Acknowledge the prior meetings you have had and what you expect to be corrected. Include what the consequence will be if the problem is not rectified. If the problem continues, give the employee a final warning. Once again, include copies of all other correspondence you have provided the employee on the subject. Specify a time period during which the problem needs to be resolved. Note that this is a final chance to correct the problem.

If you have tried everything and the employee remains a bad match despite increased supervision, training, and time, fire the person. Do not delegate this duty to someone else. Doing it yourself is not only the appropriate thing to do but also the best way to protect yourself legally. You may wish to offer severance pay to the terminated employee.

Meet with the person in private, preferably in your office. Have on hand documents (evaluations, records, or reports) that support your decision. It is important that you make it clear that the firing is a result of performance and not a personality matter. Let your employee know that the termination is not negotiable.

As this meeting will be very stressful to your employee, get right to the point. Do not show indecision. Try to maintain her or his self-esteem. Speak with confidence. Use short sentences and do not deliver a lecture. Prolonging this situation will only make it more difficult for the employee. Be firm and have the employee return all office keys, even though you will be changing the locks.

Be certain of your decision to fire the employee *before* you begin the termination interview. Do not change your mind if the employee begins begging or negotiating to keep the job. Generally this will only lead to disastrous results.

A therapist's secretary was engaging in personal telephone calls during work time, taking extended lunches, and discarding some of the mail. Despite repeated discussions about her behavior, no noticeable changes were made. The therapist called her in for a termination interview, during which the secretary became tearful and pleaded to have another chance to "prove that I can make it work."

Feeling guilty about firing her, along with concerns about possible legal ramifications for doing so, the therapist agreed not to fire this employee.

Ten days later, on the way to making bank deposits, the employee stole a large portion of the deposits and called from a pay telephone to say she was quitting.

Employees often will try desperately to avoid the unavoidable and attempt to delay the final decision. The employee must be able to get beyond the denial of the termination in order to be able to progress further. Even though the process of helping your employee accept the permanency of the termination is painful, it will be better for both of you later on. The employee can process the loss and anger more quickly. This will enable her or him to move on rather than become increasingly bitter, resentful, and possibly vindictive toward you.

Terminations must be justified. Most employees are fired for one or more of the following reasons:

1. *Layoffs.* If you are letting someone go due to slowdowns rather than employee performance, try to find the employee another job. Offer a letter of reference to help the employee in the transition.

2. *Violation of policy and procedures.* Despite availability of written documents outlining expectations of behavior, and repeated opportunities to make corrections, the employee continues to demonstrate a disregard for the rules.

3. *Dishonesty.* In particular, this may include theft, or it may be a pattern of lying.

4. *Absenteeism.* This includes chronic tardiness, abuse of sick leave, and extended lunches.

5. *Chemical dependency.* Firing can be necessary if the employee has an alcohol or drug problem that is interfering with work performance and refuses to get treatment.

6. *Poor job performance.* This includes chronic poor performance despite attempts to provide supervision, training, and counseling to bring about minimal standards.

7. *Insubordination toward supervisor or refusing to carry out a task the supervisor or employer requests.*

8. *Sexual harassment of other employees.* This can involve threatening other employees or clients in a sexual manner if they do not comply with the employee's wishes, which may be sexual.

Following the firing of an employee, always look for the educational component. Look at ways you can learn and grow from the experience. What have you learned about yourself, your office needs, or your interviewing skills?

THIRTEEN

Additional Avenues
in Private Practice

For various reasons you may at some point want to consider additional avenues of private practice. Creativity, drive, and a healthy dose of courage can enable you to establish challenging work opportunities. The following is a brief review of possible areas of expansion for your private practice.

Contracting With
Psychiatric Hospitals

Psychiatric hospitals often depend on clinicians in the community to provide contract work for inpatients. The Joint Commission of Accreditation for Hospitals (JCAH) requires that psychosocials be done on all patients by master-level social workers (MSWs). It often is more economical for the hospitals to contract with social workers to do the psychosocials than to hire additional staff. The same is true for therapy groups in the hospital. Specific groups such as psychodrama and art therapy require special training often not possessed by hospital employees. Therefore, through contracting the hospital is able to offer these groups inexpensively while simultaneously developing strong ties with allied health professionals.

In addition, clinicians with a strong outpatient practice often are able to develop consulting contracts with psychiatric hospitals. If, for example, a therapist treats a large number of sexual abuse survivors, he or she may be able to negotiate a consulting contract with the hospital to assume an administrative position on a survivors' track or unit. The hospital will expect the therapist to be instrumental in identifying patients who could benefit from the program. The therapist will be able not only to draw additional income but also to ensure name recognition through the contribution he or she makes in the treatment of this population.

General Consultation

Consultation is a tripartite, voluntary, and temporary relationship among peers in which the consultant provides either direct or indirect services to the consultee by assisting in problem solving (Dougherty, 1990, p. 10). Consultation can take place in a wide variety of arenas (Clayson, 1990, p. 352; Lewin, 1978, pp. 136-139; Morrison, 1990, p. 279; Richards, 1990, p. 87):

Business
Industry
Jury selectors
Expert witnesses
Mental health clinics
Court consultants
HMOs
Insurance companies
Self-help groups
Fraternal organizations
Community organizations
Prepromotion
Pre-job change
Prefirings/prelayoffs
Predivorce
Preretirement
Retirement
Readmission to nursing homes
Health problems/abuse
Illness of a loved one
Vacation planning
Testing and clinical assessment in schools or agencies
Precollege issues and problems for college-bound students
Prepromotion
Prework issues and problems for high school and college graduates

There are several ways to become a consultant. The first is through an existing affiliation you have with an agency. You may be able to identify a need that is not being met and offer your services as a consultant. Another way is to research and develop an understanding of an agency or group and then approach the gatekeeper with your offer of consultative services. You can then use the information you have learned to convince them of the benefit of having you assess, evaluate, and make recommendations. A third method is to get on a consulting list either with the department of social services in your state or with the federal government. If you have an all-round knowledge base with a specialization in a couple of areas, these agencies may be able to use you as a consultant.

Sending "blind" letters to organizations offering your services will not suffice. Through an inquiry call you can obtain the name of the person to whom your letter should be addressed. Typically you can obtain this information from a receptionist. The nicer you are to him or her the more likely you are to obtain valuable information (receptiveness of the individual to new ideas, needs of agency, use of consultants at present or in past). You will need to sell yourself to overcome any resistance the agencies may have and fears that you will make judgments or blame or label them. Follow-up to inquiry letters is essential. Attempt to make a short person-to-person contact. You will have a more attentive audience.

It is necessary to understand the uniqueness of each agency or group setting. Obtain this information by calling and requesting that brochures or other printed matter be mailed to you. Or, go to a public library and research anything that has been written. Talk with people you know who have had experience with the setting.

It also is important to recognize the differences between therapy and consultation. The organization, rather than an individual, is the "identified patient." If you treat the consultees like clients you will be met with contentiousness. Follow through on all commitments you make; otherwise you will lose credibility and your recommendations will be discredited.

It is necessary to address professional and ethical issues that rarely arise in traditional clinical practices. The American College of Occupational and Environmental Medicine has a guide entitled the "Code of Ethical Conduct for Physicians Providing Occupational Medical Services," which identifies 12 standards to observe in the workplace (Sperry, 1993, p. 242).

Home Evaluations for Adoptions

Home studies are required by the court for families pursuing adoption. The practitioner's role is to educate the family on the aspects of adoption, evaluate the family for appropriateness for adoption, and prepare a written report for the court reflecting his or her findings. Although states may vary as to the credentialing one is required to have to prepare such a report, often they will want a social worker with a master's degree to do the study.

Many practitioners will find this contract work appealing while maintaining a full-time job or just beginning in private practice. A considerable amount of time is required to do the home study and prepare the report.

Supervision

Supervision is a methodical practice of focusing on a therapist's understanding of theory, ability to integrate theory into practice, ability to work with organizations, diagnostic skills, and problem areas within her or his own personality that may interfere with providing treatment. Supervisors help therapists learn to avoid burnout by setting realistic goals and developing realistic limits. Supervisors help safeguard the well-being of clients. Therapists are going to want supervision, either to meet licensing requirements or to enhance their own understanding of psychotherapy and to improve their clinical skills. If you have been in practice for a while, have used supervision for yourself, and enjoy helping others grow at their own pace, providing supervision may be an option for you.

To supervise well, it is important to have a general knowledge base of many types of theoretical orientations and different employment settings, as supervisees may be employed in agencies or self-employed. When working with a therapist who is employed in an agency, it is essential that you understand the organizational structure, authority, and value system of the agency.

Ways to supervise include having the supervisee report orally on clinical interventions, provide written process recordings, or make audiotapes or videotapes. This will provide you with information necessary to teach and evaluate the supervisee's knowledge, strengths, weaknesses, and areas of growth.

Advertising your availability in local professional newsletters, contacting graduate schools, notifying agencies employing mental health professionals, and notifying colleagues of your services will be necessary in developing a referral base. Once you have a number of supervisees, explore starting a supervision group. Considerable learning can take place when sharing and problem solving with peers, and this approach also will free your time for other activities.

In many states the supervisor becomes legally responsible for the clinical actions of her or his supervisee and the welfare of the supervisee's caseload. Do not supervise unless you can accurately assess the quality of clinical care each of your supervisee's clients is receiving. If a student therapist is treating a client, obtain a consent to treatment in writing from the client(s). The consent also should include the supervisor's theoretical model of therapy and supervision (Mead, 1990, pp. 137-138). Let your malpractice insurance carrier know about a supervisor/supervisee relationship from its onset.

Teaching

Although the pay typically is not very good, the opportunity to self-promote and develop impressive credentials far outweigh the salary limitations. Careers can be expanded through teaching, especially if you possess an area of expertise. Teaching can consist of tutoring others for licensing, teaching continuing education classes, or becoming a part- or full-time faculty member of a college or university.

To get a teaching position, first obtain a copy of the curriculum offered by the college you are interested in. Then write the department head and either propose that you teach specific courses that are offered or present your idea for a new course, which you would teach. Ask for a meeting to discuss your ideas. Consider community colleges as well as 4-year colleges. Inquire about adjunct positions.

Administering to
Private Mental Health Groups

For the clinician who enjoys organizing, developing, and building practices, functioning in an administrative role may be of interest. This role would include handling the managed care paperwork as well as tracking client treatment and success (*Psychotherapy Finances,* 1991b, p. 3). Marketing may play a large role, including selecting the roles each therapist will assume, identifying creative approaches to use, and even developing a clinic newsletter. The administrator may be involved with designating office space as well as arranging for inservices and professional conferences. Monitoring the currency of professional licenses and malpractice insurance coverage also is an administrative activity.

Presenting Conferences

Once you have attained a level of expertise you can consider presenting conferences either locally or nationally. You may wish to arrange local conferences free of charge, to develop goodwill in the community and to help build your referral sources. Conferences given out of town can be primarily revenue producing.

Conferences require a considerable amount of time in preparation and development. To help ensure success, obtain mailing lists from professional organizations, secure reduced rates in a hotel for those attending from out of town, and apply for continuing educational units from professional organizations. Employ support staff to help with mailings, to assist making all preconference arrangements, and to work the day of the seminar to handle registration and address any problems that may arise during the presentation.

Another way to present is through workshops established by a speakers bureau. Speakers bureaus typically assume all of the responsibility for mailings, marketing, conference room set-up, continuing educational units, and registration. They pay the presenter a predetermined fee. The overhead risk to you is removed. Showing up and presenting is your only responsibility.

Forensic Psychotherapy

The psychotherapist's utilization of skills in the practice of law is identified as forensic psychotherapy. The psychotherapist can provide needed and valuable services to the legal profession and help assure that the needs of clients are represented fairly to the court.

Rather than working clinically with a client, the forensic psychotherapist works primarily for an attorney, court, or other institution, such as an insurance company, involved in the legal process (Wettstein, 1988, p. 1060). The client may be either a voluntary or an involuntary client of the psychotherapist. Yet, the therapist can understand the emotional stress experienced by the client, and thereby act as a buffer between the client and the attorney. The psychotherapist can help the client by providing emotional support, assist her or him in maintaining control at a critical time, and keep her or him informed of choices she or he has, thereby absorbing some of the emotional stress experienced by the client. Typical cases may include testifying in personal injury cases; testifying as an expert witness; providing evaluations in home studies, child custody, malpractice, and workers' compensation cases.

As the therapist is leaving the domain of the mental health world and entering that of the legal world, he or she must be aware of the differences between the two. One must be familiar with the legal process and language. Knowledge of the legal as well as psychiatric meaning of terms is required. The legal world is more black and white, whereas the mental health world is comprised of various shades of gray. The legal world is an adversarial one.

This is often intimidating to psychotherapists, who are accustomed to collaboration and working toward "win-win" solutions.

Expert Witness Testimony

Obviously, there are those therapists who seek forensic work, and develop a familiarity and expertise in working in the courtroom setting. However, any psychotherapist may be asked to testify as an expert witness at some point in his or her career. Expert testimony may include a variety of types of cases, from child custody and visitation, to child sexual abuse, to personal injury, to adoption, to termination of parental rights.

An expert witness is someone who has the knowledge, skill, experience, training, or education in specific areas of practice for the judge to qualify her or him as an expert. Meyer et al. (1988) list the general criteria used for determining appropriateness as an expert as the following: (a) education; (b) credentials and honors; (c) relevant experience, including previous diagnostic and intervention work and positions held; (d) research and publications, including books and articles; (e) knowledge and application of scientific principles; and (f) use of specific tests, procedures, and measurements (p. 222). An expert witness not only can address concrete facts of the case, but also can offer inferences and conclusions. These opinions can influence the judgment.

One of the most difficult concepts for the therapist to comprehend is the uniqueness of the courtroom. The legal arena is an adversarial environment. It is different from the mental health environment, in which relationships are developed, other people's integrities are protected, and professionals try to be impartial. Each attorney's responsibility is to represent his or her client, even at the expense of the other client or expert witnesses. Prior to appearing in court to testify as an expert witness it is advisable to observe a trial in progress. Observe expert witnesses so you may learn from them.

Although the attorney will be helpful and offer guidance regarding "dos and don'ts" in the courtroom, the therapist should be the one responsible for his or her own professional conduct. Issues regarding client confidentiality, giving mental health diagnoses, and professional ethics should be considered at all times. Remember to obtain consents for release of information from the clients in writing to avoid the risk of a lawsuit later on.

Remember to direct your communication to the jury. The most successful expert witnesses are those who are not intimidated by the legal process to the extent that they are rendered powerless or defensive, who speak without professional jargon, and who testify only on the facts they know.

Jury Selection
and Psychological Autopsy

Trial attorneys recognize jury selection as a highly specialized area of expertise. In selecting a jury the trial attorney must consider each juror's age, gender, occupation, religion, socioeconomic status, political ideology, and education, as well as have an understanding of how these individual variables may affect the juror's decision-making process. Psychotherapists have an understanding of psychological development and how significant life events impact a person's way of perceiving the world. Therapists also are trained to be aware of nonverbal communication and interpret this behavior. Recognizing these skills and marketing them to trial lawyers can open a new and exciting arena for psychotherapists.

Following a trial, attorneys often perform a psychological autopsy in an attempt to develop a better understanding of the jury's decision. The therapist can contract with the attorney to interview the jury. Juries usually are receptive to giving this feedback, and therapists are nonthreatening individuals with whom to speak. Questions regarding the attorney's appearance and demeanor, witness credibility, comprehension of the judge's instructions, and jury pretrial bias toward the case will be helpful feedback for the attorney.

Child Custody Evaluations

The goal in providing evaluations for the court is to offer impartial and comprehensive reports and recommendations that are both ethical and within one's area of expertise as to what the best interests of the child(ren) affected by divorce will be (Schetky, 1980). Both parents, as opposed to only one parent, should be evaluated on child custody evaluations. This provides the information required and will prevent the possibility of the evaluator over-identifying with one of the parents. However, as referrals typically come from one of the parent's attorneys, the other parent sometimes refuses to participate in the evaluation process. At times it is possible to obtain the cooperation of resistant parents if the rationale and procedures are explained thoroughly to them at the beginning. They also must be informed that there will be no confidentiality and that all relevant information will be shared with the court (Meyer et al., 1988, pp. 177-190).

To obtain work in custody evaluations, contact attorneys specializing in family law. Depending on your geographical area, the courts also may serve as a source of referrals for court-ordered evaluations.

Consultation to Personal Injury Attorneys
and Workers' Compensation

Personal injuries may arise from a variety of means, including automobile, public transportation, industrial accident, and medical malpractice. In all such cases involving serious injury, the plaintiff's attorney must establish a justifiable and credible financial claim that will meet the client's needs. Some financial claims, such as immediate expenses, are readily established. However, many short- and long-term needs of the client are unknown to most attorneys, even those who specialize in this type of litigation. This is in part because each case is unique and in part because attorneys' training and interests are in vastly different areas.

For reasons such as this, blanket claims frequently are made for "pain and suffering." This is invariably vague, unjustifiable, unsupported by facts, often unfair to both the plaintiff and the defendant, and difficult for a jury to evaluate. In fact, recent research has shown that awards for "pain and suffering" exclusively have been inadequate. The jury often feels that the plaintiff "made a killing," whereas the plaintiff feels cheated (Aiken & Rosenberg, 1984, pp. 28-32). The injured feel that no amount of money can compensate for the losses incurred.

A professional assessment of the prognosis and the current and future needs of the client is mandated. This will enable you to establish a realistic appraisal of the future requirements, cost of goods and services, and treatment required as a consequence of the injury. In addition, it will determine the extent of any emotional condition resulting from the accident. As most severe injuries require assistance in multiple systems, the psychotherapist has the educational training, day-to-day work experience, and knowledge of facilities and services available in the community. The psychotherapist also has relationships with other professionals whose services may be required for complete assessment. These professionals include physicians and occupational, physical, and speech therapists (Lenson, 1988, pp. 1-2).

It is advisable to request payment in full or at a minimum a deposit (not a retainer) for the services provided. It is unethical to accept a contingency based on the outcome of the case. You should be paid as compensation for the professional services rendered.

Once you have decided to accept the case, have worked out the payment arrangements with the attorney, and have reviewed the case material, you will want to make a list of what has already been identified as functional disabilities or losses the individual has incurred as a result of the injury. Pay close attention to the client's past medical and psychological history. Interview all significant parties, such as family, friends, employer, and church. When interviewing the client be alert for signs of malingering or any secondary gains that may exist as a deterrent to getting better. The written report you provide for the attorney must include clear, concise, accurate descriptions about the recommended goods and services; explanations about the benefits to the plaintiff; costs; and number of times the goods will need to be replaced in the plaintiff's lifetime.

The psychotherapist's understanding of and skills with networking are useful in cases such as these. The therapist may recognize a client's need for services, of which the attorney may not have been aware. The therapist can address these findings with the attorney and function as the coordinator of services, locating and contracting with other professionals to provide an assessment or treatment intervention.

I worked with a medical malpractice case in which the plaintiff suffered a subdural hematoma. As a result she became a paraplegic, was partially blind, and had difficulties in speaking and memory. I identified the previously unrecognized benefit of the plaintiff being evaluated by a rehabilitation hospital. In this advocacy role I contracted with a physical and occupational therapist to evaluate the plaintiff. Their assessments were consistent with mine and I had her evaluated at an inpatient rehabilitation unit. Not only was this helpful to the attorney, for it justified the request for an additional $100,000, but it also gave the family realistic hope for a more independent lifestyle.

In these kinds of assessments, the client is actively involved. Therefore, the client is able to maintain control at a critical time, receive emotional support, and be informed of choices.

Many cases are settled out of court. Often when the opposing attorney reviews the settlement brochure, an attempt to avoid a court appearance is made. However, the courts are full of unresolved cases, so it is critical that the therapist be prepared to go to court as an expert witness.

Nonclinical Roles With HMOs

Sank and Shapiro identified nontraditional roles that psychologists were going into in HMOs. These include administrator, organizational consultant, patient ombudsman, clinical consultant, teacher, supervisor, researcher, and primary prevention specialist, as well as clinician (Sank & Shapiro, 1979, pp. 402-408). These roles need not be viewed as available exclusively to psychologists, as other mental health providers have the expertise to provide quality services as well in these nontraditional roles.

To be successful with an HMO one must be able to balance the needs between the patient's best interests and the HMO's interests, and be able to sustain professional and ethical standards. An example of this is when the therapist must serve as a gatekeeper to mental health services. The patient's best interests may conflict with the HMO's expectation that costs be kept down.

Being involved with HMOs can enhance one's clinical private practice both by providing exposure to a large number of other mental-health-care providers and employers as well as by providing the therapist with a helpful understanding of how comfortable it would be to work within the limits an HMO requires. This includes being able to work with physicians as gatekeepers, requirements for short-term therapy, and having less control over one's practice (Kearney, 1984, p. 14).

Home Visits

Several segments of our population cannot see a psychotherapist because they either are shut-ins or otherwise lack accessibility to treatment. This includes neurologically damaged accident victims, the elderly, wheelchair-confined persons who lack transportation, parents of small infants, and those who live in rural areas.

By identifying a need in your community for a particular population to be served, you can develop a practice that caters to this group. Market yourself to physicians, hospitals, nursing homes, home health-care agencies, and medical equipment supply companies. Offer to speak at self-help groups (such as groups for persons with lupus, cancer, multiple sclerosis, or head injury). Advertise in newsletters published by the special-needs groups. Attend local conferences addressing medical illnesses.

Meeting the needs of clients by going to their home as opposed to them coming to your office can pose unique problems. Their homes offer a less sterile environment than does your office. You will not have control over interruptions. In some situations it may be unsafe for you to go to a client's home. It is also quite time consuming, as you have to travel to each client's home as opposed to them arriving at your office.

There are benefits to be had by doing home visits. Any resistance the client may have to perceived control in your office will be averted. You will be able to observe the family and their patterns of communication in their own environment. This will enable you to learn about cultural traditions, and the neighborhood in which they reside, and you will be able to integrate their environment as a part of the client system.

Telephone Therapy

When my nanny quit suddenly, I was left without child care for my 6-month-old daughter. I informed my clients that there was going to be an interruption in our regularly scheduled therapy sessions until I could hire a replacement. Realizing this could take several weeks, and not wanting to begin anew with a cross-covering therapist, several clients asked that I conduct telephone therapy sessions with them.

This is how I became drawn into the world of telephone therapy. I treated some clients on the telephone during this interim period. Some continued as telephone clients after I was back in my office. A few even continued to receive telephone therapy after I moved halfway across the country.

There is no reason that telephone therapy needs to remain in this conventional mode. In the 1990s people are under considerable financial and time pressures. They may be more hesitant to take the time from work for outpatient therapy. Yet they are commuting to work in their automobiles, often equipped with mobile telephones.

If you are comfortable with conducting therapy over the telephone, mobile phone therapy is an avenue worth exploring. You can choose to treat someone exclusively on the telephone or in conjunction with traditional therapy visits to your office.

Market this idea to a mobile telephone company in your area and suggest a joint venture. Meet with the company's marketing director to explore your idea. Suggestions include asking the mobile telephone company to offer a reduced rate for therapy. They may be receptive, as 30 minutes is a sizable block of telephone usage. (I feel the 45- to 50-minute traditional session is too lengthy for the mobile telephone.) The mobile telephone company can market your idea by including a flier detailing your services in their monthly invoices. You can offer to put together a team of psychotherapists who would agree to be "on call" for predetermined hours each week to receive calls from clients. This would enable you to offer a 24-hour service.

Bill through the client's credit card. Obtain billing information at the beginning of the session. Remember, you do not have the same relationship with your telephone clients as you do with those who walk into your office. As the commitment to paying may be reduced, payment prior to the session is important.

There are drawbacks. There is risk of a lawsuit from a driver who has an automobile accident. To help reduce your liability, include a warning on the promotional flier that in the event of emotional distress and distraction, the driver should pull off the road to a safe place. A second drawback is that telephone therapy is not an appropriate method of treating all clients. A third drawback is the risk of loss of confidentiality due to conversations being picked up by outsiders. Suicidal, psychotic, eating disorder, and other at-risk clients requiring closer monitoring are not appropriate candidates for telephone therapy. These clients need to be screened out and encouraged to come into your office. Another drawback is that some insurance companies will not reimburse for therapy that was conducted on the telephone.

Industrial Psychotherapy

The presence of psychotherapists is multiplying in the industrial sector, offering services ranging from helping managers improve their interpersonal skills so they can relate more effectively with their employees; to training, identifying, and working with chemically dependent employees; to program development. Therapists can establish counseling programs to offer employees and other programs to teach supervisors how to recognize and refer distressed workers. The psychotherapist may need to identify services in the community that can meet the employees' needs. Another role may be to work with management on its human resource policy. Psychotherapists may be expected to evaluate company policies affecting the employees and develop outplacement counseling for terminating employees. There are presently more than 117,914,000 employees in the United States (Hoffman, 1992, p. 169). They, and their families, comprise a significant population with whom to work.

Always identify the gatekeeper and elicit his or her support in your program. Without this overt and covert support, referrals will not be made to you. Because it is sometimes difficult to know who the gatekeeper is in an organization, write a letter to each vice president as well as the personnel director. Include in the letter that you will be calling in a week as a follow-up to the letter. They will then be anticipating your call and may pay more attention to your information.

In working with employees it will be important to have a clear understanding with the employer that confidentiality is necessary. If not, employees will be afraid to talk with the psychotherapist for fear of losing their jobs. Such boundaries also need to carry over into the relationship the therapist has with the other employees. Too familiar and casual a relationship between therapist and employees can result in increased discomfort with disclosing problems and asking for help. Therefore, a professional detachment must exist, which can prove to be isolating for the clinician.

In terms of consulting with managers, a therapist can engage in an intervention called "shadow consultation" (Resnick & King, 1985, pp. 447-450). The therapist closely observes a manager who recognizes that his or her behavior, beliefs, or feelings are affecting his or her proficiency in relating to others. The manager is willing to work with a therapist for the purpose of examining his or her values and behaviors more objectively than could be accomplished alone. The therapist will observe how the manager relates on the telephone and in meetings and how he or she communicates with other individuals. These observations are shared and recommendations for change are made. A strong, trusting relationship is necessary for this sort of intervention to work most efficiently. The therapist will attend meetings with the manager but assume a nonparticipatory, observer role.

Although feedback from the therapist to the manager needs to be provided on a regular, perhaps daily basis, the therapist should furnish the manager with a summary of the findings at the conclusion of their work together. This will provide the manager with written information that could be helpful in future reflections.

The therapist's different knowledge base, awareness of human needs, and skills and values used to meet goals will be beneficial to the individual she or he is working with as well as to the organization. The therapist also will need to understand the nature of the organization, its history, and its power sources. Contracting with the organization needs to be done just as it would be with a client in your office. Time will need to be allowed for the establishment of a basic trust in the relationship.

Employers habitually fail to request professional help until a need has been in existence for a period of time. When the services are requested, a great amount of pressure is often applied to resolve the problems quickly. Therefore, therapists who value and enjoy short-term treatment and crisis intervention will find the industrial setting's need for an immediate resolution compatible with their theoretical orientations (Kurzman & Akabas, 1981, p. 54).

The opportunity for entry into the field of industrial psychotherapy is vast. There are millions of employers, most of whom have pressures placed upon them from their own unresolved family-of-origin issues, as well as demanding expectations from minority groups, unions, disabled persons, and environmentalists. Therapists can enter the industrial arena and assist with indifferent systems or types of discrimination and work with these systems to better the working environment for the employee by providing reports and recommendations for changes.

Expansion With Therapists and Offices

The time may come when you question whether you should expand your practice or remain small. This may occur when your caseload is consistently high and you find you are having to place potential clients on a waiting list or are turning down referral sources. When your singular office is successful, you may assume that you can be even more successful if you take additional therapists into your office, or increase the number of offices you operate. There are pros and cons to expanding.

■ Expansion With Therapists

You can hire or contract with therapists. Hiring a therapist and guaranteeing him or her a salary may be too risky. The hiree can end up earning more than you, because his or her income is guaranteed and yours must suffer the income fluctuations that naturally occur in private practice. Also, a salaried therapist does not have the incentive to build up a referral source, leaving you to do all of the marketing and carry the burden for obtaining referrals. A guaranteed salary limits an incentive of additional income for incremental therapy sessions.

Instead, consider contracting with a therapist whom you feel not only has the experience but also will accept you in the role of supervising the practice, and will assume an active role in establishing a referral network. Most therapists negotiate a percentage agreement, whereby the therapist receives a percentage of the fees that are collected (not incurred). This is not to be confused with fee splitting, as insurance companies are clearly aware of who is providing the therapy.

A legal contract should be drawn up when working with an independent contractor. Some supervising therapists include a noncompete clause in their contract with the supervisee. For example, they may require that the therapist not practice within 20 miles of the office, should the therapist leave the practice. This is to prevent your practice from being injured by the competition. Another way to handle it is to require a cash buyout should the contractee choose to leave your practice and establish a practice nearby. (Laws regarding noncompete agreements vary by state. Be certain to check with your attorney.)

It is not a good idea to include a clause indicating that all clients remain with the practice and cannot be seen independently by therapists who leave the practice. Being forced to leave an existing therapeutic relationship would not be in the client's best interest.

When two or more therapists work in an office together it is best to have each therapist charge the same rate. This will avoid the possibility of clients feeling that one therapist is providing a better quality of service than another. It also will avoid confusion in the event that the clients are seen for cross-coverage purposes within the office.

■ Expansion Through Additional Offices

Typically, you will have more name recognition if you have more than one location. You will more than likely have greater financial resources, and the ability to survive a problem resulting in loss better than a smaller practice. However, in a large practice, spending is more difficult to control.

If your success was based on flexibility, serving target populations, and providing a high level of service, you may lose this in the growth process. With growth there is often a tendency to try to accommodate too large a market, ignoring the smaller markets that contributed to your initial success. Also, larger practices need to have more rigid rules, potentially inhibiting the ability to make quick and necessary changes.

Small practices often run smoothly because the office communication is direct and informal. Everyone understands everybody else's roles, and shares similar values and goals. Expansion requires more rigid roles, more distance between you and your employees, more professional and formalized communication within the organization. This less personalized relationship can detract from job satisfaction, with employees feeling less involved, less like their contribution is valued, and in turn requiring greater salaries and benefit packages to compensate for job dissatisfaction.

Be careful when considering expansion. Just because you are doing well does not mean you need to add another office. Many successful retail chains have succumbed due to overzealous expansion. Alternatives may be to remain in your present location and develop therapy groups that could meet the needs of your individual clients. This will in turn free time for additional clients.

Products

You may have discovered a need in your practice for specialized products that would enhance your practice. Perhaps you experimented and successfully developed such a tool for your own use. Examples may include newsletters, assessment forms, audiotapes or videotapes, or clinical aids. Such items can become an additional source of income if you market them to other practitioners. This can be accomplished through advertisements placed in professional publications or presentations made at local and national conferences.

Future Opportunities

Keep abreast of current events and political changes. Life is never static. The needs of people are forever evolving and changing. Read the newspapers and watch television with an eye for how issues are impacting your community. Anticipate how you can provide services to meet the shifting needs and concerns of others. This will enable you to keep your practice exciting and promote personal growth. It also will help others notice your practice as creative and responsive as opposed to a "me-too" type of practice.

FOURTEEN

Taking Care of Yourself

The previous chapters have focused on what you need to do to ensure the health of your practice. An equal priority needs to be given to taking care of your own well-being. If you do not take care of yourself you will not have enough energy to give to your practice. "Therapy is the most human of the arts and sciences. Some of us forget quickly that the source of our ability to touch others lies in our being human" (Goldberg, 1990, p. 797).

There is a danger that your practice can begin to run you rather than you running your practice. When this happens, stress results. Not all stress is harmful. A well-managed level of stress in our lives can "motivate, stimulate and provide the needed challenge for creativity and heightened performance" (Pelletier, 1985, p. 80). However, poorly managed stress can result in physical disorders, chemical dependency, interpersonal conflicts, burnout, or even suicide.

Stress is an inside job. Although a few changes in one's environment can be implemented to enhance a reduction in stress, most changes need to take place within each practitioner. The first step in managing stress is to recognize the sources. Various difficulties inherent in having a private practice may cause stress. In a 1984 survey of psychologists in independent practice, Nash, Noracross, and Prochaska found that the major stresses, in descending order, were time pressures, economic uncertainty, business aspects, and excessive workload (Pelletier, 1985, p. 45). As you can see, it is the day-to-day experiences that cause stress. When those stressors build up, you risk the danger of being so preoccupied that you neglect your family and/or become physically exhausted, emotionally isolated, and spiritually bankrupt.

The second step in managing stress is to identify ways to control the influences of stress. You need to develop an awareness of your own needs, how different factors can influence them, and how to maintain a healthy balance in life.

As my practice grew, I was seeing clients from 7:00 A.M. to 9:00 P.M. My husband, concerned that I was overworking, had begun to make comments suggesting that I curtail my practice. However, my investment in developing my practice prohibited me from hearing my husband. Late one night in my office I was advising a client to take care of himself and to set limits on how overextended he would allow himself to become. I realized then that although I thought I was taking care of someone else, I was really modeling a lack of limit setting. In addition, I was giving out advice to others that I was not heeding.

When you work too hard it can cause you to depersonalize your clients and develop negative countertransference. Establishing boundaries can reduce the likelihood of feeling exhausted and emotionally vulnerable. Appropriate boundaries also will be necessary in order to maintain a strong self-identity. Appropriate boundaries aid us in learning how to preserve our caring as well as ourselves.

Learn how to say no. Get control over your interruptions. Obtain an unlisted home telephone number, and do not give your home telephone number to clients. (They can always reach you through your office and service, when necessary.) Decide not to work on certain days, and stick to your decision. Learn to delegate work to others, such as housekeepers, office staff, or consultants.

Workaholism

Avoid becoming a workaholic. Workaholics have limited interests because they concentrate only on their practice. This is generally due to feelings of guilt when not producing, and tying in personal worth with what they produce. You need to have a balance in life. You need to realize that you have value regardless of what you accomplish. To enjoy "being," not only "doing," is an essential ingredient in relaxing. This entails having noncompetitive, goalless, unorganized fun. It involves socializing. Let go of the need to be in control and the need to be perfect.

Social Support

Surround yourself with personal relationships that offer social support. It will help you avoid subconsciously looking to meet those needs through clients. If personal conflicts do arise, seek to resolve them quickly, as they are likely to carry over to your work.

Clinical Expertise

Enhance your clinical skills. Feeling vulnerable due to limited training and/or clinical expertise will create stress. Often therapists are uncomfortable with certain populations or presenting problems they encounter. They continue to treat clients but feel an overwhelming anxiety due to improper training. Taking care of yourself by seeking supervision, attending conferences, continuing professional readings, and even continuing your education can enhance your confidence and hence reduce stress and a potentially negative attitude. Also, recognize what type of clients you do not like to treat. Your stress can be reduced by not accepting such clients into your practice.

Time Management

Too often clinicians feel that hectic work schedules and the pressure to keep up with deadlines on advertising, press releases, writing clinical notes, giving community presentations, and marketing contacts creates unmanageable stress. Avoid becoming a crisis junkie, moving from emergency to emergency, always reacting instead of planning. Being too busy can be a way of avoiding emotionally painful feelings or a way of obtaining some excitement, or it may be a resistance against undesirable tasks.

Schedule something personally stimulating each day so you have controlled excitement and do not need to manufacture the excitement through crises. Schedule time not only for your therapy hours but also for administrative tasks. I refer to this process as scheduling "lost hours." This includes returning telephone calls to clients and referral sources, completing paperwork, conferring with colleagues or staff, writing or preparing talks, doing bookkeeping, and so on. In other words, it is time purposely set aside for running your business.

Evaluate yourself and identify time wasters. For instance, while commuting, could you productively spend the time tape-recording notes from your sessions? Would a car telephone enable you to take care of business that otherwise would have taken place hurriedly between sessions or at home when you would prefer to relax? Would you benefit from using travel time to listen to cassette tapes addressing therapy-related topics? Or would you prefer to use the travel time to listen to relaxing music as a way to unwind from your day prior to going home?

Examine how you spend lunch. Do you skip lunch? You should not, as maintaining a healthy diet is an important ingredient in your emotional and physical well-being. Consider using lunchtime to meet with a colleague or a potential referral source. Perhaps you may wish to use lunch as a time to rest.

Waiting, be it in your office for a late-arriving client or at the office of a potential referral source, can be time well spent by returning telephone calls or reading correspondence, articles, or books.

Written Communications

Writing letters can be unnecessarily time consuming, further adding to your stress. Anticipate the need by developing form letters for the most common correspondence you will need. This may include thank-you notes for referrals, requests to be included as a provider with a third-party payer, as well as marketing letters. Then, you need only make minor adjustments and personal touches to your established letter each time you use it. This will save you time, reduce the need for repetitive work, and help you avoid the tendency to procrastinate.

Organization

Organize. Start with a clean desk. Clutter on your desk will offer distractions and may contribute to feelings of being overwhelmed. Create a daily "to do" list of things you need to do each day. Cross them off after they are completed. This will give you a sense of accomplishment. Start each day doing the task you least like. This will reduce feelings of guilt at not addressing the work that has to be done, which contribute to stress.

Realistic Goals

Establish realistic goals. Avoid becoming greedy or unethical. Determine how much time you need to contribute each day or week to your family, spirituality, physical exercise, and social needs so you have balance in your life. Avoid the trap of becoming a hypocrite, expecting yourself always to be available for clients while advising clients to have a life outside of work. Give yourself permission not to be perfect.

Monotony

Avoid monotony, which can lead to stress. Work on a variety of projects, alter your work schedule, schedule something positive each day, and be certain to have spontaneous as well as structured times.

Childhood Messages

Look at unhealthy "tapes" from childhood that may be influencing your stress level. Were you taught that you had to be productive to have worth? If so, you are at risk of becoming a workaholic. Were you told you needed to be perfect? If so, you are going to feel guilty when relaxing and not accomplishing anything specific. It is important to be able to sit back and relax. If these childhood messages are negatively influencing your adult behavior then you need to examine which messages no longer serve you well and discard them.

Isolation

Combat feelings of isolation. Schedule time to meet with other therapists. Opportunities exist through lunches, conferences, and peer supervision groups.

Developing and maintaining a private practice in psychotherapy entails dealing with professional and personal issues not encountered in other, nontherapy professions. A private practice can create strong feelings: fear, insecurity, anger, ambivalence, and anxiety. It is important that you learn to identify what is behind these feelings, as they may be at the source of your stress. Once you can identify these feelings you can go about making necessary changes in your beliefs and behaviors. Making changes may be difficult because it entails making changes in yourself that previously were not necessary. Change is often difficult. It means letting go of something familiar.

Because of the unique and inherently demanding qualities of running a private practice, it will be necessary to continuously evaluate how the practice is affecting you personally as well as how it is affecting your values, goals, and ability to meet your spiritual, social, and physical needs. This process must take place on an ongoing basis, year after year. There are no "shoulds" to follow with regard to deciding how to care for yourself while maintaining a private practice. Rather, there is simply a need to develop an awareness of your personal needs.

Maintaining a private practice is a fluid process. Therefore, whatever decisions you make may need adjustment. Your private practice may be influenced by changes in your personal life as well as by changes in the direction your practice is growing. Continue to identify what is personally and professionally important to you. It will help focus the growth of your practice. It also will help with managing your feelings. You may find the process of committing to paper your goals for a lifestyle as well as professional accomplishments to be helpful. Review this material frequently to ensure that you are not straying too far off track.

As I stated earlier, I am not advocating an avoidance of stress. Stress can be highly motivating and exciting. It can bring about positive challenge and growth. Periods of stress, however, must be accompanied by periods of relaxation and personal renewal. Hart notes that during high stress periods we should plan for recovery so we can recuperate. This might mean allowing extra sleep, cutting back on some activities, or increasing the amount of relaxation exercises one does (Hart, 1988, p. 120). If we take care of ourselves we will be able to continue to function at a high capacity level for years, as well as to provide good role models for our clients.

Plan for Retirement

Despite the glossy pictures we see in the media about how relaxing retirement is, many find it to be a stressful, uncomfortable experience. Retirement may not be gratifying unless you prepare for it properly. When you are focusing on building a career, little attention is typically directed toward ending it years later. Whereas you may plan for retirement financially, you may tend to fall short on emotional preparation. When our grandparents retired, they typically died within a few short years. Now we can expect to find ourselves living many healthy, productive years following our retirement.

Finding areas of interest outside your career will help you to develop relationships, grow in various ways, and receive enjoyment once you cease working. These pursuits need to take place during your working years so the transition into retirement can be emotionally easier. As the experience of loss creates stress, it will be vital to have other supports and strengths from which to draw.

References

Aiken, T. J., & Rosenberg, S. (1984, Fall). The Canadian connection: Proving special damage in the catastrophic injury case. *Trial Diplomacy Journal, 7,* 28-32.

Barker, R. L. (1984). *Social work in private practice.* Silver Spring, MD: National Association of Social Workers.

Beigel, J. K., & Earle, R. H. (1990). *Successful private practice in the 1990s.* New York: Brunner/Mazel.

Besharov, D. J. (1985). *The vulnerable social worker: Liability for serving children and families.* Silver Spring, MD: National Association of Social Workers.

Bly, R. W. (1991). *Selling your service.* New York: Henry Holt.

Burns, L. M. (1989). The medical secretary. In *Webster's new world secretarial handbook.* New York: Simon & Schuster.

Canter, M. B., & Freudenberger, H. J. (1990). Fee scheduling. In E. A. Margenau (Ed.), *The encyclopedic handbook of private practice* (pp. 217-232). New York: Gardner Press.

Clayson, D. (1990). Teaching. In E. A. Margenau (Ed.), *The encyclopedic handbook of private practice.* New York: Gardner Press.

Cohen, R. J., & Mariano, W. E. (1982). *Legal guidebook in mental health.* New York: Free Press.

Conlee, G. (1990). Using marketing as a tool for practice development. In E. A. Margenau (Ed.), *The encyclopedic handbook of private practice.* New York: Gardner Press.

Department of Treasury, Internal Revenue Service. (1990). *Publication 535: Business expenses* (Catalog Number 15065Z). Washington, DC: Government Printing Office.

Dorpat, T., & Boswell, J. (1963). An evaluation of suicidal intent in suicide attempts. *Comprehensive Psychiatry, 4,* 117-125.

Dougherty, A. M. (1990). *Consultation.* Pacific Grove, CA: Brooks/Cole.

Ethics Committee of the American Psychological Association. (1987). Report of the Ethics Committee: 1986. *American Psychologist, 42*(7), 730-734.

Everstine, L., Everstine, D. S., Heymann, G. M., True, R. H., Frey, D. H., Johnson, H. G., & Seiden, R. H. (1990, September). Privacy and confidentiality in psychotherapy. *American Psychologist, 35*(9), 828.

Feldman-Summers, S., & Jones, G. (1984). Psychological impacts of sexual contact between therapists or other health care practitioners and their clients. *Journal of Counseling and Clinical Psychology, 52*(6), 1055-1058.

Freud, S. (1913). On beginning the treatment: Further recommendations on the technique of psychoanalysis I. In J. Strachey (Ed.) (1958), *The standard edition of the complete psychological works of Sigmund Freud, Vol. 12* (pp. 111-144). London: Hogarth.

Goldberg, C. (1990). Mistakes of the seasoned therapist. In E. A. Margenau (Ed.), *The encyclopedic handbook of private practice.* New York: Gardner Press.

Greenburg, S. L., & Greenburg, J. H. (1988). Malpractice litigation: Fears and facts. *Psychotherapy in Private Practice, 6*(1), 61.

Hare-Mustin, R. T., Marecek, J., Kaplan, A. G., & Liss-Levinson, N. (1979, January). Rights of clients, responsibilities of therapists. *American Psychologist, 34*(1), 7.

Hart, A. (1988, April). *Adrenalin and stress.* Irving, TX: Word.

Hiratsuka, J. (1990, February). Managed care: A sea change in health. *National Association of Social Workers News, 35*(2), 3.

Hoffman, M. S. (Ed.). (1992). *The world almanac and book of facts 1992.* New York: Scripps Howard.

Hogan, D. B. (1979). *The regulation of therapists.* Cambridge, MA: Ballinger.

Hyatt, J. (1990, October). The parent trap. *Inc.,* 49-62.

Jackson, R. A. (1991, August 16). *Open Minds* finds non-psych docs treat many MHSA patients. *Managed Care Outlook,* p. 5. (Biweekly newsletter available from Capitol Publications. Alexandria, VA.)

Johnson, K. L. (1988). *Subliminal selling skills.* New York: American Management Association.

Kachorek, J. (1990). Record keeping. In E. A. Margenau (Ed.), *The encyclopedic handbook of private practice.* New York: Gardner Press.

Kearney, M. (1984, Summer). Confidentiality in group therapy. *Psychotherapy in Private Practice, 2*(2), 19-20.

Keith-Spiegel, P., & Koacher, G. P. (1985). *Ethics in psychotherapy.* Hillsdale, NJ: Lawrence Erlbaum.

Kissel, S. (1983). *Private practice for the mental health clinician.* Rockville, MD: Aspen Systems Corporation.

Knapp, S., & VandeCreek, L. (1987). *Privileged communications in the mental health professions.* New York: Van Nostrand Reinhold.

Kriss, J. P. (1975). On white coats and other matters. *New England Journal of Medicine, 292*(19), 1024-1025.

Kurzman, P., & Akabas, S. H. (1981, January). Industrial social work as an arena for practice. *Social Work, 24*(1), 54.

Lenson, E. S. (1988, August). *Expanding social work roles—The social worker as an expert consultant to trial attorneys.* Paper presented at the 27th annual International Conference for the Advancement of Private Practice of Clinical Social Work, Cape Cod, MA.

Lewin, M. H. (1978). *Establishing and maintaining a successful professional practice.* Rochester, NY: Hatherleigh.

Manbeck, H. F., Jr. [assistant secretary and commissioner of patents and trademarks], & Samuels, J. M. [assistant commissioner for trademarks]. (1992, February). *Basic facts about trademarks.* Washington, DC: Department of Commerce, Patent and Trademark Office.

Margolin, G. (1982, July). Ethical and legal considerations in marital and family therapy. *American Psychologist, 37*(7), 794.

Mead, D. E. (1990). *Effective supervision.* New York: Brunner/Mazel.

Meyer, R. G., Landis, E. R., & Hays, J. R. (1988). *Law for the psychotherapist.* New York: Norton.

Morrison, J. K. (1990). Techniques for expansion. In E. A. Margenau (Ed.), *The encyclopedic handbook of private practice.* New York: Gardner Press.

National Association of Social Workers. (1987, June). *Professional social work recognition.* Silver Spring, MD: Author.

National Association of Social Workers News. (1991, March). *Vol. 36*(3), p. 5.

Pelletier, K. R. (1985). *Healthy people in unhealthy places: Stress and fitness at work.* New York: Delta/Seymour Lawrence.

Perlin, M. L. (1988). The basis of medical malpractice. In F. Flach (Ed.), *Psychiatric risk management.* New York: Hatherleigh.

Practice Builder. (1984a, February). Vol. 2(2), p. 4. (Obtain from Alan L. Bernstein, publisher/executive director, 2755 Bristol Street, Suite 100, Costa Mesa, CA 92626-5909, (714) 545-8900.)

Practice Builder. (1984b, March). *Vol. 2*(3), pp. 6, 8.

Practice Builder. (1984c, May). *Vol. 2*(5), pp. 4, 5.

Practice Builder. (1984d, August). *Vol. 2*(8), pp. 4, 6.

Practice Builder. (1984e, September). *Vol. 2*(9), p. 7.

Practice Builder. (1984f, November/December). *Vol. 2*(11), p. 2.

Practice Builder. (1985a, February). *Vol. 3*(2), p. 9.

Practice Builder. (1985b, March). *Vol. 3*(3), p. 5.

Practice Builder. (1985c, October). *Vol. 3*(10), p. 6.

Practice Builder. (1985d, November/December). *Vol. 3*(11), p. 9.

Practice Builder. (1988, July). *Vol. 6*(7), pp. 3, 11.

Practice Builder. (1989a, January). *Vol. 7*(1), pp. 4-5.

Practice Builder. (1989b, September). *Vol. 7*(9), p. 2.

Practice Builder. (1991, September). *Vol. 9*(9), p. 6.

Price Waterhouse. (1992). *Retirement planning adviser.* New York: Pocket Books.

Private Practice Update. (1991, Spring). Quarterly newsletter, Charter Hospital, Kingwood, TX, p. 1.

Psychotherapy Finances. (1991a). *Vol. 16*(14), p. 5. (Obtain from Ridgewood Financial Institute, Ridgewood, NJ.)

Psychotherapy Finances. (1991b). *Vol. 17*(8), p. 3.

Psychotherapy Finances. (1991c). *Vol. 17*(10), p. 2.

Psychotherapy Finances. (1992a). *Vol. 17*(12), p. 1.

Psychotherapy Finances. (1992b). *Vol. 18*(2), pp. 4-6.

Reamer, F. (1987, September). Informed consent in social work. *Social Work, 32*(5), 425-429.

Reamer, F. G. (1989, September). Liability issues in social work supervision. *Social Work, 2*(5), 445-447.

Resnick, H., & King, J. (1985, September-October). Shadow consultation: Intervention in industry. *Social Work, 30*(5), 447-450.

Richards, D. L. (1990). *Building and managing your private practice.* Alexandria, VA: American Association for Counseling and Development.

Rosenberg, N., Butzen, J., & Butzen, P. (1984). *Preferred provider organizations: A manual for psychotherapists.* [Prepared for the California Society for Clinical Social Work.] Sacramento, CA: Society for Clinical Social Work.

Rozovsky, F. A. (1986). *Consent to treatment: A practical guide.* Boston: Little, Brown.

Sank, L. I., & Shapiro, J. R. (1979). Case examples of the broadened role of psychology in health maintenance organizations. *Professional Psychology, 10,* 402-408.

Schetky, D. B. E. (1980). *Child psychiatry and the law.* New York: Brunner/Mazel.

Schrier, C. J. (1980, November). Guidelines for record-keeping under privacy and open access laws. *Social Work, 25*(6), 452-457.

Schwartz, G. (1989, May). Confidentiality revisited. *Social Work, 3*(3), 225.

Smith, B. D. (1990, August). *How insurance works.* Malvern, PA: Insurance Institute of America.

Sperry, L. (1993). *Psychiatric consultation in the workplace.* Washington, DC: American Psychiatric Press.

Talbott, J. A., Hales, R. E., & Yudofsky, S. C. (Eds.). (1988). The American Psychiatric Press textbook of psychiatry. Washington, DC: American Psychiatric Press.

Tardiff, K. (1989). *Concise guide to assessment and management of violent patients.* Washington, DC: American Psychiatric Press.

Weitz, R. D., & Samuels, R. M. (1990). The sale and purchase of a private health-service-provider psychology practice. In E. A. Margenau (Ed.), *The encyclopedic handbook of private practice* (pp. 384-390). New York: Gardner Press.

Wettstein, R. M. (1988). Psychiatry and the law. In J. A. Talbott (Ed.), *The American Psychiatric Press textbook of psychiatry.* Washington, DC: American Psychiatric Press.

Wilson, S. J. (1978). *Confidentiality in social work: Issues and principles.* New York: Free Press.

Woody, R. H. (1988). *Protecting your mental health practice.* San Francisco: Jossey-Bass.

Wright, R. H. (1981, December). What to do until the malpractice lawyer comes: A survivor's manual. *American Psychologist, 36*(12), 1536.

Recommended Reading

Beigel, J. K., & Earle, R. H. (1990). *Successful private practice in the 1990s.* New York: Brunner/Mazel.

Brodsky, S. L. (1991). *Testifying in court.* Washington, DC: American Psychological Association.

Freudenberger, H. J., & North, G. (1986). *Women's burnout: How to spot it, how to reverse it, how to prevent it.* New York: Penguin.

Gallessich, J. (1982). *The profession and practice of consultation.* San Francisco: Jossey-Bass.

Gray, D. A., & Cry, D. G. (1987, September). *Marketing your product: A planning guide for small business.* Bellingham, WA: International Self-Counsel Publishers.

Hallman, G. V. (1992). *Financial planning for retirement.* New York: McGraw-Hill.

Keith-Spiegel, P., & Koacher, G. P. (1985). *Ethics in psychology.* Hillsdale, NY: Lawrence Erlbaum.

Kissel, S. (1983). *Private practice for the mental health clinician: Seven business headaches.* Rockville, MD: Aspen Systems Corporation.

Klien, H. (Ed.). (1991). *The Psychotherapy Finances guide to private practice.* Hawthorne, NJ: Psychotherapy Finances.

Lakin, M. (1991). *Coping with ethical dilemmas in psychotherapy.* Elmsford, NY: Pergamon.

Mannino, F. V., Trickett, E. J., Shore, M. F., Kidder, M. G., & Levin, G. (Eds.). (1986). *Handbook of mental health consultation.* Rockville, MD: National Institute for Mental Health.

Margenau, E. A. (Ed.). (1990). *The encyclopedic handbook of private practice.* New York: Gardner Press.

Meyer, R. G., Landis, E. R., & Hays, J. R. (1988). *Law for the psychotherapist.* New York: Norton.

Perlin, M. L. (1988). *Mental disability law: Civil and criminal.* Charlottesville, VA: Kluwer.

Porter, S. (1991). *Planning your retirement.* New York: Prentice Hall.

Richards, D. L. (1990). *Building and managing your private practice.* Alexandria, VA: American Association for Counseling and Development.

Sadoff, R. L. (1975). *Forensic psychiatry.* Springfield, IL: Charles C Thomas.

Shilling, D. (1986). *Be your own boss.* New York: Penguin.

Shuman, D. W., & Weiner, M. F. (1982). The privilege study: An empirical examination of the psychotherapist-patient privilege. *North Carolina Law Review, 60,* 893-942.

Slovenko, R. (1966). *Psychotherapy, confidentiality and privileged communications.* Springfield, IL: Charles C Thomas.
Stone, A. (1984). *Law, psychiatry & morality.* Washington, DC: American Psychiatric Press.
Szykitka, W. (Ed.). (1978). *How to be your own boss.* New York: New American Library.
Woody, R. H. (1988). *Protecting your mental health practice.* San Francisco: Jossey-Bass.

Index

Abandonment, 190-191
Absenteeism, employees and, 222
Abuse victims, 132
Accountant, 51-52
  corporations and, 19
  home office and, 33
  purchased practices and, 15
  secretary meeting with, 215
Accounting period, 73
Accounting software, 111-112
Accounts payable, 109
Accounts receivable, 109
Addictive dependency, 184, 222
Administrative activities, time for, 6-7
Administrative role, 227
Adolescent therapy group, 140, 150
Adoptions, home evaluations for, 225-226
Advertising, 28, 164-181
  accounting for, 75
  billboards, 175-176
  brochures, 170-172
  direct mail, 166-167
  free, 177-180
  group practice and, 11
  magazines, 169
  newspapers, 168-169
  position, 176
  promotional items, 181
  radio, 173-174
  television, 174
  Yellow Pages, 172-173

Advertising agencies, 176
Agencies, supervisees in, 226
Akabas, S. H., 236
Alarm system, 48
Alcohol screening services, 150, 175
American Medical Association, 93
Analytical thinking, 7
Answering machine, 13, 28, 190
  answering service versus, 40
  secretary and, 210
Answering service, 13, 28, 190
  answering machine versus, 40-41
  politeness and, 164
  secretary and, 210
  tax deductions and, 75
Appearance, 5
Appointment book, 54-55
Appointment cards, 46, 47
Appointments:
  missed, 46, 107-108
  scheduling with computers, 42
  secretary scheduling, 210
Articles, in newspapers, 178
Art therapy, 223
Assessment sheet, referrals and, 141-142
Assets:
  intangible, 15
  retirement, 196
Attire, 5, 182
  court and, 126
  employees and, 207

Attorneys, 52-53
    corporations and, 20
    insurance company and, 116
    lease and, 33
    purchased practices and, 15
    selecting, 124
Audiotapes, 238
Audit(s):
    insurance, 94
    IRS, 74, 81, 113
Auditory people, 161
Autonomy, desire for, 1-2

Bad debts, write off of, 76, 104-105
Balance sheet, 72
Bank accounts, 112-113
Bank deposits, 74, 112, 213
Bank service charges, 75
Bank statements, 74
Bartering fees, 103
Battered clients, 132
Beigel, J. K., 101
Benefits, employee, 30
Besharov, D. J., 118
Billboards, 175-176
Billing, 86-88
    appointment book and, 54-55
    credit card, 234
    delinquent accounts and, 103-107
    employee assistance programs and, 98
    exclusive provider organizations, 100
    health maintenance organizations and, 98
    hospitals and, 102-103
    insurance, 91-96
    managed care and, 100-102
    missed appointments, 46
    preferred provider organizations, 98-100
    secretary and, 211-212
Blackmail, 95
Bly, R. W., 159
Bonuses, 75, 217-219
Bookkeeping, 108-112
    computers and, 42
    records, 73-74
    systems, 51
Books, 75
Boswell, J., 130
Boundary issues, 192-193
    employees and, 207

fees and, 83, 104
therapeutic contract and, 189
work day and, 7
Brochures, 36, 166, 167, 170-172
Budget, 8
Bulk mailings, 166
Bureaucracy, latitude from, 3
Burglar alarm, 75
Burnout, 240
Burns, L. M., 211, 212, 214
Business:
    asking for, 157, 161
    setting up, 21-53
Business cards, 44-46
    direct mail and, 167
    in waiting room, 36, 37, 44
    other people's, 42, 44, 163
    tax deductibility of, 75
Business deductions, 74-76
Business organization, type of, 17-20
Business overhead expense insurance, 50
Business records, 73
    purchased practices and, 15
    See also Bookkeeping
Business skills, 2
Butzen, J., 99
Butzen, P., 99
Buying a practice, 14-17

Canceled checks, 74
Cancellation policy, 46, 59, 83, 107
Canter, M. B., 84, 86
Capital, partners', 72
Capitation, 101
Car expenses, 75
Cash:
    insuring against loss of, 48
    payments in, 88
    receipt log, 73
C corporations, 19
Central air conditioning, 35
Certified Alcohol and Drug Abuse Coun-
    selor, 151
Certified public accountant (CPA), 52
Check, bouncing, 90, 111
Checkbooks, 73
Checking accounts, 112
Chemical dependency:
    employees and, 222

insurance and, 57
training, 151
Child abuse, 134, 187
Child custody evaluations, 90, 230
Childhood messages, 244
Child Protective Services, 124
Children:
  at risk, 123, 132, 134
  keeping files of, 68
Churches:
  presentations at, 147
  referrals from, 145
City taxes, 79, 209
Claim forms, 91
Claims-made policy, 115-116
Clayson, D., 224
Cleaning service, 36, 39
Clergy, referrals from, 145
Client(s):
  accessibility to, 190
  access to records, 56
  battered, 132
  billing, 86-88
  child-abusing, 134
  contacts through current, 154
  continuing nonbenefiting, 192
  correspondence, 68
  feedback and, 164
  financial situation, 84-85, 97
  following up with, 163
  hospitalized, 102-103
  litigious, 135
  locating office near, 30
  maintaining contact with, 162
  newsletters for, 180
  noncompliant, 122, 190, 191
  number of, 6
  patients information packet, 59-63
  professional, 85
  purchased practices and, 15
  reviewing records with, 66
  secretary receiving, 210
  selectively choosing, 3, 14
  social setting and, 192
  suicidal, 129-131
  transferring, 190
  trusting relationship with, 121
  value differences and, 185
  violent, 122, 123, 132-134
  welcoming new, 162
  well-paying, 85
Client intake forms, 56-63
Client records, *see* Clinical records
Clients Seen List, 86-87
Client tax deductions, 80-81
Clinical experience, 7, 121, 242
Clinical expertise, 242
Clinical notes, 63-67
  attorney and, 52
  client requests for, 56
  confidentiality and, 186
  insurance companies and, 94
  legal requests for, 52, 56
Clinical offices, furnishing, 37
Clinical records, 54-70, 211
  access to, 56, 66-67
  confidentiality and, 55
  ethical issues and, 194
  group practice and, 11
  lawsuits and, 116
  maintaining, 212-213
  old, 67-68, 211
  purchased practices and, 15
  reasons for termination in, 191
  storing, 211
  subpoenaed, 55, 56
Clinical skills, 7
Clothes, *see* Attire
Codes:
  DSM-III-R, 91
  missed appointments, 96
  Physicians Current Procedural Terminol-
    ogy, 57, 93
Cohen, R. J., 118
Cold calls, 155-159
Collection agencies, 104
Colleagues, treating, 192
Commitment of client, 131, 133
Communication skills, 5
Community, awareness of issues in, 13
Community agency, transfer of client to, 84
Community papers, 168
Community support groups, 70
Competition, 136, 138, 162, 183
Computers, 28, 42
  accounting on, 52, 111-112
  insurance and, 48
  management system, 112
  security and, 36
Conferences, 1-2, 242

fees for, 8
group practice and, 11
presentations at, 146, 227-228
Confidentiality, 124, 185-187
    clinical records and, 55
    court and, 229
    employees and, 207, 214
    industrial psychotherapy and, 235
    insurance and, 91
    managed care and, 102
    soundproofing and, 35
    suicidal clients and, 130
Conlee, G., 165
Consent form, 55, 59-63, 141, 188-189
Conservative style, 5
Consolidated Omnibus Budget Reconcili-
    ation Act (COBRA), 49-50
Construction, office, 34-35
Consultants, setting up private practice
    using, 51-53
Consultations, with other professionals, 8
Consulting:
    general, 224-225
    with psychiatric hospitals, 223
Contempt of court, 188
Continuing education units, 175, 228
Contract(s):
    lease and, 33
    liability and, 118
    loans, 28
    managed care firm, 101-102
    partnerships and, 19, 237
    purchased practices and, 15
    selling practice and, 16-17
    therapeutic, 130, 189-190, 191
    with psychiatric hospitals, 223-224
Contracted services, 75
Conventions, 75
Copayment, 85, 94-95
Corporations:
    pension plans and, 201
    taxes and, 72
Correspondence, see Letter(s)
Countertransference, 126, 193
County taxes, 79
Couple counseling, 83, 151
Court:
    attending, 125-127
    attire in, 126
    child custody evaluations, 230

commitment by, 131
expert witness and, 228, 229
forensic psychotherapy and, 228-229
jury selection and, 230
privileged communication and, 188
psychological autopsy and, 230
testimony in, 53
See also Legal issues
Court order, 124
Creative skills, 2, 7
Credentials, 21-28, 91, 121
Credibility:
    advertising and, 165, 166
    personal image and, 182
Credit card:
    business expenses on, 74, 113
    payment using, 105, 234
Creditors:
    corporations and, 19
    partnership and, 18
    sole proprietorship and, 18
Credit report, 105
Crimes:
    disclosure of, 123
    insurance against, 48
Criminal investigations, 187
Crises, 6, 40
Cross-coverage, 9
    abandonment suits and, 190
    partnerships and, 30
    preferred provider organizations and, 99
    supervision and, 118
Cross-referrals, 96
Current Procedural Terminology (CPT) code
    list, 57, 93

DSM-III-R, V codes in, 91
Dangerous situations, 129
Debts:
    attorney and, 52
    write off of, 76, 104-105
Defensiveness, employees and, 206
Defined benefit pension plan, 199
Degree, on stationery, 44
Delinquent accounts, billing and, 103-107
Delivery, 36
Dependency needs, 192
Depositions, 124, 125
Depreciation, deduction for, 75, 76

Diagnoses:
  clinical notes and, 66
  insurance and, 91, 92, 95, 177
Diagnostic Related Grouping (DRG) system, 177
Dictation, clinical notes, 65
Direct mail, 166-167
Disability insurance, 50
Disbursements, books, 73
Dishonest employees, 222
Dishonest therapists, 116
Doctor-patient privilege, 123
Documentation, 64. *See also* Clinical notes
Dorpat, T., 130
Dougherty, A. M., 224
Drawings, in ads, 169
Dress, *see* Attire
Dropouts, 163
Drug screening, 150, 175
Dual relationships, 192
Due reasonable care, 117
Duty to warn, 122, 123, 134, 187

Earles, R. H., 101
Education requirements, 21, 91
Emergencies, 129
  partnerships and, 30
  phone calls about, 40, 210
  privileged communication and, 187
Emotional injuries, money damages for, 114
Emotional isolation, 8
Emotional stability, 7
Employee(s):
  benefits, 46
  compensation record, 73, 110, 111
  confidentiality and, 207
  corporations and, 19
  defensiveness and, 206
  evaluation of, 217, 218
  firing, 219-222
  hiring, 204-208
  liability for, 29, 115
  managing, 215-219
  personnel records and, 77, 208-209, 219
  policy and procedure manual and, 29-30, 208
  qualifications, 214-215
  retirement plans for, 197-201
  rewards for, 217-219
    self-esteem and, 206
    tasks, 209-214
    taxes and, 73, 77, 209
    workers' compensation for, 48-49
Employee Assistance Programs (EAPs), 98, 118, 153
Employee dishonesty insurance, 48
Employee Withholding Allowance Certificate, 209
Employer Identification Number (EIN), 73, 209
Employment Eligibility Verification Form (I-9), 77
Employment application, 205
Employment taxes, 77
Entertaining, 75
Entrepreneurs, 4, 5-6
Equal employment opportunity, 29, 208
Equipment, 15, 35-43
Equity insurance, 51
Estate planning, 52, 196, 202-203
Estimated taxes, 76
Ethical issues, 123, 184-195
  abandonment, 190-191
  availability of records, 194
  boundaries and, 192-193
  consulting and, 225
  continuing nonbenefiting clients, 192
  contracts and, 189-190, 191
  group therapy and, 194
  hospitalization and, 193-194
  informed consent and, 188-189
  premature termination, 190-191
  secretary and, 214
  sexual misconduct, 193
  supervision and, 195
  value differences, 185
  See also Confidentiality; Privileged communication
Ethics committee, 116
Evaluations:
  adoptions, 225-226
  child custody, 230
  employee, 217, 218
  free, 150
Evening hours, 13
Everstine, D. S., 185, 187
Everstine, L., 185, 187
Exclusive Provider Organizations (EPOs), 100

Expenses:
    daily summary of, 111
    monthly, 28
Expert witness, 90, 125-127, 228, 229
Explanation of Insurance Benefits, 93, 213

Families:
    access to client records, 194
    fees and, 83
    home office and, 32
    home visits and, 233
    loans, 28-29
    practice's effects on, 8
    suicidal clients and, 130, 131
Federal income tax, 76, 77-78
Federal Insurance Contribution Act (FICA),
    76
Federal Payroll Tax Returns, 77
Federal Unemployment Tax Act (FUTA), 78-
    79
Fees, 59
    agency policies, 1
    bartering, 103
    billing, 86-88
    collection of, 88-90, 95, 212
    for courtroom appearances, 127
    for depositions, 127
    inability to afford, 190-191
    insurance paying, 91-103
    marketing and, 150
    missed appointments and, 107-108
    payment sources, 90-97
    private pay, 90-91
    raising, 85-86
    reasonable and customary, 91, 92
    renegotiating, 97
    reviewing records with clients and, 66
    secretary and, 212
    setting, 82-86
    sliding scale, 83, 84-85
    third-party reimbursement, 97-103
Female clients, sexual misconduct and, 193
File cabinet, 37
Files, see Clinical records
Final diagnosis, documentation of, 66
Financial advisor, 197
Financial compensation, 2
Financial issues, 8-9, 88
Financial policies, 83

Financial rewards, 4
Financial statements, 51
Financial status, 28-29
Financing, start-up, 8
Firing employees, 219-222
First impressions, 4-5
Fliers, 36
Forensic psychology, 126, 228-229
Forms, 69, 92
401-K plan, 200
Fraud, 116
Free advertising, 177-180
Free services, 150
Freud, Sigmund, 88
Freudenberger, H. J., 84, 86
Frey, D. H., 185, 187
Friends, treating, 192
Fringe benefits, 207
Full-time practice, 13
Furnishings, 2, 15, 35-38, 75, 133
Future, planning for, 6. See also Retirement
    planning

Gatekeeper, HMOs and, 233
General ledger, 86
General liability insurance, 47
General practice, 14
Gifts, 75, 123, 163
Goals, realistic, 243
Goldberg, C., 240
Goodwill, 15
Governmental funding, 3
Governments, consulting lists, 225
Gratification, ability to defer, 7
Greenburg, J. H., 121, 123
Greenburg, S. L., 121, 123
Group practice, 10-13
Group supervision, 226
Group therapy, 83-84
    ethical issues and, 194
    in hospital, 223
    seating for, 38

Hales, R. E., 114
Handouts, public talks and, 146
Handwritten clinical notes, 64-65
Hare-Mustin, R. T., 189
Hays, J. R., 117, 125, 126, 229, 230

Health, 5
  stable, 7
  start-up financing and, 9
Health-care costs, 98, 100
Health Care Financing Administration
  (HCFA) 1500 claim form, 57, 92-93
Health insurance:
  for self and staff, 49-50, 77, 207
  See also Insurance
Health maintenance organizations (HMOs),
  98, 153, 172, 232-233
Heat/electricity, 28
Heymann, G. M., 185, 187
Hiratsuka, J., 100
Hoffman, M. S., 235
Hogan, D. B., 118
Hold-harmless clauses, 12, 100, 118
Home evaluations, for adoptions, 225-226
Home office, 3, 31-33, 75
Home visits, 233
Hospital(s), 153
  affiliation with, 154
  billing and, 102-103
  contracting with, 223-224
  discharge from, 191
  group practice and, 11
  hold-harmless clauses, 118
  marketing to, 176-177
  medical, 177
  referrals and, 151, 176-177, 193
  visits to, 9
Hospitalization of clients, 123
  insurance and, 57, 92
  involuntary, 131
  privileged communication and, 188
  voluntary, 130-131
"Housekeeping" issues, 83
Hugging, 122, 193
Hyatt, J., 29

Image, marketing and, 182
Immigration and Naturalization Service
  (INS), 77
Incentive program, 217-219
Income:
  bank accounts, 112
  books, 73
  potential, 8
Income taxes, 15, 209

Indemnification clause, 102
Independence, 8
Individual retirement accounts (IRAs), 197
Individual retirement annuity, 197
Industrial psychotherapy, 235-236
Informed consent, 59-63, 91, 188-189
Injury:
  disability insurance and, 50
  employees and, 48-49
  liability insurance and, 47
Inquiry call, 162
Inservices, 151
Insubordination, 222
Insurance billing, 28, 88, 91-103
  assigning benefits to therapist, 59
  audits and, 94
  calling, 94
  confidentiality and, 91, 187
  correspondence and, 68
  diagnoses and, 95, 177
  expired or nonreimbursing, 97
  forms, 92, 211, 213
  limited policy, 84
  phone calls and, 91-92
  preferred providers and, 98-100
  refusal to pay and, 83
  rewards for collecting money, 219
  sharing information and, 124
  slow pay and, 7
  verification of benefits, 57-59
Insurance for practice, 21, 46-51
  corporations and, 19
  disability, 50
  employee dishonesty, 48
  fraud, 95, 96
  group, 10
  health, 49-50, 207
  home office and, 32
  liability, 47, 115-116, 123
  life, 51
  malpractice, 49
  property, 47-48
  workers' compensation, 48-49
Intake forms, 56-63
Intangible assets, 15
Integrity, level of, 3-4
Interest rate, loans, 28-29
Internal Revenue Service:
  audits, 74, 81, 113
  publications, 20, 71, 72, 75, 78, 111, 209

International Association of Employee Assis-
  tance Program Professionals, 152
Interviewing job applicants, 205-207
Interviews, radio, 179
Involuntary commitment, 123
Isolation, 8, 12, 244

Jackson, R. A., 140
Job description, 205
Job satisfaction, 217
Job security, 2
Johnson, H. G., 185, 187
Joint Commission of Accreditation for Hos-
  pitals, 223
Joint sessions, group practice and, 11
Journals, 74, 168
Jury selection, 230

Kachorek, J., 122
Kaplan, A. G., 189
Kearney, M., 187
Keith-Spiegel, P., 188, 192
Keogh plan, 198-199
Kinesthetic individuals, 161
King, J., 235
Kissel, S., 196
Kissing, 122, 193
Knapp, S., 185
Koacher, G. P., 188, 192
Kriss, J. P., 5
Kurzman, P., 236

Landis, E. R., 117, 125, 126, 229, 230
Lawsuits, 114-117
  notification of, 116
  prevention of, 121
Layoffs, 222
Lease, 33-34
Ledger, 74, 110-111
Ledger cards, 88, 104, 105, 106, 109
Legal and accounting services, 28
Legal issues, 114-128
  employee termination, 220-222
  See also Court
Legal situation, clinical notes and, 63, 65, 66
Leggett v. First Interstate Bank of Oregon,
  186

Letterhead, 44
Letter of reference, 222
Letters, 5, 68-69
  acknowledging referrals and, 142
  consultant sources, 225
  direct mail, 166
  employee warnings, 219
  form, 243
  potential referral sources, 144-145
  secretary generating, 211
  termination, 67, 192
  to new clients, 162
  to new contacts, 157
Lewin, M. H., 224
Liability:
  attorney and, 52
  contracts and, 118
  in supervision, 117-118
  keeping old files and, 67-68
  malpractice, 49
  preferred provider organizations and, 100
Liability insurance, 47, 115-116, 123
License number, on stationery, 44
Licenses, 21, 91, 121
Life insurance, 51
Lighting, 39
Limits, setting, 191
Liss-Levinson, N., 189
Litigious clients, 135
Loans, 19, 28-29
Location
  multiple, 238
  office, 30-33
Locks, changing after terminating employee,
  221
Long-term disability insurance, 50
Loss, taxes and, 72
Lying employees, 222

Magazines, 36, 75, 157, 169, 178
Mail, secretary handling, 213
Mailing lists, 42, 147, 166-167
Major medical health insurance, 49-50
Malicious acts, 116
Malpractice, 8, 37, 49, 114, 125-127
  clauses for, 118-121
  clinical notes and, 66
  components of lawsuits, 117
  corporations and, 19

group practice and, 12
managed care and, 102
preventing suits, 121-123
privileged communication and, 187
supervision and, 227
testifying in court and, 232
Managed care, 100-102, 172, 227
hold-harmless clauses, 118
referrals and, 152
Managerial skills, 2
Marecek, J., 189
Mariano, W. E., 118
Marketing, 5, 7, 136-183
advertising, 164-181
client feedback and, 164
cold calls, 155-159
computers and, 42
conferences, 146
correspondence, 68
free advertising and, 177-180
goals and objectives, 137-139
group practice and, 11
home visits, 233
newsletters and, 180
open house and, 180-181
part-time practice and, 13
personal image and, 182
products, 238
psychiatric hospitals, 176-177
public talks, 146-150
referral lists and, 151-153
referrals and, 137, 139-155
second office, 34
selling your services, 159-162
stationery and, 43-46
telephone and, 158-159, 164
telephone therapy, 234
Marketing consultants, 176
Marketing skills, 2
Marketplace, understanding, 140
Marriage, preparing for, 151
Marriage and family therapists, state certifying bodies, 23-24
Master-level social workers, 223
Mead, D. E., 227
Meal expenses, 75
Media, working with, 141
Medical expense, 80-81
Medical hospitals, marketing to, 177
Medical insurance, 49, 91-103

Medicare, 96
Medication consultations, 140
Mental health, 7
Mental health examination, 123, 130
Mental health groups, administering to private, 227
Mental-health-related services, funding for, 3
Meyer, R. G., 117, 125, 126, 229, 230
Mileage, 75
Minorities, start-up financing and, 8, 9
Minors:
parental consent and, 122
privileged communication and, 187
Missed appointments:
calling, 163
code, 96
Mobile telephone therapy, 234-235
Money-purchase pension plan, 198-199
Monotony, 244
Monthly operating expenses, 28
Morrison, J. K., 224
Music, waiting room, 35, 36, 39

Name recognition, 169, 174
Naming, practice, 43
Negative transference, 190
Neglect, 117
Neighbors, treating, 192
Networking, 151, 154, 232
open house and, 181
solo practitioners and, 12-13
New client packet, 59-63
Newsletters, 238
Newspapers, 141, 168-169, 178
Niche, finding, 139
No shows, calling, 163
Noncompete clause, 12
Noncompliant behavior, clinical notes and, 66

Occurrence policy, 115-116
Office:
construction of, 34-35
furnishings and equipment, 2, 35-43, 133
in home, 3, 31-33, 75
lease and, 33
location of, 30-33
organization of, 5, 243

second, 34
soundproofing, 32, 33, 34, 35
subletting, 13
Office expansion, 236-238
Office hours, 3
Office supplies, 28, 42-43, 75
Ogilvy, D., 168
On call, 9
Open house, 180-181
Operating expenses, 28
Organization, as "identified patient," 225
Organizational skills, 6
Others, danger to, 134
Overhead:
    disability insurance and, 50
    group practice, 10
    part-time practice and, 13
Overtime, 30

Packaged sessions, 151
Pagers, 13, 40, 41-42, 75, 190
Paperwork, 54-70
Parenthood, juggling demands of, 3
Partnership, 18-19, 237
    policy and procedure manual and, 30
    taxes and, 72, 76
Part-time practice, 13
Pay increase, 217
"Payment contract," 105
Payment plan, 104, 105
Payments due, 36
Payment sources, 90-97
Payroll records, 109, 111, 209
Payroll taxes, 75, 76, 77
Peers, sharing with, 226
Pegboard systems, 111
Pelletier, K. R., 240
Pending files, 42-43
Pension plans, 196-201
Percentage payment, subleasing and, 31
Perlin, M. L., 114-115
Personal image, marketing and, 182
Personal injury attorneys, 231-232
Personal issues, 244
Personal leave, 207
Personal life, 9, 192-193
Personal qualifications, 5
Personal relationships, 241-242
Personal retirement deductions, 76-77

Personal satisfaction, 4
Personal telephone calls, 215, 221
Personnel records, 77, 208-209, 219
Petty cash, 73, 112
Photocopier, 37
Photograph, 169, 170, 171
Physicians:
    cold calls and, 155
    referrals and, 140, 145
    working under supervision of, 96
Physicians Current Procedural Terminology
    (CPT) codes, 57, 93
Play therapy supplies, 75
Policy and procedures manual, 29-30, 208,
    221, 222
Political clout, group practice and, 11
Position advertising, 176
Postage, 75
Postcard tips, 172
Practice, see Private practice
Practice experience, 21
Preferred Provider Organizations (PPOs),
    98, 152-153
Prescriptions, 130
Presentations, 139, 146-150, 160, 175, 227-
    228
Presenting problem, clinical notes and, 66
Press releases, 178
Preventative custody, 133
Private mental health groups, administering
    to, 227
Private pay, 90-91
Private practice:
    attraction of, 1-9
    autonomy and, 1-2
    buying versus starting a new, 14-17
    credentials and, 21-28
    full versus part time, 13-14
    general partnership, 18-19
    group versus solo, 10-13
    legal aspects of, 114-128
    professional corporation, 19
    selecting options in, 10-20
    setting up, 21-53
    sole proprietorship, 17-18
    specialized versus generalized, 14
Privileged communication, 53, 55, 123, 185,
    187-188
Privileged information, 125
Pro bono cases, 84

Procedures manual, 29-30
Products, specialized, 238
Professional activities, documented, 21
Professional certifying examination, 21
Professional contacts, 13
Professional corporations, 19
Professional counselors, state certifying bodies, 22-23
Professional goals and objectives, 137-139
Professional groups, marketing to, 139
Professional journals, 75
Professional literature, 123
Professional materials, 38
Professional meetings, 1-2
Professional organization, 28
 malpractice insurance and, 49
 liability insurance and, 115
Professional presentation, 4-5
Professionals, as clients, 85
Profits:
 purchased practices and, 15
 sole proprietors and, 17
 taxes and, 72, 74
Profit-sharing retirement plan, 198
Prognosis, documentation of, 66
Progress notes, 213
Promotional items, 181
Property insurance, 47-48
Provider directory, 101-102
Provider number, 93
Psychiatric hospitals, 102-103, 153, 193-194
 contracting with, 223-224
 marketing to, 176-177
Psychodrama, 223
Psychological autopsy, 230
Psychological tests, 38
Psychologist-patient privilege, 123
Psychologists, state certifying bodies, 24-26
Psychosocials, social workers and, 223
Public service announcements, 178
Public speaking, 5, 146-150

Quality of care, clinical records and, 64

Radio, 141, 173-174, 179
Reamer, F., 117, 118
Reasonable and customary charges, 91, 92
Receipts, for cash, 88

Receptionist, hiring, 204-208
Recommendations, documentation of, 66
Records, 54-70, 122
 bank, 112-113
 billing, 86-88
 bookkeeping, 108-112
 business, 73-74
 insuring against loss of, 48
 See also Clinical notes
References, employees, 207
Referrals, 117, 122, 137, 151-153
 accepting all, 150
 acknowledging, 141-144
 asking for, 157, 161
 cold calls and, 155-159
 contacting potential, 144-145
 development of, 139-155
 documentation of, 66
 fees charged, 84, 85
 group practice and, 10-11
 hospitals and, 176-177, 193
 maintaining, 162-164
 managed care and, 101
 part-time practice and, 13, 14
 paying for, 96
 purchased practices and, 15
 specialists and, 14, 191
 taking to lunch, 163
 to other practitioners, 140, 190-191
 value differences and, 185
Release of information form, 11, 59-63, 141-143
Religious agencies, 139
Religious beliefs, 122
Rent, 28, 31, 75
Repair people, 36
Reply card, postage-paid, 167
Resnick, H., 235
Resource file, 70
Responsibility, delegating, 6
Retirees, start-up financing and, 8-9
Retirement planning, 52, 196-203, 207, 245
Rewards, for employees, 217-219
Richards, D. L., 32, 224
Risk, retirement plans and, 201-202
Rosenberg, N., 99
Routine, freedom from, 2
Rozovsky, F. A., 188-189

Safe-deposit box, 75
Safety issues, 129-135
Salaries, 28, 207, 217
Salary-deferral retirement contribution, 197
Salespeople, 36
Samuels, R. M., 15
Sank, L. I., 232
Savings accounts, 73, 112
Schetky, D. B. E., 230
School counselors, 59
　　cold calls and, 155
　　referrals from, 142-143, 145
Schools, release of information and, 142-143
Schwartz, G., 186, 187
S corporations, 19, 72
Season, starting business, 28
Seating, 37-38
Secretarial area, furniture, 36-37
Secretary:
　　billing and, 211-212
　　collecting payments, 88, 89
　　confidentiality and, 214
　　fee discussions, 83
　　fee quotes and, 212
　　hiring, 204-208
　　mail and, 213
　　qualifications, 214-215
　　tasks, 209-214
　　See also Employee(s)
Security:
　　computers and, 42
　　lease and, 33
Security deposits, 28
Seiden, R. H., 185, 187
Self:
　　belief in, 4
　　taking care of, 240-245
Self-appraisal, 4
Self-confidence, 4
Self-defense, 133
Self-employment tax, 76-77
Self-esteem, employees and, 206
Self-help groups, 70, 139
Self-injury, 123
Self-mailer, 166, 167
Selling practice, 14-17, 68
Selling services, 159-162
Seminars, 174-175
Sexual harassment, by employees, 222
Sexual misconduct, 115, 193

Shapiro, J. R., 232
Sick leave, 207
Simplified employee pension (SEP), 197
Single-premium deferred annuity, 201
Sliding fee scale, 83, 84-85
Small claims court, 104
Smith, B. D., 49
Smoking, deterring, 36
Social groups, 139
Social life, 5
Social Security (FICA), 76-77, 200-201, 209
Social setting, encountering clients in, 192
Social support, 241-242
Social workers:
　　adoption reports and, 226
　　psychosocials by, 223
　　state certifying bodies, 26-27
Society's values, 3
Sole proprietorship, 10-13, 17-18
　　taxes and, 71-72, 76
Soundproofing, 32, 33, 34, 35
Speakers bureau, 228
Specialist, 3, 122, 153-154
　　consulting as, 225
　　fees and, 83
　　referrals to, 191
SS-4, 209
Standard of care, 117, 122
Start-up costs, 8, 28
State-by-state listing, certification and, 22-27
State competency exams, 21
State income taxes, 79, 209
State unemployment insurance, 78-79
Stationery, 43-46
Stock, professional corporation, 19
Stress, 5, 7, 240-241, 245
Sublease, 13, 31, 33
Subpoena, 55, 56, 124-125, 187
Success, belief in, 4
Suicidal clients, 129-131
Superbill, 111
Supervision, 8, 12, 117, 190, 195, 226, 242
Supplies, 28

Talbott, J. A., 114
Tangible assets, 14-15
Tarasoff v. Regents of the University of California, 122
Tardiff, K., 133

Target benefit pension plan, 199-200
Tasks, prioritizing, 6
Tax-deferred annuities, 201
Tax-deferred retirement plans, 196-200
Taxes, 28, 71-81
    accountant and, 51-52
    bookkeeping for, 111
    business deductions, 74-76
    business entity and, 71-72
    business records and, 73
    client deductions, 80-81
    corporate, 19
    employee, 73-74, 209
    federal income, 77-78
    filing forms for, 74, 80
    home office and, 31, 32-33
    local, 79
    Medicare, 78
    partnership and, 18, 19
    payroll, 77
    purchased practices and, 15
    self-employment, 76-77
    Social Security, 78
    state, 79
    unemployment, 78-79
Taxpayer identification number, 73
Teaching, 227
Telephone, 28, 75
    availability by, 190
    consultant sources, 225
    employee's demeanor and, 204-205
    etiquette, 164
    home office and, 32
    marketing and, 158-159, 164
    personal calls, 215, 221
    personal image and, 182
    secretary and, 209-210
Telephone book, 55, 172-173
Telephone message book, 210
Telephone numbers, state certifying bodies,
    22-27
Telephone system, 39-40
Telephone therapy, 234-235
Television, 141, 174, 179-180
Termination of therapy, 191-192
    documentation of, 66
    inability to pay and, 97
    letter, 67, 192
    managed care and, 102
    noncompliant patients, 122

    premature, 190-191
    problem employees and, 204, 205
Termination of employees, 219-222
Term life, 51
Testing equipment, 38
Theft, employees and, 222
Therapeutic alliance, 95-96
Therapeutic contract, 130, 189-190, 191
Therapist(s):
    availability of, 190
    charging, 122
    danger to, 132-134
    expansion with additional, 237
Third-party reimbursement, 21, 28, 97-103
Time management, 242-243
Toastmasters, 5
Tort law, 114
Toys, 37, 38
Trademark, 43
Training employees, 215-216
Transcription, 213-214
Transference, 190
    juries and, 126
    selling practice and, 16
Travel expenses, 75
Travel time, 242
Treatment, rationale for, 122
Treatment plan, clinical notes and, 66
True, R. H., 185, 187
Trust, 67, 121
    access to records and, 194
    marketing to new clients and, 182
    secretary and, 215
    sexual misconduct and, 193
12-step meetings, 70
Typing, 213-214

Unemployed, counseling for, 151
Unemployment taxes, 78-79, 209
Urine analyses, 150
Utilities, 75
Utilization review, 99, 101

Vacation, 2, 190, 207, 215
Value differences, with clients, 185
VandeCreek, L., 185
"V" codes, 91
Vendorship law, 91

Verbal communication skills, 5
Verification of Insurance Benefits, 57-59,
    92, 94
Videotapes, 238
Violent client, 37, 122, 132-134
Visually-oriented people, 161
Voice mail, 41
Voluntary agencies, 139

W-4, 209
Waiting room, 35, 36, 170
Weapons, 130
Weitz, R. D., 15
Wettstein, R. M., 228
Wills, 202-203
Wilson, S. J., 187, 188
Women, start-up financing and, 8, 9

Woody, R. H., 56, 116, 117, 123
Workaholism, 241
Workers' compensation, 48-49, 209, 231-232
Working, enjoyment of, 6-7
Work structure, 6
Wright, B., 165
Wright, R. H., 116
Written communication, 5, 243. *See also*
    Letters
Written consent, 189

Yellow Pages ads, 172-173
Yudofsky, S. C., 114

Zip codes, targeted, 166-167
Zoning laws, 31

About the Author

Eileen S. Lenson is a psychotherapist with more than 15 years of clinical experience. A much sought-after lecturer, she has presented papers nationally as well as internationally, has been a frequent guest on radio talk shows, and speaks at local events within her community. She also has written on a variety of mental-health-related topics. She has taught at George Washington University Medical School on bioethics and health-care issues. Prior to developing her private practice, she worked as a medical social worker and supervisor and provided consultation to attorneys concerned with personal injury and malpractice cases. A graduate of the University of Maryland School of Social Work and Community Planning, she has been licensed as a social worker in Virginia, Texas, and Maryland; is a Board Certified Diplomate in Clinical Social Work and an Academy Certified Social Worker; and is certified in Trauma Resolution Therapy and trained in Clinical Hypnosis. She has built private practices from the ground up in three widely diverse regions of the country.

DATE DUE

Demco, Inc. 38-293